The Secret Trial of Imre Nagy

The Secret Trial of Imre Nagy

Alajos Dornbach

Foreword by
János Radványi

PRAEGER
Westport, Connecticut
London

Library of Congress Cataloging-in-Publication Data

The Secret trial of Imre Nagy / [edited by] Alajos Dornbach ; foreword by János Radványi.
p. cm.
Includes index.
ISBN 0-275-94332-1 (alk. paper)
1. Nagy, Imre, 1896-1958—Trials, litigation, etc. 2. Trials (Political crimes and offenses)—Hungary—Budapest. 3. Hungary—History—Revolution, 1956. I. Dornbach, Alajos.
KKF41.N34S43 1994
943.905'3—dc20 94-16459

British Library Cataloguing in Publication Data is available.

Library of Congress Catalog Card Number: 94-16459
ISBN: 0-275-94332-1

First published in 1994

Praeger Publishers, 88 Post Road West, Westport, CT 06881
An imprint of Greenwood Publishing Group, Inc.

Printed in the United States of America

The paper used in this book complies with the Permanent Paper Standard issued by the National Information Standards Organization (Z39.48-1984).

10 9 8 7 6 5 4 3 2 1

Contents

CONCLUSION

APPENDICES

Foreword

János Radványi

In this important book, Deputy Speaker of the Hungarian Parliament Alajos Dornbach presents readers with long-awaited documentary evidence of the secret trial of Imre Nagy, the leader of the 1956 Hungarian Revolution, and a group of his associates. It is a book of historic significance—at once a tribute to individual courage in the face of insuperable odds and a crushing indictment of the abuse of human rights in a communist dictatorship.

In his capacity as an attorney for the Historical Justice Committee in Hungary in the 1980s, Dornbach was both participant and observer in the protracted political and legal battles that cleared the way for the rehabilitation of Imre Nagy and other martyrs of the revolution. His incisive essay on the communist judicial system and practice serves as an introduction to the hitherto top-secret transcripts from the Nagy trial, which in turn are rounded off by Professor György Litván's historical background chapter. Taken together, these pages offer a rare look at the ways in which the post-revolution regime fashioned "legal means" to subvert the popular will and stamp out resistance against their totalitarian rule. The proceedings serve also as a grim reminder, if any is needed, that for decades under Soviet domination, the bosses of the world's communist parties constituted the most brutal mafia in contemporary history, a force geared at all times to retribution in the service of preserving the *pax sovietica*.

The editor, Alajos Dornbach, fulfills an important task in facilitating the Western reader's comprehension of the complexity of events in Hungary in 1956 and Nagy's role in them. Until now, Nagy was perhaps best remembered in Washington, Paris, London, and Rome as the Hungarian premier who held office during a turbulent revolution in October 1956, fell out of favor in the communist camp, and, like so many before him, met an untimely end. What few outside the Soviet sphere realized was that even before his death Nagy had become a symbol of personal freedom and national independence not only in Hungary but throughout Eastern and Central Europe. And even fewer, inside or outside

Hungary, knew of the sufferings and humiliation Nagy and the other leaders of the crushed revolution had to bear.

As a matter of fact, most Hungarians learned about Nagy's trial only on June 16, 1958, when Radio Budapest, the official broadcast organ of the communist government, sternly announced: "The Hungarian legal authorities have concluded proceedings in the case of the leading group of persons who, on October 23, 1956, started a counterrevolutionary armed uprising against the legitimate order of the Hungarian People's Republic." The speaker went on to report that the People's Tribunal of the Supreme Court of the Hungarian People's Republic had found all the defendants guilty. Imre Nagy and three of his close associates (Pál Maléter, Miklós Gimes, and József Szilágyi) had been sentenced to death and five other co-defendants either to life or to long prison sentences. No appeals would be forthcoming. The death sentences had been carried out.

These documents prove that although the charges were carefully drafted and revised over several months to compound the allegations against the accused and the trial itself was conducted after several calculated delays, the accusers knew their efforts had fallen short. What was at first doubtless conceived as a show trial was in the end reduced to complete secrecy; and before the trial and its outcome were announced the hanged men were laid to rest in unmarked graves and all traces of the sordid executions were obliterated.

The documents also prove that behind its oft-acclaimed facade of "liberal policies and practices," János Kádár's regime reverted to the methods and fabrications of the Stalinist Rákosi period. While it is true that the extremity of Kádár's measures resulted in part from the pressure of hard-liners in the international communist movement, they also reflected Kádár's personal conviction that a *memento mori* was needed to maintain communist rule in Hungary.

The news of the judicial murder of the leader of the Hungarian Revolution and his associates was received with stunned and sullen silence in beleaguered Hungary. But elsewhere in the world it prompted a surge of demonstrations against the Soviet Union and the Hungarian communist regime. Political leaders from London to New Delhi expressed outrage. Intellectuals saw in the executions the beginnings of a revival of the Stalinist terror. Students in Paris held protest meetings; angry demonstrators in the Scandinavian countries, in Bonn, and elsewhere shattered windows at Soviet embassies. The State Department in Washington issued a statement to the effect that the Soviet Union and the Soviet-imposed regime in Hungary had violated every principle of decency and must stand in judgment before the conscience of mankind. The United Nations Special Committee on the Problem of Hungary pointed out that the secret trial and executions clearly contradicted solemn assurances which János Kádár had made to the U.N. on behalf of the Hungarian government. Indeed, the wave of indignation was such as to bring into open question the matter of Soviet reliability in international politics. U.S. President Dwight D. Eisenhower, British Prime

Minister Harold Macmillan, and French President Charles de Gaulle now let it be known that they no longer considered the circumstances favorable for a summit conference, despite Soviet leader Nikita Khrushchev's persistent urging that such a meeting was needed to "strengthen peaceful coexistence."

But by September 1959, as happened so many times during the Cold War, human rights protest gave way to superpower diplomacy. In that month President Eisenhower hosted at his retreat in Maryland the same Khrushchev who had demanded exemplary punishment for the Hungarian "rebels." There, "in the spirit of Camp David," the two leaders pledged that "all outstanding international questions should be settled . . . by peaceful means through negotiation." Reportedly, the Nagy trial and the executions were subjects carefully avoided during the talks. The Hungarian drama had had its hour upon the international stage. How quickly, it seemed, the world could forget.

In Hungary and elsewhere in Eastern and Central Europe, however, the Hungarian Revolution had ignited a flame of hope, and after the flame receded a stubborn spark still burned. That spark would not die. Nearly three decades later it would flare again, and this time its fire would spread north and east and south to join new fires until the whole world knew that *change* was happening and the political landscape would never be the same.

For diplomatic historians, for students of East Central European politics, and for laymen alike, the Nagy trial documents bear eloquent testimony to the historical fact that in crucial times courageous men will come forth and put their lives on the line to end oppression. Sometimes—not often, alas—such deeds bear wondrous fruit. Without the ultimate sacrifice of Imre Nagy and his associates, Hungary probably would not be a parliamentary democracy today. Beyond question Nagy ultimately contributed to the downfall of the Soviet empire. And as an irony of history, Nagy's courage and steadfast belief in human values may even have paved the way for a reconciliation between Russia and Hungary. For during his November 11, 1992, visit to Hungary, Russian President Boris Yeltsin visited the grave of Imre Nagy to pay his respects. There he acknowledged that under the communist system relations between Budapest and Moscow were oppressive and unfavorable to Hungary, but he expressed his hope that future cooperation between the two nations would be harmonious and friendly. Many of the Hungarian observers marked that occasion as truly a turning point in history.

Preface

Alajos Dornbach

The secret criminal proceedings in which Prime Minister Imre Nagy, József Szilágyi, Miklós Gimes, and Pál Maléter were sentenced to death in 1958 and then summarily executed shocked public opinion at the time and have since generated much interest in Hungary and abroad. Even after the co-defendants who survived were released from prison, only minor facts about the trial became known, and those only in very restricted circles, because not even the persons who had been sentenced were allowed to read the verdict to acquaint themselves with the bulk of the evidence. In 1989 the documents became accessible at last, the case was reviewed, and the Supreme Court acquitted Imre Nagy and every one of his fellow defendants. A great deal more professional labor will be needed before we can fully evaluate the more than one hundred thousand pages of case evidence and sort out the various versions of the court records (yes, it is clear the records have been manipulated again and again). Nevertheless, we thought the publication of four basic documents—the original indictment, the trial verdict, the procurator's motion that led to the trial review of 1989, and the subsequent acquittal resolution—would prove enlightening to many readers, even in the absence of an analysis of all the material.

As the lawyer who participated in the review process, I was afforded the honor of overseeing the publication of these documents.

I should like to express deep gratitude to the surviving trial defendants, as well as to the relatives of those defendants who were executed and of those who are now deceased, for granting their permission to publish the documents.

In 1957 Frederick A. Praeger, publisher, obtained a copy of the original mimeographed document written by Imre Nagy during his forced retirement in 1955-1956 after he had been ousted form his position as premier and expelled from the Central Committee. The document, published by Praeger under the title *Imre Nagy on Communism: In Defense of the New Course,* was a crushing indictment of the Hungarian Rákosi satellite regime. Imre Nagy's friends who printed the same work clandestinely in Hungary are belatedly expressing their thanks to Frederick A. Praeger. I am especially happy that Praeger Publishers, even though Frederick Praeger is no longer associated with the company, has agreed to undertake the publication of this volume. I am grateful to the staff, especially editor Dan Eades, for the patience and understanding assistance in seeing the book through publication.

Thanks are due also to the following persons who lent cooperation in this endeavor:

To György Litván, historian and director of the '56 Institute, for his insights into the political background of the trial and for his contribution of the chapter that concludes this volume. In 1956 György Litván belonged to Imre Nagy's circle. He was sentenced to six years in prison after the defeat of the revolution. In 1988 he became a founder and leader of the Historical Justice Committee, which from its inception demanded a review of the Imre Nagy trial.

To János Radványi, historian and professor at Mississippi State University, who arranged for the publication of this book in the United States. In the early 1960s János Radványi headed the Washington Embassy of the Hungarian People's Republic. He participated in formulating and communicating positions adopted in international political circles that led to the release of most of the political prisoners who were thrown into prison following the defeat of the revolution. The Hungarian state security apparatus initiated an investigation into his activities, but he succeeded in emigrating. He was sentenced in absentia to death on fabricated charges; the charges were dismissed and the sentence annulled only in 1990.

To János Rainer and János Bak, historians and associates of the '56 Institute, for compiling a brief biography for each of the defendants.

To Éva Pálmai and Ervin Dessewffy, who undertook the very difficult task of translating into English the procurators' motions and the sentences of the court. Their task was made all the more arduous by the prolix and arid bureaucratic language of the 1958 documents, and by the differences in terminology and structure between the Anglo-Saxon and Hungarian legal systems. Their translation was professionally revised by Árpád Erdei, professor at Eötvös Loránd Law School, Budapest, who also translated the introductory and concluding chapters for this volume. Special thanks also to style editor Carol Norton of California, and research assistant Tan Tsai of the Center for International Security and Strategic Studies at Mississippi State University.

To the Soros Foundation, which generously supported the research of this work and covered the costs of translation.

To the Earhart Foundation, which contributed to the desktop publishing work and style editing expenses.

To Erzsébet Nagy, the daughter of Imre Nagy, and to my friend Miklós Vásárhelyi for their valued trust. With one exception, all the defendants or their representatives commissioned me to serve as legal representative in the review process. In January 1988 Miklós Vásárhelyi, with my collaboration, petitioned for a formal review of the case at the Supreme Court, at that time unsuccessfully. In 1989, however, as head of the legal section of the Historical Justice Committee and as empowered legal council, I was privileged to represent those sentenced in the Nagy trial as well as those convicted in many other political terror trials. Collectively, these cases, chief among them the trial of Imre Nagy, the prime minister who presided during the 1956 revolution, have provided the most moving experience I have known in more than thirty years of active legal practice.

I believe the documents from the Imre Nagy trial contained in this volume stand as a lesson for all who care about the rule of law and the principle of judicial independence.

August 1993, Budapest
Alajos Dornbach

Abbreviations

ÁVH (Államvédelmi Hatóság)
State Security Agency: political police force, essentially independent of the government, operating under the direction of the top Party leadership and of Soviet advisors, and having jurisdiction over practically everything.

Be (Büntető Eljárási Törvény)
Criminal Procedure: Act 1 of 1973 on criminal procedure.

BHÖ (Hatályos Anyagi Büntetőjogi Szabályok Hivatalos Összeállitása)
Official Compilation of Substantive Criminal Law Provisions in Force: since after 1945 the Penal Code was not given a new Special Part, the provisions of penal law were compiled in that collection.

Bp (Büntető Perrendtartás)
Code of Criminal Procedure (not in force any more).

Btá (Büntető törvénykönyv általános része)
General section of the Criminal Code: Act 2 of 1950.

DISZ (Demokratikus Ifjusági Szövetség)
Democratic Youth Alliance: the only youth organization in the 1950s amalgamating the earlier youth groups.

FKP (Független Kisgazda Párt)
Independent Smallholders' Party.

IM (Igazságügyi Minisztérium)
Ministry of Justice.

KTBTK (Katonai Büntető Törvénykönyv)
Military Criminal Code.

MÁV (Magyar Állam Vasutok)
Hungarian State Railway.

MDP (Magyar Dolgozók Pártja)
Hungarian Workers' Party.

MÉFB (Magyar Értelmiség Forradalmi Bizottsága)
Revolutionary Committee of Hungarian Intellectuals: a group of organizations (Writers' Association, Journalists' Association, etc.) under the influence of the reformist opposition in the party.

MEFESZ (Magyar Egyetemi és Főiskolai Egyesületek Szövetsége)
Federation of Hungarian University and College Associations: functioning until the establishment of the DISZ in 1950, reestablished at Szeged University on October 16, 1956.

MKP (Magyar Kommunista Párt)
Hungarian Communist Party; in 1949 it forced fusion with the Social Democratic Party; from that time on: Magyar Dolgozók Pártja (Hungarian Workers' Party).

MSZMP (Magyar Szocialista Munkáspárt)
Hungarian Socialist Workers' Party: the new Hungarian communist party established on November 4, 1956, which adopted the name of the Hungarian communist party operating between the two world wars.

NÉKOSZ (Népi Kollégiumok Országos Szövetsége)
National Association of People's Colleges: organization of colleges, established after World War II and dissolved in 1949, providing free higher education to students of worker and peasant parentage.

SZDP (Szociáldemokrata Párt)
Social Democratic Party.

SZKP (Szovjet Kommunista Párt)
Soviet Communist Party.

SZÖVOSZ (Szövetkezetek Országos Szövetsége)
National Federation of Cooperatives.

TTIT (Társadalom és Természettudományi Ismeretterjesztö Társulat)
Society for the Propagation of Social and Natural Sciences

Papers and magazines mentioned in the text:

Irodalmi Ujság	Literary Gazette
Kis Ujság	Little Gazette
Magyar Honvéd	Hungarian Soldier
Magyar Közlöny	Hungarian Gazette
Magyar Nemzet	Hungarian Nation
Magyar Szabadság	Hungarian Freedom
Magyar Világ	Hungarian World
Müvelt Nép	Cultured People
Október Huszonharmadika	October 23rd
Szabad Nép	Free People
Szabad Szó	Free Speech
Sziv Ujság	Heart Gazette
Vengria	Hungarian

The Secret Trial of Imre Nagy

Introduction

Administration of Justice in the Party State and the Trial of Imre Nagy

Alajos Dornbach

I

Legal order is built on good laws, on respect for the law, and on courts that apply the laws fairly. However, it is only when the courts are independent of the other branches of government that they can satisfy the requirement of fairness. An important distinguishing factor among various systems of government is the position they take with respect to judicial independence.

The administration of justice in Hungary before the communist takeover was fairly evenhanded by European standards of democracy, in spite of the fact that the establishment of civil institutions was incomplete. Legal education in Hungary had a long and honorable tradition, and the administration of justice was regulated by modern laws, including the laws governing judicial procedure. However, after World War II, the Hungarian justice system, as it operated vis-à-vis the developed democracies, was destroyed. The damage of those years will take a long time to repair.

Communist dictatorship eradicated judicial independence everywhere it held sway, and—like all totalitarian systems—degraded the administration of justice to an instrument of social oppression and intimidation. Hungary was no exception. There the communists, relying at first on the strength and support of the Soviet occupation army, gradually increased their influence. Then in 1949 they abolished the multiparty system and thereby achieved dominance and introduced a Soviet-style single-party dictatorship.

Very soon they gained control over the courts as well. They got rid of the "bourgeois elements," that is, the judges who were reluctant to serve the interests of those in power, particularly the criminal court judges. The resulting shortage of judges was overcome by the appointment to the bench of young peasants and workers without law degrees, indeed often lacking even secondary school degrees, but loyal to the Communist Party. All that was required of the new appointees was that they complete a training course of a few months.

It was relatively easy to induce these raw but ideologically committed recruits and the intimidated older judges who remained in office to accept the principle that for the courts, the primary source of law resided not in written laws but in a "revolutionary legal awareness of the working people." The administration of justice was proclaimed to be an instrument of class struggle; hence the courts avowedly became a means of terrorization against the class enemy, the former exploiting classes. In practice, the regime would employ judicial terror not only against the so-called exploiters but also against members of the "ruling classes," against workers and peasants, and even against its own loyal supporters. For in fact the ruling minority perceived itself able to maintain its power only through the use of intimidation and terror, and through forcing unconditional obedience from its supporters by periodic decimation of the ranks.

In the years after 1949, an unprecedented campaign was initiated to employ the justice system against anyone who in any manner showed aversion to those in power. Thereafter tens of thousands were sentenced to imprisonment for political reasons every year, and even more were held in internment camps without court order. Spectacular show trials were held, mostly on the basis of trumped-up charges; many people in leading political or business management positions were sentenced to death or imprisonment, and countless ordinary citizens fell victim almost by chance to the machinery of terror. In the more important cases Communist Party officials decided not only who should prosecute and who should try the case, but also what charge should be leveled and what sentence imposed. Even in the smallest provincial towns it was common for local party chiefs to instruct the courts as to precisely what judgment to render in a given case.

Intimidation was used against judges as well. We know of judges who acquitted the accused against Party instructions and were summarily arrested, and later imprisoned. It was a fortunate judge who proved unreliable and was merely discharged from his position. Even so, such a discharge carried grave career consequences: for years the offender was allowed only a blue-collar job, for most employers would not dare employ anyone in disfavor with the political police. In sum, in the years following 1949, judicial independence was for all practical purposes eliminated.

Attorneys also were subject to terror and intimidation. The rights of defendants and their counsel were grossly violated: during a trial, defendant and counsel were often denied access to the documents of investigation, and it was common for defendant and counsel to meet for the first time in the courtroom during the trial. Defense attorneys often were not allowed to confer with their clients or, if so allowed, could meet only in the presence of the investigating officer, who immediately attached a report of the conversation to the case file.

In some cases the charges were made known to the defendant only in the courtroom, and in the so-called accelerated proceedings defendants were convicted and sentenced without the court taking any evidence, solely on the basis of recorded testimony taken during investigations, with no court hearing of witnesses and no opportunity for the defense to present evidence.

Many attorneys were arrested, imprisoned, and expelled from the Chamber of Attorneys simply because they tried to exercise their rights as defense counsel in political trials. The autonomy of chambers of attorneys was abolished, persons serving the interests of the political police were appointed to head them, and all chambers were placed under control of the minister of justice. With opportunities to pursue the legal profession extremely limited, some of the intimidated attorneys proved all too willing to cooperate with the authorities. In one memorable case, for example, an attorney appointed by the court to defend the accused in a major political show trial began his closing argument by saying, "I cannot find words to express my indignation at the depravity of my client."

In political cases, especially, investigators brutally mistreated suspects and often even witnesses, and confessions were elicited through torture and blackmail. Confession so derived was deemed by the court to be sufficient evidence for a judgment of guilt even if the defendant withdrew his confession during the trial on the protest it was made under duress. For the most part, however, the show trial defendants performed during their trials like dutiful pawns, readily confessing to the most absurd charges.

The reason for such behavior becomes clear upon examination of some of the elements of just one case in point: the infamous Standard show trial of 1949. In 1988 this writer, acting as an attorney, initiated the review of that trial, which arose in late 1949, out of criminal proceedings brought against the managers of the Budapest plant of ITT-ISEC (International Telephone and Telegraph Corporation-International Standard Electric Corporation, or Standard, as it was commonly known). The charges were sabotage, espionage, and treason; the proceedings were brought to enable a state takeover of the plant, which was the largest European installation of the American-owned ITT-ISEC. The general manager and a number of his associates were arrested on the concocted charges and convicted in what was to become one of the first major show trials. The general manager and one of his associates were sentenced to death and later executed. The other defendants were sentenced to long terms of imprisonment, and the factory was taken into state ownership.

The case proved a paradigm of show trials. When, after a year of being stalled by officials, this writer was permitted to see the file on the investigation, he got a shock. The file documented the process of constructing false charges with cynical candor, revealing gross legal violations perpetrated by investigators and duly reported to their superiors, and detailing discussions of just what charges against which (clearly innocent) persons might be made to seem most credible.

The notes of one of the investigating officers make it clear that the defendants first denied the acts they were charged with, but after the "harder methods" suggested by a Soviet advisor were employed they broke down and confessed. The harder methods meant physical and mental duress: beatings, starvation, inhumane prison conditions, and threats of the same treatment for family members unless the defendants cooperated. The records of the trial were prepared in advance and taught to the defendants in the form of questions and answers, and several rehearsals were held in the presence of the judge. The presiding judge was prohibited from asking questions not included in the prepared list lest the defendants become confused and depart from the script.

One of the investigating officers warned his superiors after the investigation was completed that the defendants' cooperation in playing their roles could be ensured only if they received continuous harsh treatment during the whole period before the trial. Another investigator suggested that if treatment alternated between extreme harshness and clemency the defendants would be so grateful for the latter they would abandon their opposition completely. One of the defendants, a loyal communist, was made to believe that his death sentence was only a fake, a necessary pretense in the struggle against the American imperialists, that afterward he would be able to work in the Soviet Union for a few years under an alias, and then be freed. But, perhaps just to be on the safe side, this defendant, too, was tortured along with all the others.

In the Standard case the public trial was held in the presence of Western journalists. No one in the audience who was the least bit informed, of course, believed it when the defendants admitted, even asserted their guilt; but part of the public at large was naive enough to be roused to wrath against the defendants, while another part was intimidated by the whole display.

There were relatively few show trials, and they were conducted as a sort of theater performance. Most of the political cases, however, were dealt with in secret hearings with the public completely excluded. It was quite common for people simply to disappear. Quite often even the closest relatives of those taken away had no information as to why their loved ones were arrested and what was their subsequent fate. Not only was no information given out, but those who tried to make inquiries were threatened and relatives of those who had disappeared were fired from their jobs as "hostile elements" and forced to move to places far away from the cities. In many cases it was only years, sometimes many years, later that relatives learned about the secret trials.

In June of 1953, when the reform communist Imre Nagy was appointed prime minister of Hungary, the central leadership of the Hungarian Workers' Party brought a historic resolution. That resolution acknowledged that unlawful proceedings had been conducted for years and show trials had been based on trumped-up charges, and it ordered the review of about three hundred trials. As a statement of policy change, the resolution is on a par with the famous address by Nikita Khrushchev in February 1956 to the Twentieth Congress of the Communist Party of the Soviet Union. However, since in the Hungarian case it was not a mere few dozen communist leaders declared responsible for the violations but also a vast apparatus, the conservative forces within the party managed to prevent publication of the full document until 1989, and after 1956 the process of reviewing the trials ground to a halt. In 1962 a few more cases were reviewed, but it was only in 1989 that the work of review was generally resumed.

Until 1989 communist leaders spoke in generalities and euphemisms about "victims of the cult of personality," that is, about persons convicted and sentenced in the preconceived trials and in political trials in general, but actually only a very few of those victims had been rehabilitated and then only partially.

After June 1953 legality improved to some extent, to be sure. The survivors of the major show trials were—with little publicity, almost surreptitiously—released from prison. A few dozen judgments, mostly those brought against communist leaders on the basis of concocted charges, also were reviewed formally, and the defendants were acquitted, but this was done without publicity. And even after the reformer Imre Nagy was ousted from office by orthodox Muscovites in the spring of 1955, an increasing dissatisfaction among the population together with Soviet advisement of caution had the effect of discouraging show trials, and actually allowing the review of preconceived trials to continue, albeit with some reluctance.

II

The Hungarian communist policy of administering justice after 1956 differed significantly from the policy before that date. Both policies became milder with the passage of time: in the first case the softening came after 1953; in the second, from the mid-1960s onward. The first period, the Stalinist era, began with an appalling number of politically motivated trials. Between 1949 and 1953, in a country of ten million, as specified in the June 1953 resolution, courts rendered some 280,000 judgments purely on the basis of political considerations. It was common for people to be convicted and sentenced for events that never took place, on the basis of wholly fabricated evidence. The primary aim of these trials was intimidation to enforce social compliance.

After 1956 the political aim was different, and accordingly the political methods were different, too. Now the main aim was retribution. The communist leaders, the investigators of the secret political police, and the procurators and judges controlled by them attacked with uncontrolled fury those who had participated in the revolution. Many of the avengers were motivated by the personal fear and humiliation they suffered during the days of revolution when they hid to save their lives or perhaps faced an angry crowd directly. The whole machinery of terror was directed against those who had participated in any way in the revolution. However, the earlier practice of imprisoning Communist Party members on false charges in the interest of general discipline was not resumed.

The Executive Committee of the Hungarian Socialist Workers Party (HSWP)—the inner circle of Hungarian communist leaders—dealt with the issue of reprisal for participation in the revolution in a secret meeting on April 2, 1957. At that meeting János Kádár declared: "Taking the experience of the past into account, we must not invent anything, we must take facts known to hundreds of thousands as a point of departure." The reason was quite clear: in 1953 the trade secrets behind the unlawful proceedings had been exposed (they were already known to a major part of society in any case, thanks to the great numbers who had experienced them at first hand), and then, in the summer of 1956, a few of the earlier show trials were publicly reviewed and the violations of law acknowledged. Thus, for example, László Rajk, the one-time communist minister of the interior, who was executed in 1949, and his associates were posthumously acquitted, and it was admitted that they had been tried on spurious charges and convicted and sentenced on the basis of confessions obtained by torture. Their ceremonial reburial on October 6, 1956, just two weeks before the outbreak of the revolution, had occasioned a demonstration by a crowd of a hundred thousand. János Kádár knew perfectly well that even his own followers would be reluctant to endorse the earlier methods. This self-restraint, of course, did not mean that the courtrooms became temples of Justitia. The old violations of law flourished in other forms: where once masses of people were convicted on the basis of information that was wholly fabricated, now factual information was distorted and, on the basis of distorted facts, false inferences were made as to the aspirations of the defendants and the role they played in events. Thus, for example, if a man had made a speech to an angry crowd during the days of the revolution with the intent of calming the participants, and if criticism of the communist regime had been a part of the speech, in a fortunate case he might be sentenced to several years in prison for inciting a riot; in a less fortunate case he would be sentenced to death for "active participation in a conspiracy aimed at subverting the people's democratic order of state." A number of highly regarded people were executed on such charges.

János Kádár, who was one of the many Hungarian communist leaders with personal experience of the prisons of the Stalinist period, tried fervently to make society and the world believe that the regime after 1956 was not the same as the Stalinist system obtaining before the revolution. In fact, the most compromised of the local Stalinist leaders disappeared from the political scene after 1956 (they had to emigrate to Moscow, for, owing to their unpopularity, the Soviets thought them unsuitable for any further political role at home), but the machinery of oppression was the same as that of the early 1950s.

The crushing of the revolution was followed by an unprecedented wave of reprisals, in spite of János Kádár's repeated promises of immunity for the participants of the revolution. The courts sentenced more than 22,000 people to imprisonment, and even greater numbers were interned, or kept in confinement for a varying periods without any court order. More than 300 people were executed without any court sentence. Many revolutionaries were arrested and executed on the spot by the Soviets. We know from the records of cemeteries in Budapest that more than 1,200 people died from acts of violence during the fighting.

It was also a form of reprisal that masses of people were fired from their jobs for their participation in the revolutionary events; for years thereafter these people could not find jobs suited to their skills. Students were expelled from colleges and universities. More than two hundred thousand people fled the country, many of them solely to escape the reprisals.

Particularly during the first period and mostly in the provinces, arrested persons were brutally abused and usually not even a semblance of legality was observed. Any critical or anticommunist remark made during the days of the revolution was sufficient grounds to be called to account. Hundreds of thousands felt unsafe.

Most of the retaliatory cases were tried by the courts in utmost secrecy: in many cases the relatives were not told why a defendant was sentenced to death and executed; they were merely informed of the fact. Many of them learned only in 1989 precisely what charge formed the basis for the death sentence and execution of a relative. The possibility of viewing the file of the deceased opened only in the spring of 1989.

To illustrate the arbitrary way in which courts dealt with ordinary citizens, let us consider the case of Géza Pásztor, a young worker who was sentenced to life imprisonment for complicity in murder. He served twenty years in prison and, as a consequence of the brutalities he suffered during the investigation, was released as an invalid. According to the accusation this young worker, a member of the armed national guard during the revolution, took part in arresting a relatively unknown, low-ranking communist functionary and escorting him to a police station. According to the accusation and the judgment, the arrested functionary had "obviously" been executed subsequently. The court accepted as fact the assumption contained in the accusation and, without any further evidence, convicted Pásztor. It could not be clarified who initiated the arrest, or who asked the young national guardsman, on the scene by chance, to help escort the prisoner to the police station. Although the identity of the "victim" was known, the court did not attempt, despite repeated motions by the defendant and his counsel, to clarify what had happened to the prisoner. In 1990, in the process of reviewing the case, this writer determined without difficulty from the central records of the police that the "victim" defected to the West in January 1957. The judgment was brought by the same People's Court division, Dr. Ferenc Vida presiding, that would convict Imre Nagy and his associates. Dozens of similarly baseless judgments came to light in 1989 and 1990.

Young soldiers and workers were sentenced with particular harshness; indeed, these occupations accounted for the majority of those executed. The smaller number of intellectuals who took part in the fighting, as well as others who were relatively knowledgeable and informed, were better equipped to present an effective defense.

When it was proved of someone that he had participated in armed combat, or he admitted participation, the sentence, usually a death sentence, was imposed for attempted murder, even if there was no proof that he had so much as inflicted a wound. There were soldiers attached to organized units who were ordered by their commanding officers to engage in armed resistance at the beginning of the Soviet invasion. Almost without exception these soldiers were executed.

By a policy unprecedented in the history of civilized states, the burial place of the executed was kept secret from relatives. At sites where it was possible to guess from certain rumors that executed persons lay buried, as happened in the case of Lot No. 301 of the New Public Cemetery in Budapest, relatives who tended the presumed graves were harassed by the police until the late 1980s. The tributes left at the graves were destroyed and the visitors were pestered.

This writer headed the section of the Historical Justice Committee that was granted official permission to search for the graves and to disinter and identify the victims. Masses of relatives requested the identification and decent reburial of the remains.

III

It is worthwhile to take a look at how those in power tried to facilitate the work of the apparatus of reprisal.

Law Decree No. 28, entering into force on December 11, 1956, and Decree No. 6/1956 (XII.11) Korm. introduced the so-called summary court process. Courts following the summary process were attached to the military courts and empowered to bring judgment within seventy-two hours after the arrest of the defendant in cases involving a serious crime against public order and security and in cases involving possession of firearms or ammunition without a license. The charge was presented orally by the procurator who collected the evidence, and the court imposed a sentence of either death or life imprisonment. In cases involving juveniles it was possible to impose lighter sentences; for example, in the case of one Peter Mansfeld, an apprentice arrested for participating in armed fighting, the court postponed final sentencing until the defendant reached the age of majority, for the death penalty could not be imposed on a person under eighteen.

In death penalty cases these special proceedings also allowed the same judge who pronounced sentence on a defendant to decide upon any subsequent petition for clemency. According to the constitution, in regular proceedings a decision on clemency in the case of a death sentence belonged within the competence of the Presidential Council of the Hungarian People's Republic, a body acting for the head of state. Thus the summary court provision on the right of granting clemency was unconstitutional from the outset.

On January 15, 1957, Law Decree No. 4/1957, on accelerated proceedings, entered into force. It contained provisions similar to those of the statute on summary proceedings, but extended the scope of special competence of the court to include cases of conspiracy against the state, mutiny, and treason, and the rules became applicable by courts outside the military as well.

On March 22, 1957, the Penal College of the Supreme Court (the body of judges who dealt with criminal cases tried before the Supreme Court), took a position concerning the interpretation of the radio address of November 4, 1956, at the beginning of the second Soviet invasion, in which János Kádár had promised immunity for the participants in the events if they would lay down their arms. The Penal College found that Kádár's statement could not be considered even as a mitigating determinant in individual cases since it did not constitute a declaration of amnesty, for an amnesty could be declared only by the collective head of state, the Presidential Council.

On April 6, 1957, Law Decree No. 25/1957, on the establishment of the People's Court Division of the Supreme Court, entered into force. This court division, composed of four lay people's judges and one professional judge, was accorded a special competence to conduct trials under the rules of the accelerated penal proceedings, and its judgments could not be appealed. The people's judges were to be "elected" by the collective head of state, the Presidential Council; in fact they were nominated by the political police and the party leadership.

The People's Court Division did not operate in its original form for long, for on June 15, 1957, Law Decree No. 34/1957, concerning "People's Court Divisions and the regulation of certain issues of the judicial organization and criminal procedure," entered into force. This decree ordered the institution of People's Court Divisions at all county courts as well as at the Supreme Court level, authorizing the use of the rules of accelerated proceedings by every division. In addition, fundamental changes were introduced to the code of criminal procedure. For the appellate process, in the case of a first-instance judgment brought by a People's Court, the modification rendered ineffective the criminal law provision on the prohibition of reformation *in peius*, according to which an appellate court could not impose a more severe penalty in a case where a defendant or his counsel merely appealed for a lighter sentence. In the People's Court proceedings there were some tragic cases in which a defense counsel appealed a first-instance judgment in order to gain a reduced sentence for a client only to have the People's Court Division of the Supreme Court impose a more severe sentence—the death penalty.

The right of defendants to choose their own defense counsel also was restricted. From that time on, before military courts and in cases of political significance as determined by the minister of the interior and the minister of justice, only attorneys whose names appeared on a list approved by the minister of justice could act as defense counsel. These restrictions on choice of defense counsel remained in force until the end of the 1980s. During the last years of the regime many lawyers of undeniable integrity had their names entered into the list, but in the initial period only those loyal to the regime were allowed to act in political trials.

The great wave of reprisal came to an end in August 1962. At that time the leaders most compromised by their activities before 1956 (Mátyás Rákosi and his associates) were expelled from the Communist Party, and at the same time the political police investigators who had committed the gravest violations of law before the revolution were also dismissed from service. The Kádár leadership gradually consolidated their positions after crushing the revolution, and the more secure they felt in their power the less repressive the system became. Political prisoners sentenced to relatively short terms were granted reduced sentences through amnesty as early as 1959 and 1960. A major general amnesty was declared in March 1963: all persons imprisoned after 1956 were released with the exception of those sentenced for murder or treason. (It is another story that many of those imprisoned for murder or treason had been convicted on totally unfounded and arbitrary grounds.)

The 1963 amnesty was motivated primarily by foreign policy considerations. After 1956, the U.N. General Assembly kept the "Hungarian Question," that is, the crushing of the revolution and the unprecedented reprisals that followed, on its agenda for consideration and debate before the world forum. The aim of the regime was to remove this embarrassing issue from the U.N. agenda. For this reason, when the general amnesty was declared the secretary general of the U.N. was invited to Hungary to check on its implementation.

From the mid-1960s, the communist leadership that bore the hallmark of János Kádár made strenuous efforts to achieve peace at home and respect abroad. This is why the "soft dictatorship" that ensured a privileged position for Hungarian society within the Soviet bloc gradually came into existence. Hungary became "the most cheerful barrack in the camp." But the machinery for the administration of justice remained unchanged, even though some personnel changes were effected. Thus, for instance, around the mid-1960s the unschooled cadre-judges were obliged to enroll in law school correspondence courses to get their law degrees, and those unable to meet the requirements were removed from the judiciary. Professionalism was gradually gaining place in judicial work. But the old reflexes did not disappear. Those in power could not give up their old habits.

Although in decreasing numbers, there still were political trials, conducted, if possible, with the exclusion of the public, in the greatest possible secrecy. For example, in 1968, János Radványi, former Hungarian ambassador to Washington, was secretly tried and convicted in absentia and sentenced to death for espionage and treason. Back in 1962 he had mediated between the Hungarian state and party leadership on the one hand, and the U.S. State Department officials on the other, in order to remove the so-called Hungarian Question from the U.N. agenda. Radványi brought assurance from the Kádár government that those political prisoners who were jailed after the crushing of the 1956 revolution will get amnesty. In exchange the Americans promised to exercise influence at the U.N. General Assembly to end the yearly recurring debate on the Hungarian Question and to get Hungary's credentials at the world body recognized. Radványi's action was successful. Nevertheless, he later was suspected of espionage and treason by the orthodox communist leaders, and was recalled to Budapest for "consultation." In the meantime, however, he cut his ties with the Kádár regime, and attained asylum in the United States. It was only in 1990 that he found out he had been under sentence of death in Hungary for more than twenty years. (in 1990, the case was reviewed by the Supreme Court and János Radványi was acquitted on a finding of absence of criminal offense.)

IV

One can learn a lot about the nature of the system from the way its evaluation of the revolution and the role of Imre Nagy and his associates changed over time and from the eventual rationale behind its decision to review the Nagy trial.

For more than twenty-five years after the judgment and sentencing in the trial of Imre Nagy were made public, those in power would speak of Nagy only in tones of vituperation. The *samizdat* publications present in Hungary in ever-increasing numbers from the late 1970s dealt more and more with the role of Imre Nagy and his associates in the revolution, and foreign publications on the revolution in numbers sufficient to fill whole libraries were also finding their way into the country. In such circumstances, those who represented the regime found it necessary to come up with some more refined value judgments.

The first to do so was János Berecz, one of the key figures of the HSWP leadership, who, at a television roundtable conference on the thirtieth anniversary of the revolution, characterized Imre Nagy not as a conscious counterrevolutionary but as someone who had been caught up by events against his own intentions and, in the final analysis, played a counterrevolutionary role. This represented a considerable change from earlier assessments, particularly the one included in the court judgment. It was, however, out of the question that the idea of reviewing the case could be officially raised, or that any of the interested parties could be allowed to inspect the records of the trial.

The activities of the democratic opposition in Hungary increased gradually from the early 1980s on. Members of the opposition made an attempt at a fair and objective assessment of the 1956 revolution through occasional improvised university lectures and organized conferences held in private homes. It was a momentous event when at a conference, in addition to other items on the agenda, Ferenc Donáth or Miklós Vásárhelyi or Árpád Göncz (Göncz, now the president of the republic, had been sentenced to life imprisonment after 1956) was scheduled to describe his personal memories of the revolution and the trials. During those years dedicated historians and sociologists systematically interviewed surviving participants and eyewitnesses of the revolution lest they carry their knowledge of the events to the grave.

In January 1988, Miklós Vásárhelyi, the single co-defendant in the Nagy trial still living in Hungary at the time, attempted to initiate a retrial of the Imre Nagy case with the assistance of this writer. After several months of stalling, the authorities still refused to permit him to see the records of the case or even the judgment convicting him. Their only concession was to allow him to read a short summary of the judgment prepared for the purpose by one of the Supreme Court judges. The summary included the most important elements of the judgment relating to Miklós Vásárhelyi but in mere outline form. Eventually Vásárhelyi's petition for retrial was denied by the Supreme Court, and the Presidential Division of the Supreme Court dismissed his appeal against that decision in late 1988. By the time of the appellate decision, however, Károly Grósz, then first secretary of the HSWP, had already promised that the reburial of Imre Nagy and his associates would be allowed.

Like many other martyrs of the revolution, Imre Nagy and four of his co-defendants were secretly buried after their execution, and the efforts of their relatives to ascertain the precise location of their graves remained unsuccessful for thirty years. It was only on the basis of vague rumors that graves believed to be theirs were located and tended by the bereaved, and then the secret political police destroyed the visitors' tributes and tried to obliterate even the slightest traces of the graves. The growing number of visitors at the cemeteries on the anniversaries of the revolution were routinely harassed by the police from the late 1970s onward.

June 16, 1988, was an important date in the history of the growing protest: hundreds of demonstrators went on an organized pilgrimage to the presumed graves of the executed. The police had learned of the preparations for the demonstration, and warned the organizers repeatedly, finally hinting that although a commemoration within the cemetery wall would not be interfered with, any incident outside the wall would be prevented. For they also knew that demonstrations were planned not only at the grave sites but also in the center of the city at the memorial to the executed prime minister of the revolution of 1848, Lajos Batthyány, which was situated about two hundred meters from the parliament building.

Hours before the planned event hundreds of police blocked the targeted areas and the surrounding streets. Nevertheless, several hundred citizens advanced to hold the ceremony. Police assaulted the demonstrators, who had swelled to some two thousand people, and who protected the speakers with their own bodies. The demonstration moved on to the television building, then to downtown Vörösmarty Square, where it was finally dispersed by brutal police action. Several organizers and participants were arrested. (It must be added that the arrested persons were released the same evening and no criminal proceedings were initiated against them.)

The establishment of the Historical Justice Committee (HJC) on June 5, 1988, was another major element in the chain of events. The HJC was composed of relatives of those executed in connection with the Imre Nagy trial, surviving co-defendants, and a group of intellectuals who had suffered imprisonment after 1956. At that time the organization was established informally with the single public demand that the reburial of the executed should be permitted and their role in the revolution reassessed.

A month later, in July 1988, the HJC legally and formally transformed itself into an association and formulated its demands more broadly and explicitly: it demanded exploration and disclosure of all politically motivated legal violations perpetrated by the authorities after 1945, and legal, moral, and political restitution for all those persecuted by these violations. A copy of the association's demands was sent to every member of the government and every member of the National Assembly. The authorities forbore to recognize the existence of the organization until January 1989, and no newspaper was allowed to write about it. Meanwhile, the organization on behalf of and in cooperation with the relatives began a campaign to have the remains of Imre Nagy and his associates unearthed and ceremonially and publicly reburied.

When the HJC gained official recognition in January 1989, it was acknowledged as a negotiating party and allowed to publish notices in the form of paid advertising to offer its services in locating the graves of persons executed in the reprisals after 1956 and unearthing and identifying the remains. An astounding number of relatives came forward, and they were interested not only in the location of the graves and the reburial of the dead but also in learning the reasons for the executions and seeing the trial records.

Half a year passed after Károly Grósz made his promises concerning the burials of Imre Nagy and his co-defendants before their relatives were officially informed that the reburial would be permitted. This time the authorities acceded to the wish of the relatives and the HJC that the burial should take place publicly, on June 16, 1989, the thirty-first anniversary of the execution. The cause for the delayed permission came to light only during the disinterment process: it was a serious question where the graves were located because no written records were available; hence the young investigators appointed to locate them were at a loss. Those who had been involved in the burials were either dead or claimed to know nothing. After more than half a year of investigation, however, the circumstances of the executions and the burials came to light.

The executions were carried out in the early hours of June 16, 1958, in a section of the largest Budapest prison, the so-called Transit Detention House, where all executions in Budapest at that time took place. Before the execution, strict regulations were introduced in order to limit to an absolute minimum the number of people who would know what was happening. The bodies of the executed were placed in primitive coffins and buried at the scene, next to the gallows, in the yard of the so-called Small Detention House.

For reasons still unknown, one night in 1961 the coffins were unearthed in utmost secrecy and immediately reburied in Lot No. 301 of the neighboring New Public Cemetery, the usual burial site for executed convicts or deceased prisoners whose bodies remained unclaimed by relatives. This also was the place of interment for dead animals from the zoo. Lot No. 301 was situated in the remotest corner of the cemetery, in an area overgrown with brush and weeds and for the next thirty years deliberately left so. The cemetery records revealed fictitious names for the human remains buried there. The investigators were helped in their search when by chance they located a retired cemetery worker who in turn had heard a prison guard talk of knowing where Imre Nagy was buried. The worker had memorized the location. Eventually—after many false starts—the likely graves of Imre Nagy, Géza Losonczy, Pál Maléter, and Miklós Gimes were determined and the disinterred remains were positively identified by medical experts and anthropologists using the most modern scientific methods. The exhumation took place in April 1989.

It was characteristic of the political conditions of the time that some of those present at the exhumation, including this writer acting as the head of the legal section of the HJC and as attorney for the relatives, received threatening phone calls from anonymous night callers.

In the chain of the events it was a momentous development when, in February 1989, Imre Pozsgay, then a minister without portfolio, a member of the leading body of the HSWP, and the head of the committee appointed to evaluate the previous historical period, declared that the events of October 1956 were to be considered a justified "popular uprising" and not a "counterrevolution." Although numerous publications by historians and publicists had earlier challenged the official position on the revolution of 1956, Pozsgay's announcement came as a surprise, and its effect was sensational.

The pace of events speeded up. Soon it was admitted that the outcome of the trial of Nagy and his associates had been preconceived by the prosecution, and the leading body of the HSWP ordered a review of the case. Party Secretary General Károly Grósz, however, declared with special emphasis that in his opinion, the review should not be taken as a de facto political rehabilitation of Nagy and the others. This assertion drew an enormous public uproar, which caused the secretary general to reconsider his position. Finally, Grósz announced on television that the judicial review of the trial would have to be completed before the solemn funeral service took place on June 16. In May the documents of the case, top-secret until then, were declassified and from that time on available to the relatives, the survivors, and their attorneys.

V

From the documents published in this volume, the reader may learn what charges and what circumstances led the court to convict and sentence Imre Nagy and his associates after the revolution had been crushed, and what considerations led the court thirty years later to declare their innocence. The judgment of acquittal analyzes the violations of law in the judgment of 1958 in great detail. Still, it is not without interest to go beyond the judgment of acquittal and to survey some elements of the trial and the 1957-1958 investigation which do not come to light in the present documents.

On November 3, Pál Maléter, the minister of defense in the Nagy government, was at the Soviet headquarters in Tököl negotiating with the Soviet command for the withdrawal of Soviet troops from Hungary. It was a surprise even to his Soviet counterpart, a general, when in the middle of negotiations conducted in a cordial atmosphere, General Serov, the omnipotent KGB chief, rushed into the conference room with a detachment of heavily armed soldiers and arrested Maléter and the members of his delegation.

On November 4, 1956, in the early hours of the day of the decisive second Soviet invasion, Prime Minister Imre Nagy protested against the Soviet occupation in a radio address, asked for the help of the free world, and then, accepting the Yugoslav offer, sought political asylum together with some of his close associates at the Yugoslav Embassy in Budapest. Among the associates who fled to the embassy and remained there with Nagy until November 22 were Ferenc Donáth, Miklós Vásárhelyi, József Szilágyi, and Géza Losonczy, all of whom would be named co-defendants in the coming trial.

The embassy building was immediately surrounded by Soviet tanks in a move to put pressure on the Yugoslavs and their entourage to force Nagy and his associates to leave the compound. Thereafter the embassy was subjected to a veritable blockade: those who tried to enter were insulted, several of them even arrested, and the building was fired upon (one embassy official was killed). Finally, the Yugoslav and Hungarian governments reached an agreement whereby Nagy and his associates and their family members would be allowed to leave the compound and return to their homes unharmed.

On November 22 a bus arrived to take them home. The bus containing Nagy and his group was stopped by the Soviets as it pulled out of the compound. Yugoslav diplomats who protested were manhandled, and the Hungarian group was taken to the Soviet-held Mátyásföld barracks near Budapest, where they were detained as prisoners. At the barracks attempts were made to persuade the prisoners to cooperate with János Kádár in return for immunity from prosecution, and to induce Imre Nagy to officially resign as prime minister. After these attempts failed, on the next day, November 23, Nagy and several of his associates and their families were deported to Snagov, Romania.

The Soviets and the Hungarian internal security forces soon arrested Sándor Kopácsi and Miklós Gimes as well. Zoltán Tildy and Ferenc Jánosi were arrested much later, obviously as a result of a later decision.

During the first few weeks after November 4, arrests were made mostly by Soviet military police, and the military prison in Gyorskocsi Street also was controlled by them. During that period the guards and the interrogators as well were mostly Soviets. It was only gradually, in early 1957, that the Soviets let the newly organized Hungarian political investigative apparatus and guards take over these tasks. But Soviet advisors remained and operated in the prison building. Some sources have suggested that Soviet advisors played a role in directing the investigation against Imre Nagy and his associates. Although we have no written documents confirming this supposition, such had been the practice in earlier years. By now it is common knowledge that the Soviet advisors had offices in the building of the political police, but the documentary evidence of their operations was carefully removed and destroyed. (Similarly, although the records of the investigation in the above-mentioned Standard case of 1949 contain numerous references to consultations with Soviet advisors, there is no more direct evidence of their activities in those documents, either.)

As György Litván notes in his analysis (see pp. 369-370), it was entirely on the basis of political considerations that the authorities decided who would be the co-defendants in the Imre Nagy trial. The actual activities of the defendants in the case were not so closely connected as to justify bringing them to court together, for more than one of them had much looser revolutionary connections with Nagy than many others who were called to account in separate trials. Obviously, the case of Imre Nagy was originally intended to be a show trial and the defendants were selected as representatives of the various circles that were seen as responsible.

It is interesting to note that the investigations against General Pál Maléter and Chief of Police Sándor Kopácsi were completed quickly, and the act of accusation against them was filed with the Budapest Military Court as early as February 28, 1957. The court actually set their trial date for March 8. The trial, however, was not to be held, because one of the political police investigators removed all the records of the case from the court, leaving only one copy of the written act of accusation in the court file. The other records disappeared.

János Kádár repeatedly declared that no criminal proceedings would be brought against Imre Nagy and his associates for their activities. It is known, however, that during March 21-27, 1957, when Kádár visited Moscow, he had a personal conference with Nikita Khrushchev and they agreed that Nagy and his group would be put on trial. On March 27 and during the following days, the defendants were arrested in Snagov and taken into custody. At first they were held in a prison in Bucharest. Then, on April 17, 1957, they were secretly flown to Budapest, where they were kept in solitary confinement in the prison on Gyorskocsi Street for eleven months.

Meanwhile, an amazingly large investigative force carried out the investigation. In the first half of 1957 the investigation churned out more than one hundred thousand pages, forming eighty-three volumes, which would constitute the dossier for the trial. The inquiries extended not only to the defendants in the Nagy trial but to all the leaders of the revolution, that is, to all the more important political figures.

It was the political police who decided who the co-defendants in each political trial should be. In each case they made "recommendations" as to when, against whom, and for what offense an accusation should be preferred. They also named the judge, the lay assessors, the procurator, and the court clerk, and in most cases they even determined where and when the trial should be held (supplying the exact address of the court building and the number of the courtroom). In their recommendations the investigators more than once explained why a certain judge would be best for a particular case. The courts followed these recommendations without exception. In each case, during the whole trial, the political police investigators were present: they wrote reports for their superiors of everything said during the trial, and in such a report one can also find remarks by a superior, in more important cases by the minister of the interior, showing the date (usually soon after the trial) when that official saw the report. More than once an investigator assessed the work of a judge, reporting on how well he performed his job.

The interrogation of the defendants went on endlessly. Each of the defendants in the Imre Nagy case was questioned dozens of times. The records from the interrogations of Imre Nagy alone account for several hundred pages, and there were numberless confrontations. The aim was to obtain from each defendant statements detrimental to the other defendants, and in connection with those statements to order new confrontations that would turn the defendants against one another. To overcome the resistance of the defendants by physical and psychological means was the obvious goal. Imre Nagy and József Szilágyi protested repeatedly and forcefully against the boorish tone and the generally harsh treatment employed during the investigations. Fragments of a documentary film that have been found show clearly that the defendants grew thin and their physical state deteriorated during the period before the trial. From the way the questions of the interrogators were formulated it is clear that the investigating officers acted with undisguised hatred and hostility toward the subjects.

The records of the interrogations are relatively accurate; that is, they contain more or less what the defendants were allowed to say, because otherwise they would have refused to sign. And for the investigators, only signed records had any value.

We know of physical abuse only in the case of Géza Losonczy, who in consequence succumbed in prison on December 21, 1957. The medical records and the autopsy report made accessible in 1989 render the fact of physical abuse in this case indisputable. Losonczy suffered a complete nervous breakdown with manifest symptoms of psychosis. He accused himself of acts against imaginary persons, his behavior was unmanageably erratic, and it was clear that no court judgment could be based on his statements. When he went on a hunger strike he was brutally punished. Several of his ribs were broken; he died while being force-fed.

The investigation essentially was completed during the first days of August 1957. No interrogations of any importance were conducted after that. In fact, the chief investigator prepared a very lengthy written act of accusation dated August 17, 1957, which lacks only the signature of the procurator. In that document Géza Losonczy is named as defendant no. 2. Obviously there were political reasons for not sending the records of the completed investigation to the court for almost half a year. The summer of 1957 was not seen by the communist leaders as an apt time for the trial of Imre Nagy to be accepted by the party and by society. The tone of the official statements concerning Nagy's role was changing along with the increasing consolidation of the position of the leadership. At the beginning, János Kádár had promised immunity from prosecution for Nagy and his associates, and then gradually stressed more and more the responsibility, later even the guilt of Imre Nagy. Finally, at a session of the Central Committee of the HSWP on December 21, 1957, he proposed that "the legal process must be allowed to take its unhampered course" against those arrested. At that meeting the Central Committee agreed that the Imre Nagy case should go to trial. It was a coincidence that Géza Losonczy died that very day. Still, a new written act of accusation had to be prepared. The new document, dated January 28, 1958, is a largely verbatim version of the one dated August 17, 1957. In place of the deceased Géza Losonczy, however, General Béla Király, the commander of the national guard, who by that time was living abroad as an emigrant, is named as defendant no. 2.

According to the trial records, proceedings in the case of Imre Nagy and his associates started on February 5, 1957, with the separation of the case of General Béla Király, commander of the national guard, who had fled abroad. Under the code of criminal procedure this meant that the court would try the case of Béla Király separately at a later time. As it turned out, the accusation against Király was never tried. The reason is not known, but one may make an assumption. In 1952, Király had been sentenced on first instance to death, on appeal to life imprisonment, on a conviction of espionage and an offense against the state. He was released from prison in the fall of 1956. When he was subsequently appointed commander of the national guard by Imre Nagy, the Supreme Court, on a remedial petition by the procurator general, acquitted him of the 1952 charges. Then in January 1957, the procurator general filed a remedial petition against the judgment of acquittal. On the basis of that petition the Supreme Court, relying on procedural errors, declared the acquittal decision null and void and brought the judgment of 1952 back into force. At any rate, in the fall of 1989 the procurator general closed down the proceedings against Király, which had been interrupted in February 1957, by terminating the investigation owing to an absence of criminal offense. (It is a separate issue, but worth mentioning, that it was on the initiative of this writer that the procurator general filed a remedial petition for the second time against the judgment brought in 1952 in the case of Béla Király; on the basis of that petition the Supreme Court again acquitted Király for the absence of any criminal offense. But on June 16, 1989, when Király delivered his address at the reburial ceremony for Nagy and the others, there was still a valid sentence of life imprisonment outstanding against him—only he did not know about it. He did not learn until the fall of 1989 that the judgment of 1952 had been brought back into force in January 1957.)

According to the code of criminal procedure in force in 1958, a prepared act of accusation had to be presented to the court together with the dossier of the investigation. It was after this requirement was satisfied that the president of the court appointed the presiding trial judge. The written act of accusation in the Imre Nagy case was dated January 28, 1958, but the first court hearing was set for February 5 and 6, 1958. It was between those dates—January 28 and February 5—that the accusation had to be presented, the presiding judge and the other members of the panel assigned, and the documents of the investigation studied by the assigned judges. Hungarian criminal procedure employs the principle of judicial examination, whereby it is the presiding judge and not the procurator or defense counsel who first examines the defendants and the witnesses; thus the judge must know well the facts and findings of the investigation in order to be able to ask questions. Given the more than one hundred thousand pages contained in the investigation document, it is evident there was no chance for the judiciary panel to study the material properly in the time allotted. Rather, the investigative authority had to "prepare" the presiding judge, calling his attention to those parts most useful to him. The presiding judge was Dr. Zoltán Radó. He presided over the trial only on February 5 and 6, 1958. On February 6, the trial was adjourned, and when it was continued in June 1958, Dr. Ferenc Vida presided. It is noteworthy that in 1989 the widow of the since-deceased Dr. Radó told representatives of the press that her husband had himself been a victim of unlawful trials, because he had been forced to try the Imre Nagy case and certain others that put him under so much stress he suffered a heart attack and died.

In February 1958 the trial began in utmost secrecy. It became known only years later, after Miklós Vásárhelyi and Ferenc Donáth were released from prison, that it was abruptly interrupted on February 6 and resumed only in June. Until 1990, the reason for the interruption was a subject of speculation. But from the documents now accessible we know that on February 6, at the request of János Kádár, the Central Committee of the HSWP ordered the interruption because the Soviet leaders thought a trial of Imre Nagy would jeopardize the chances of a Soviet-initiated East-West summit. For this reason, to the great glory of judicial independence, the party leadership decided the trial was to be adjourned indefinitely.

The majority of the witnesses interrogated during the investigation and heard during the trial were themselves in jail either under arrest or serving sentences. More than once the timing of events was calculated to ensure that a person was called to testify as a witness just a few days before the scheduled date of his own trial. The witnesses were given to understand that by incriminating others they might improve their own situation.

The trial was held in the political police prison building on Gyorskocsi Street.

A special trial room was built for the purpose, with very tight security to ensure secrecy. One political police technician who learned by chance that the trial of Imre Nagy was in progress was sent to prison for years because no one felt confident of his discretion.

Only attorneys registered on a special list could serve as defense counsel. They were not allowed to leave the court building for the duration of the trial. They were instructed to tell their relatives and partners that they would be out of town on a case for several days. They were prohibited from carrying any document related to the case out of the courtroom, and they were not allowed to enter the case into their own office records. Even the notes they took during the trial were confiscated. Each of them was given a notebook with his name on it to be used for taking notes; the attorneys' notebooks are still attached to the court file.

However, for complete veracity, one exception must be reported. Nagy and his family insisted that instead of the appointed attorney, Dr. Imre Bárd should act in Imre Nagy's defense, and with considerable reluctance the authorities agreed. Dr. Bárd, whose name was on the approved list, acted with complete dedication and perfect integrity. As is borne out by the records of the trial, he used every possible argument for his client and did everything a bona fide professional could do in this sort of case. The outcome can in no way be blamed on him. Indeed, Imre Bárd was so shattered by the experience that a few days after the trial ended he had a heart attack and died.

The conduct of the trial was arbitrary in the extreme. The presiding judge severely limited the opportunities for the defense to prevent its case. But it was in the preparation of the record of the trial that the court showed itself most egregiously unfair. According to the law of criminal procedure, the record of a trial does not need to be signed by the defendant, only by the members of the court and the record keeper, and the record need not provide a complete verbatim transcript of all utterances made during the trial. But what happened in this case is unbelievable. The hearings were fully recorded on tape and a shorthand record also was taken. Neither the tapes nor the shorthand records are now available in full. But the typed transcript from the tape recordings is available, and it is almost complete (the statements of several defendants made on the right of last word are missing even here). In the preparation of the official trial record, the transcript was carefully edited in two phases: long parts were left out, and certain other parts were altered through rephrasing. As a result of such editorial changes, Nagy's statements of June 9, 1958, which, together with his statements made on February 5, account for fifty-one pages in the tape transcript, have been reduced to only three and a half pages in the final record. The statements of the other defendants were similarly hacked and twisted before they were put into the final record. As a consequence, in certain passages it is difficult to determine what any defendant said at any given point in the proceedings.

We need to say a few words about the deportment of the defendants during the trial. Imre Nagy and József Szilágyi maintained they were not guilty throughout the trial and tried to refute the charges with admirable perseverance. Neither of them could have had any illusion as to their fate. Indeed, Nagy had already made it clear in memoirs he wrote while in Snagov that he knew what to expect and he did not want to do anything to avoid it. Reading his statements during the proceedings, one has the impression he was speaking not so much to the investigators or the court as to posterity. His reasoning was realistic, sound, and professorial precise. He remained calm at all times, his manner polite and dignified, even when addressing the judges who displayed such prejudice and malevolence toward him. He had the strength to explain with dignity after the judgment was pronounced why he would not ask for clemency.

József Szilágyi, according to the records and the recollections of other defendants, displayed emotions close to anger; he did not defend himself, he attacked. He asserted that János Kádár and the other members of the Kádár leadership should be put in the dock next to him and demanded that those persons be called at least as witnesses. His statement on the right of the last word, a veritable disquisition on the evils of the prevailing regime, was interrupted by the presiding judge at least ten times with the warning that he was there to defend himself and not to accuse others. Earlier, during the investigation, Szilágyi had sent lengthy handwritten petitions to the authorities declaring his none too flattering opinions of the Soviet and Hungarian communist leaders. This pattern of behavior meant his fate was sealed early on. His conduct in the courtroom on February 5 and 6, 1958, made it doubtful whether the trial could continue in an orderly fashion. When the trial was adjourned indefinitely on February 6, the procurator moved immediately to separate the case of József Szilágyi from the others and his trial was over in three days: the evidentiary process was superficial, with only a brief and perfunctory examination of witnesses. Judgment was pronounced on April 22, imposing a death sentence. The sentence was implemented on April 24. The fact that József Szilágyi was sentenced to death in a separate trial came to light only after Ferenc Donáth and Miklós Vásárhelyi were released from prison.

The other defendants tried to behave sensibly during the trial in order simply to survive the proceedings. After eleven months of solitary confinement spent in the shadow of the gallows, nobody could be reproached for that. It was characteristic, however, that none of the defendants was willing to compromise when it came to fundamentals: not one of them admitted participation in the alleged conspiracy which the interrogators and the court were seeking to prove. And the whole travesty of justice could have meaning only if the defendants were to make such an admission and the court could then make it public. No, this idea failed because as far as the most important facts were concerned, every defendant insisted up on speaking the truth. In late 1956 and early 1957, each defendant was offered immunity in exchange for compromises. But each accepted responsibility for what he had done without at the same time betraying the cause of the revolution. The fact that some of the defendants who braved the ordeal of the proceedings admitted some measure of personal guilt and spoke of contrition in their addresses on the right of last word, can hardly be seen by anyone as a cause for indignation.

VI

According to Hungarian laws on criminal procedure, a final court judgment may be reviewed by applying one of two so-called extraordinary remedies: retrial, or remedial petition. Retrial of a case may be ordered if it appears that a repetition of the whole judicial process is justified in the light of new evidence. The process of remedial petition, initiated on the basis of a petition that can be submitted only by the president of the Supreme Court or the procurator general, enables the Supreme Court to examine whether the judgment brought in the original case was in accordance with the law on the basis of the evidence available at the time the judgment was rendered. The judicial authorities resorted to the latter in the Imre Nagy case if for no other reason than that, thirty years after the original judgment, retrial *de novo* would not make much sense inasmuch as most of the original participants were no longer living. (Four defendants had been executed; some of the other defendants and many of the witnesses had died.) It was the task of the procurator general to prepare the remedial petition and submit it to the Supreme Court. To the great glory of the "independent" Hungarian courts, up to May 1989 the records of the trial were kept at the Ministry of the Interior, inaccessible without the official consent of the Ministry even to the procuracy or the court. After the documents were declassified, the procurator general was desperate enough to display on television the written materials of the trial—more than one hundred thousand pages contained in eighty-three volumes—by way of demonstrating that the procuracy would need several months to survey the records and prepare the petition. It was obvious that the promise of party Secretary General Károly Grósz of concluding the trial review before June 16, 1989, the day of the funeral, would be impossible to fulfill. In the event, the retrial was held on July 7, 1989.

The question naturally arises as to what extent the principle of judicial independence was observed in the remedial proceedings of 1989. In the spring of that year, in response to HJC demands and to pacify the public, the compromised judges of the past who had passed death sentences during the post-1956 reprisal period were removed from the courts. But a number of the remaining judges had participated in reprisal trials, or in political trials in the period after 1956, although they had not handed down death sentences. The seven-member Presidential Division of the Supreme Court which was to acquit Miklós Vásárhelyi was still denying his request for retrial in the fall of 1988. Probably it could not do otherwise at the time. Also on a somewhat discordant note, it was by courtesy of the party leadership that the Supreme Court was in the position to review the judgment brought in 1958. Although the illegality of that judgment was obvious to most members of society, it would be charitable indeed to presume that all seven members in the Presidential Division of the Supreme Court were led purely by professional conviction when they voted for the judgment of July 7, 1989. One's doubts concerning the independence of judges might seem less justified had the seven judges of the Presidential Division never been obliged to satisfy the expectations of persons in power.

The role of the office of the procurator general is even more doubtful. Some of the procurators employed there—including some who would play a role in the later review of the case—sent a letter in February 1989 to the leaders of the HSWP protesting Imre Pozsgay's classification of the events of October 1956 as a popular uprising and stressing that the "counterrevolution" designation was still correct. The antipathy felt by some procurators toward the reevaluation of the trial was evident. It was not by chance that after the trial records became accessible to the general public, journalists got hold of fragmentary statements that seemed to put some of the defendants in an unfavorable light. (The newspapers published parts of statements taken out of context which, lacking clarifying commentary, could only lead to distorted inferences.)

We must recognize that both the judgment of acquittal of July 7, 1989, and the remedial petition that served as its basis are lopsided, owing to the positions and personal limitations of the participating procurators and judges. According to the code of criminal procedure, on the basis of a remedial petition the court may examine only whether or not the judgment attached to the petition was lawful according to the law of the time it was brought.

In 1958, the People's Court Division of the Supreme Court convicted Imre Nagy and his associates for offenses "aimed at the subversion of the people's democratic order of state." The Presidential Division of the Supreme Court in the judgment of acquittal of 1989 found that the defendants had not wanted to subvert the people's democratic order of state, and that the conduct forming the basis of the accusation had been in every respect in accordance with the law. This assertion is, however, only half true. In 1958, the "people's democratic order of state" encompassed not only the constitution but a mass of laws relating to the system of state institutions. In its stated principles, the constitution could be considered modern enough: because it sententiously guaranteed the basic human rights, it seemingly met most of the main international criteria for a document of fundamental law. But the laws on the system of institutions not merely did not ensure the effectuation of basic human rights but created a system of institutions that trampled on them. During the last days of the revolution, the acts of the defendants in the Nagy trial were directed, beyond any doubt, at eliminating of the system of institutions of the "people's democratic order of state," in other words, at "subversion of the people's democratic order of state." Their acts, however, were not in conflict with the fundamental provisions of the constitution, in fact served the effectuation of constitutional principles and historical progress. For this reason an important element was missing from the acts, namely, danger to society. And that factor should have precluded guilt even under the laws of 1958.

Neither the apparatus of the procurator general, which prepared the petition, nor the Presidential Division of the Supreme Court, which brought the judgment of acquittal, had the courage to declare that the laws on the system of state institutions and, in general, "the people's democratic order of state" had been in conflict with the Hungarian constitution in force, and that for this reason any activity aimed at subverting that order of state could not have been classified in 1958 as a criminal offense because it could not be construed as a danger to society. Instead, the Presidential Division of the Supreme Court tried to prove that the defendants in fact had not intended to subvert the system; they had only tried to reform it. Even should this assertion prove true for some acts of the defendants, the roles and aims they adopted during the last days of the revolution served the purpose of subverting the regime. But the political climate in Hungary in 1989 simply did not make it possible for the court to declare honestly. The political struggle was still unresolved. The majority of society still worried about a possible leftist return to power. The Soviet Union was still intact, and many feared that the forces of orthodoxy would resort to violent measures.

An examination of how the prerequisites for ensuring judicial independence might best be established in a period of transition from dictatorship to democracy could serve as a fascinating topic for a separate study.

It is well-known that the funeral held on June 16, 1989, for the executed Imre Nagy, József Szilágyi, Pál Maléter, and Miklós Gimes, and for Géza Losonczy, who died in prison, was attended by a crowd of some two hundred thousand people. The ceremony commemorated not only the five martyrs of the Nagy trial but all the other victims of the revolution. At the Heroes' Square in the heart of Budapest, which could accommodate such a crowd, organizers constructed a catafalque and placed upon it a symbolic coffin for the martyrs of the revolution. By agreement with the relatives, the HJC meanwhile had reburied the remains of Imre Nagy and his fellows at the place where they were found, in Lot No. 301. This has become a place of national pilgrimage. The grave of each executed person buried there has been identified and properly defined, and the remains of executed persons who were buried in other places have been brought and buried here. This is the place where the powerful monument by sculptor György Jovánovics, dedicated to all martyrs of the revolution, has been placed.

By an irony of fate, János Kádár died on the same date (July 6, 1989), and at the same hour, when the Presidential Division of the Supreme Court began its retrial of the case of Imre Nagy and his associates. János Kádár seized power from Imre Nagy on November 4, 1956, and, helped by Soviet tanks, ran the country until 1988. His persona and the role he played are fraught with contradiction, and it will take some time for historians to arrive at a true picture of this man. By now we have found documents proving that Kádár advocated having Nagy and his associates called to account and dealt with severely—presumably at least in part because Nagy otherwise would have posed a continuing challenge to the legitimacy of Kádár's own power. The documents also prove Kádár's personal responsibility in the policy of reprisals. At the same time, it is beyond question that Kádár deserves credit for his role in the process of societal reconciliation, and that the reform process, which faltered several times but still made Hungary the "most cheerful barrack" in the Soviet camp, was inseparately bound up with his personal influence.

For the sake of candor it must be mentioned also that the funeral of János Kádár drew a crowd of about one hundred thousand people. This fact alone suggests the extent to which the country had been divided by the events of the past few decades.

VII

Finally, the attitudes authorities evinced toward publicity are rather instructive. The Nagy trial was filmed. Most of the film footage, however, could not be found; there remains only an abridged version prepared for propaganda purposes, mostly with a narrator providing the audio accompaniment. This version, intended for the general public, is not very effective for the purposes of the producers, so it is not surprising that it was never released. Although the defendants are shown at their weakest moments during the trial, there is no doubt they would have elicited popular sympathy. The film was made with a view to manipulating opinion: not a single statement in it is presented in context, the voices of the defendants shown can be heard only for one or two sentences, and the alleged purport of their statements is read by the narrator. Naturally, what the narrator says is not what the trial record shows.

The day after the deportation of Imre Nagy and his colleagues to Romania, on November 23, 1956, a brief communiqué was issued by the government. After that there was no further official statement until June 1958. Until then the most the public could surmise from official statements was based on János Kádár's earlier promise of immunity. On June 17, 1958, the day following the executions, the government issued a lengthy communiqué, which reported the conclusion of the trial, the responsibility of Imre Nagy and his associates as determined by the judgment, and the sentences and executions. Most of the population was stunned.

The way in which the defendants' relatives who remained in Romania were informed of the judgment was inhuman. They knew nothing about the trial, had received no news of the relatives returned to Hungary. They were herded without explanation into a room where copies of the newspapers of June 17, 1958, containing the government communiqué, were placed on a table before them. They learned of the judgment and the executions by reading those papers. The wives and children of the defendants were allowed only later to return to Hungary, where they suffered poverty and stigmatization.

It is not without interest to mention the afterlife of the trial records and the investigation file. The documents were held in special archives at the Ministry of Interior until May 1989, inaccessible to relatives and researchers alike. But they were kept continuously alive. In all political cases, including the Nagy case and the Standard case, the organs of the Ministry pursued a curious procedure.

Each dossier had a precise name index that listed all the names of persons mentioned in the file together with notations of important data about those persons. It recorded any criminal proceedings conducted against a person, the outcome of the proceedings, and the page numbers in the file where the person's name was mentioned. There was space for added comments, where a death of a person might be recorded. Both the Standard and the Nagy dossiers contain index notations of the deaths of numerous persons (mostly witnesses and persons mentioned in testimonies and other statements). Such notations were made as late as 1987.

The documents are now housed in regular judicial archives and being processed by researchers.

In conclusion, let me quote the answer of Imre Nagy to the question put to him by the presiding judge after the pronouncement of judgment whether he would apply for clemency. He replied as follows:

> If the honored People's Court Division pleases, I should like to explain my position in connection with the petition for clemency. The death sentence which the honored People's Court Division has imposed on me I, for my part, deem unjust. I consider its rationale unfounded; therefore, although I know there is no possibility of appeal, I cannot accept it. My only consolation in this situation is my conviction that sooner or later the Hungarian people and the international working class will exonerate me of the grave charges the burden of which I now must bear, in consequence of which I must give my life, but which I must accept. I believe the time will come when, in a less disturbed atmosphere, with a clearer horizon, on the basis of a better understanding of the facts, justice can be done in my case, too. I believe I am the victim of a serious error, a judicial error, and I shall not ask for clemency.

Alajos Dornbach
attorney,
Deputy Speaker of Parliament

Documents of the Imre Nagy Trial

Act of Accusation Against Imre Nagy and His Associates January 28, 1958

Top-secret!
Office of the Procurator General—No. 07092/1957
To the President of the Supreme Court of
the Hungarian People's Republic, Budapest

ACT OF ACCUSATION against Imre Nagy and his associates, for conspiracy aimed at subverting the people's democratic order of state[1] and for other crimes.

I

In October 1956, hostile elements opposed to the people's democratic system, with the active support of the imperialists, launched a counterrevolutionary attack with the purpose of subverting the Hungarian People's Republic, the people's democratic order of state. The counterrevolutionary bandits embarked on a course of terrorism and violence right from the start. On the morning of October 24, they bestially murdered communists and other progressive citizens at the Radio and elsewhere. Murderous white terror raged in Budapest and in the provinces. During these days, 234 communists and other progressive-minded patriots fell victim to the counterrevolutionary terror. Manhunts and lynching were the order of the day, and there were anti-Semitic demonstrations and pogroms[2] at a number of locations. The counter-revolutionaries were preparing for the coordinated annihilation of the forces loyal to the people's rule. Throughout the country, there were mass arrests of communists, of those working for the county and city councils, and of members of the armed forces. By November 4, more than three thousand people had been arrested, and their mass execution[3] was to be carried out within days. Tens of thousands of people were put on various death lists.

Actively participating in the counterrevolutionary terror, the fascist book burnings, and the destruction of Soviet monuments were the around seventeen thousand political and common criminals set free by the counterrevolution. Organized into armed bands in significant numbers, they provided the core of the counterrevolutionary insurgent forces. Once the armed attack was under way, the establishment and stabilization of the counterrevolution's government, military organs, and political organs began. The reactionaries started to eradicate the organs of the people's democratic order of state: the county and city councils, the armed forces, and the leading force of the people's democratic system, the party. In their place, they put counterrevolutionary "committees," and organized armed insurgents into a so-called national guard. Within days, nearly seventy diverse political organizations were established, the majority of them blatantly aiming at a bourgeois restoration. The activities which the enemies of the people's democratic system engaged in concurrently with their unbridled chauvinistic, nationalistic, and incendiary propaganda were aimed at causing the country to secede from the socialist camp, and change sides to join the capitalists. In all this, the counterrevolution's purpose was to establish the preconditions of its final consolidation: the total annihilation of the socialist forces and the capitalist restoration that could then follow. The destruction and disorder wrought by the counterrevolution caused more than twenty billion forints of damage to the Hungarian People's Republic.

The comprehensive examination of the counterrevolutionary events of October has established that Imre Nagy, Géza Losonczy, Miklós Gimes, Ferenc Donáth, Sándor Kopácsi, and József Szilágyi had leading and commanding roles in planning and setting off the counterrevolution, and that Ferenc Jánosi, Miklós Vásárhelyi, and others took part in these activities. The persons listed had been carrying on coordinating and leadership activities already quite some time prior to the outbreak of the counterrevolution, with the purpose of undermining the people's democratic order of state. After the outbreak of the counterrevolution, they allied with Pál Maléter, and with the overtly reactionary Zoltán Tildy and Béla Király.

On the basis of data at our disposal, it has been established that, along with Imre Nagy and his faction, the official circles and the propaganda and intelligence organizations of the imperialist states played a decisive role in planning and launching the counterrevolutionary attack of October, as did the remnants of the hostile classes still present in considerable numbers within the country.

In the period preceding the counterrevolutionary attack, the imperialist intelligence and propaganda organizations stepped up their work of subverting the Hungarian people's democracy, in order to cause the country's secession from the socialist camp and to bring about a capitalist restoration.

The Hungarian sections of the imperialist propaganda organizations had been reinforced about a year to a year and a half prior to the October events. Within the American propaganda organization Radio Free Europe, it was the section dealing with Hungary that had the largest staff. In the period preceding the October attack, they sent counterrevolutionary leaflets into the country in over three million copies.

The Budapest embassies of the U.S.A., of Britain, and of other states played a significant part in organizing the imperialist subversion and hostile propaganda activities directed against Hungary. In their subversive activities, they counted absolutely on the situation that Imre Nagy and his faction had created. On a number of occasions, certain diplomats of the U.S. Embassy recommended to their superiors appropriate ways of exploiting the advantages of the situation created by Imre Nagy and his faction. An American intelligence agency going by the name of Strasbourg "University" worked out a concrete program inciting to insurrection as early as September 1956. Adolf Berle, one of the directors of the so-called Radio Free Europe Committee, stated in a propaganda document smuggled into the country that "liberation movements have started" in Central Europe, and that "we shall simply do away with communism, as the impediment to a twentieth-century revolution."

In order to prepare for the counterrevolutionary attack, way before the October events, the imperialists provided military training to fascist émigrés in various camps in West Germany and Spain, under the direction primarily of American officers. A number of these units were dispatched to Hungarian territory at the time of the counterrevolution.[4] In the course of the investigation of the counter revolutionary crimes, it was proven that the armed groups' infiltration from Austria started simultaneously with the disarmament of the border guards at Mosonmagyaróvár and Hegyeshalom. These groups were armed with rifles without stocks, pistols, and hand grenades. On October 29, an armed group of 130 crossed the border, consisting of Hungarians who had previously escaped to the West. A truck full of armed civilians crossed the border at Rábafüzes, and headed for Budapest. From the camp maintained at Zindorf by Caritas, a so-called relief organization, a large group of traitors set off for Hungary during the counterrevolution. Radio Free Europe broadcast strategic advice from the American Colonel Bell to the Hungarian insurgents, calling for partisan action in Transdanubia.

Arms and ammunition were sent into the country disguised as Red Cross donations. On November 1, 1956, a West German Red Cross convoy of twenty cars and sixty-three people arrived in Hungary, equipped with a shortwave radio transmitter for maintaining contact with Bonn.

Leading émigré traitors engaged in a whole range of counterrevolutionary activities. On October 28, 1956, Béla Varga, chairman of the so-called Hungarian National Committee, announced that he "and members of the committee were in direct contact with the leaders of the Hungarian revolt."

On October 29, Miklós Horthy turned to the leaders of the three imperialist great powers and demanded intervention on behalf of the counterrevolution.

The remnants of the hostile classes within the country also accelerated their actions against the Hungarian People's Republic in the period preceding the October counterrevolutionary attack. Especially active were the leaders of the former bourgeois parties and members of the Horthy regime's armed organi zations, who saw the activity of Imre Nagy and his group as leading to a situation in which their hopes for a capitalist restoration would soon be realized, and organized an extensive network of illegal groupings to promote this end. In the course of their activities, these illegal groups comprised the hostile classes, and established contacts with the imperialist intelligence organizations which gave them guidance and which also provided financial support for their activities. At the time of the October armed insurrection, the illegal groups increased their activities. Disguising their true objectives, they set up so-called revolutionary committees. They made their way into the most important positions of the so-called national guard, in order to secure their counterrevolutionary military power and realize their criminal goals.

II

Regarding the activities of the hostile faction organized and led by Imre Nagy, the investigation has established the following:

Quite some time before the outbreak of the counterrevolutionary attack, Imre Nagy organized an exclusive circle consisting of reactionary intellectuals, the enemies of the people's democratic order of state. Géza Losonczy, Ferenc Donáth, Miklós Gimes, Miklós Vásárhelyi, Ferenc Jánosi, József Szilágyi, Sándor Kopácsi, and others comprised the core of this circle. The coterie that developed around Imre Nagy engaged in criminal activity against the Hungarian People's Republic continuously as of late 1955. The members of the coterie maintained and organized illegal contact with one another. In the interest of taking over power, they exploited the legal avenues but also made use of every possible illegal means.

To coordinate their activities, in the course of 1956, they periodically gathered at the homes of some members of the group, where, besides exchanging political views, they discussed various concrete operations of the planned attack.

The guidelines that Imre Nagy had worked out and put into writing quite some time prior to the counterrevolution formed the ideological basis of the group's criminal objectives.

To support their activities, the hostile group rallied the reactionary intelligentsia and other elements hostile to the people's democratic order of state. In addition, they tried to draw young people under their influence, especially those with a nationalistic orientation.

It has been established that the organized activity of this treasonous faction was behind a number of those maneuvers which public opinion had been misled to believe to have been spontaneous. Thus, for instance, the so-called "writers' memorandum"[5] of 1955 was the result of direct and concrete organizing on the part of Imre Nagy and his associates, with the participating writers playing but a secondary role. The authors of the incendiary articles, commentaries, and poems which appeared in 1956 were either themselves members of the treasonous faction—thus, for instance, Gyula Háy and Zoltán Zelk—or were written by people with whom members of the faction had prearranged the lines of attack. They had close ties to the leaders of the Petőfi Circle,[6] and manipulated the circle's activities to suit their own objectives. The most incendiary debates were chaired and the hostile comments were prearranged by members of the faction.

The party resolution of July 1956 brought a certain lull in the group's hostile activity; there were a few weeks of hiatus. Soon, however, Imre Nagy was demanding that the hostile activities be continued forthwith, in consequence of which an integrated attack started up, surpassing that of the previous period.

By this time, the intensified activity of the hostile faction was connected to the organization of mass demonstrations, and planning for the power takeover was on the agenda.

Imre Nagy and the treasonous group he led made full use of the support of the imperialists and of the domestic reactionaries in their subversive bid for power.

Numerous documents prove that the imperialist circles were using the tactic of making the situation created by Imre Nagy and his faction the basis of an attack on the people's democratic order of state. In July 1956, the West German *Die Welt* observed, in connection with the insurrection in Poznan, that "the same objective preconditions exist in Hungary." The French *Combat* published an article to the same effect, with the title "Prerevolutionary Fever in Hungary." The Swiss *Die Tat* published an article entitled "Imre Nagy Is Biding His Time" in September 1956, and Radio London had a lengthy program in praise of Imre Nagy, entitled "Imre Nagy's Evident Political Future." A few days later, the Voice of America announced: "Imre Nagy will soon again be holding an important position." In October 1956, the Agance France Pocss Wire Service (AFP) noted: "Imre Nagy's readmission to the party is, without a doubt, a step along the way to his return to power." Any number of reports of this kind appeared in the bourgeois press.

The various members of the group played significant parts in organizing the demonstration that introduced the armed counterrevolutionary attack of October 23. It was through Gábor Tánczos, one of the leaders of the Petőfi Circle, that Géza Losonczy directed the organization of the demonstration which developed into an armed counterrevolutionary attack.

Imre Nagy and his treasonous faction considered the armed forces of the counterrevolution to be the allies who would enable them to take over power, and concurrently, to put their hostile plans into action. The purpose of the faction's activities was to use provocation, falsification, pressure, and petitions to frustrate the steps aimed at annihilating the counterrevolution. To camouflage their alliance with the reactionaries, they tried to present the attack on the people's democratic order of state as a "democratic movement."

Imre Nagy and his faction came into power in overt and unequivocal alliance with the reactionaries. Their treasonous activities were aimed at destroying the basis of the dictatorship of the proletariat. The annihilation of the government organs of the People's Republic was started on a nationwide scale. Leadership was assumed by the so-called Revolutionary Committee, whose hostile activities were decisively influenced by the two committees organized by the treasonous faction, the "Revolutionary Committee of Intellectuals," and the "National Committee." While communists were being persecuted and counterrevolutionary terror raged throughout the country, on October 31 Imre Nagy made, among others, the following announcement to an audience of several hundred gathered at the Parliament: "We are living the first days of our freedom and independence" (*Magyar Szabadság*, November 1, 1956, vol. 8, p. 18).

Their attempts to cause the country to secede from the socialist camp were totally in keeping with the imperialists' goals. The identity of interest between the treasonous faction and the official circles of the imperialist powers, and their interconnectedness, is shown by the statements made by Eisenhower and Secretary of State Dulles as reported in the October 26, 1956, issue of the *New York Herald Tribune*, in which they declared that "government which fulfills the promise attached to Imre Nagy will certainly enjoy the complete economic support of the United States."

The counterrevolutionary leadership headed by Imre Nagy introduced a whole series of traitorous measures jeopardizing the country's independence, ones completely in keeping with the plans and objectives of the treasonous émigré bourgeois circles in the imperialists' pay. It was common knowledge that Károly Peyer, Ferenc Nagy and other émigré leaders had voiced their conviction that a preferable tack, from the point of view of the Western powers, was for Hungary's secession from the socialist camp "to be accomplished by a group that can call itself communist."

Imre Nagy and his faction counted on the imperialists' support. It was in this spirit that Zoltán Tildy suggested to the traitorous Ferenc Nagy during the October days that he use his influence to get Radio Free Europe to endorse the Imre Nagy government. It was for this same reason that Géza Losonczy called on the Western journalists to back the Imre Nagy government during the counterrevolution. It was likewise Géza Losonczy who, flagrantly betraying the interests of the working class, conducted talks with Prince Löweinstein—the representative in Hungary, at the time, of renascent German fascism and of the West German capitalists supporting it—about the possibility of establishing diplomatic relations, and of financial support for the country. In his capacity as the order of state's press and radio representative, Losonczy gave Löweinstein permission to make a statement on Hungarian Radio without consulting with the order of state. Löweinstein's broadcast was sheer propaganda: he applauded the Hungarian events, and promised the Imre Nagy government the West German capitalists' financial support. (Löweinstein's radio address, vol. 12, p. 493; Losonczy's autograph notes, vol. 12, p. 494.)

Imre Nagy and his associates did everything in their power to obstruct the domestic socialist forces, who engaged the help of the Soviet armed forces in their defense of the people's rule. Following the formation of the Revolutionary Workers' and Peasants' government, in close alliance with the retreating reactionaries, they continued their attack. The members of the group were not loath to engage in illegal organizing, to distribute incendiary leaflets, and to use other hostile means to obstruct the order of state's efforts to restore order, put down the counterrevolution, and start up production. (Albums 1 to 12: 1—The antecedents of the armed counterrevolution of October 23, 1956. The demonstration of October 23. 2—The beginning of the counterrevolution/armed insurrection. Treason in the armed forces. The organization of the counterrevolutionary armed forces. 3—The armed attack on the Radio of October 23, 1956. 4—Bloody counterrevolutionary provocation in front of the Parliament on October 25, 1956. 5—Counterrevolutionary attack on the prisons. The liberation of political and common criminals and their counterrevolutionary activities. 6—Armed counterrevolutionary attack on party and order of state buildings. The defilement of monuments, red stars, and flags. 7—Counterrevolutionary terrorism against communists and other progressive individuals. 8—The activities of bourgeois parties, "revolutionary committees," and other counterrevolutionary organizations during the counterrevolution. 9—The leaflets and printed matter published during the counterrevolution. 10—The role played in the Hungarian counterrevolution by the intelligence agencies of the imperialist states and the Western Hungarian émigrés. 11—The attempts made by the counterrevolutionary forces to dissever Hungary from the socialist camp. 12—Statistical data on the material damage caused by the counterrevolution.)[7]

III

The personal activities of the defendants: The coordinating and leadership activities of Imre Nagy in the ideological planning of the counterrevolution consisted in his having—in the course of 1955-1956, considerably prior to the armed counterrevolutionary attack—established an exclusive circle with the purpose of engaging in hostile activities. His plan was to place the members of his group into positions of leadership should he come to power, and to carry out his hostile policies with their help.

Ten to twelve months prior to the counterrevolutionary attack on the People's Republic, Imre Nagy elaborated in writing his plan for annihilating the basis of the dictatorship of the proletariat, that is, his plan for the country's secession from the socialist camp. He had these writings reproduced, and distributed them to members of his circle with the assignment to illegally circulate them among their acquaintances. It was to this end that Géza Losonczy, Miklós Gimes, and Miklós Vásárhelyi, as well as other members of the group and their acquaintances, concerned themselves with Imre Nagy's studies. László Kardos, a member of Imre Nagy's circle, sent the studies containing the hostile views to the West via a secretary at the British Embassy in Budapest, a certain Cope, with instructions to have them circulated in printed book form.[8] The bourgeois propaganda and intelligence organizations have, accordingly, been circulating the illegally supplied incendiary writings far and wide in the West, as well as illegally sending it into Hungarian territory. (Five basic principles of international relations and the matter of our foreign policy, vol. 7, p. 139; statement of Miklós Vásárhelyi, vol. 3, pp. 34-35.)

Of the members of Imre Nagy's group, Losonczy, as well as Donáth—with Imre Nagy's concurrence—exploited to the utmost the possibilities which the operation of the Petőfi Circle offered to disseminate their hostile views, and popularize the person of Imre Nagy. Among the leaders of the Petőfi Circle, Imre Nagy maintained personal contacts with Balázs Nagy, who has since escaped to the West. In June 1956, Imre Nagy received the draft of Szilágyi's planned speech to the Petőfi Circle for his information and comments. Imre Nagy concurred in the text of the proposed destructive speech, and sent Szilágyi one of his pamphlets to use in the speech. (Statement of József Szilágyi, vol. 33, p. 30; pamphlet drawn up by Imre Nagy, vol. 33, pp. 363-375.)

With Imre Nagy's knowledge, Géza Losonczy played a significant role in choosing the topics discussed by the Petőfi Circle, and personally prepared hostile speeches on a number of occasions. Losonczy had discussed with the journalists Tibor Mérai and Miklós Gimes ahead of time the demagogic and hostile speeches given by them. Losonczy and Haraszti had agreed with Tibor Déry, one of the members of the group, on the content of his speech to the Petőfi Circle, in the course of which Déry expressly formulated the faction's hostile objectives when he declared, among other things, that no problems would be solved until "our critique extends to our entire ideological system." Déry, in the course of his reactionary speech with its extremist attack on the order of state, said also the following, with a view to win over the young people: "I ask the young people not to forget their predecessors, the March youth, who are often called the youth of '48. I'd like us to have a youth of '56 as well." Imre Nagy, too, knew the content of Tibor Déry's speech before he ever delivered it.

In the second half of 1956, the group led by Imre Nagy carried out maneuvers directed at mobilizing all hostile elements. At the September 1956 general assembly of the Writers' Association, writers belonging to the group took over the executive posts of the association. They exploited the mood of the general assembly to place it, as well as the journal of the Writers' Association, the *Irodalmi Ujság*, totally in the service of Imre Nagy and his faction, and made the latter into the chief organ of the attack on the state. In order to widen the hostile influence they had acquired through their manipulation of the Petőfi Circle, they organized a NÉKOSZ reunion. Imre Nagy personally attended the reunion of the members of the Györffy College organized in October 1956. After the counter revolution was put down, the leading core of the illegal conspiracy of intellectuals active against the Revolutionary Workers' and Peasants' government consisted of former members of the Györffy College. At the time that the reunions were being organized, as early as the summer of 1956, Géza Losonczy, one of the most active members of the group, was already giving voice to the notion of overthrowing the order of state by force. In the summer of 1956, in an interview with an Israeli journalist, he declared that he would not rule out the possibility of the people's overthrowing the order of state in Hungary, and if it came to that, that would suit him fine. Losonczy added: "This is my personal opinion, and probably the opinion of my political friends as well." (Statement of Géza Losonczy, vol. 9, pp. 158-160, and vol. 9, pp. 187-190; of Ferenc Donáth, vol. 1, p. 193; and of Ferenc Jánosi, vol. 35, pp. 25-28; final judgment in the criminal proceedings against Tibor Déry and his associates.)

In the second half of 1956, concurrently with their maneuvers to organize the mass support necessary for their takeover of power, Imre Nagy and his faction, in preparation for the takeover, established illegal contacts with certain leaders of the former SZDP. In September 1956, at the home of the writer Dr. Lajos Hatvany, Géza Losonczy and Sándor Haraszti had secret discussions with Anna Kéthly about her participating in the "prospective" Imre Nagy government. Imre Nagy personally held similar discussions with the right-wing social democrat, István Erdei. In the course of the discussion, Erdei declared that he had been empowered by Anna Kéthly to seek out Imre Nagy. (Statement of Géza Losonczy, vol. 9, pp. 223-234; statement of Sándor Haraszti, vol. 2, pp. 227-249.)

On October 22, 1956—the time when the activism to which the treasonous group had inspired the elements opposed to the people's democracy entered the phase of direct action, and the party and government leaders were abroad—Imre Nagy and the members of his group organized an illegal gathering on the premises of the SZÖVOSZ. They agreed to work out the program of the "prospective" Imre Nagy government. (Géza Losonczy's autograph notes, vol. 7, pp. 354-356; statement of Zoltán Vas, vol. 3, pp. 92-109; statement of Ferenc Donáth, vol. 13, pp. 304-341; statement of Miklós Gimes, vol. 17, p. 283.)

On October 23, 1956, at 11 a.m., Imre Nagy, Géza Losonczy, Ferenc Jánosi, Sándor Haraszti, Miklós Gimes, and Szilárd Ujhelyi held another illegal meeting at the home of Géza Losonczy. On the basis of his telephone conversations with Gábor Tánczos, the leader of the Petőfi Circle, Géza Losonczy informed those present of the mood among the students and the preparations being made for the demonstration planned for that day. The leaders of the traitorous group assessed the planned demonstration as their opportunity to come into power. At the illegal meeting, they agreed to take over power, agreed on the personnel changes to be made in the party and the government leadership, and on placing members of their faction in party and government offices.

In the course of the illegal meeting, Imre Nagy declared that he wanted to be prime minister and not—as some members of the group suggested—first secretary of the party, for "that's how (he was) known to the people." Imre Nagy and his group also agreed that Imre Nagy would assume the office of prime minister only if the personnel changes planned in the top leadership took place. The participants at the meeting declared that they considered themselves bound by the resolutions brought, and in view of the accelerated pace of political events, would hold meetings on a daily basis. (Statement of Miklós Vásárhelyi, vol. 36, pp. 242-247; statement of Miklós Gimes, vol. 1, pp. 285-286; statement of Szilárd Ujhelyi, vol. 9, pp. 193-199; Géza Losonczy's autograph notes, vol. 3, pp. 130-150.)

On October 23, 1956, the reactionary elements launched an armed attack on the Hungarian People's Republic.

Imre Nagy, as president of the Council of Ministers, conducted a two-faced policy with the purpose of safeguarding the reactionary forces and escalating the counterrevolution, thereby frustrating the measures taken by the order of state to annihilate the counterrevolutionary gangs.

On October 26, 1956, Imre Nagy, taking advantage of his position of power, arbitrarily lifted the curfew imposed on the recommendation of the defense council. He prevented the implementation of the martial law instituted against the armed insurgents, which he himself had been the one to sign.

He openly stated in front of the members of the group that—contrary to the party's and the order of state's official stand—he considered the armed attack launched by the reactionaries to be a "democratic mass movement." (Documents pertaining to the declaration of martial law, vol. 8, pp. 25 and 27; minutes of the Central Leading Body, vol. 7, p. 51; statement of Ferenc Jánosi, vol. 35, pp. 38-40; statement of Jenő Hazai, vol. 3, pp. 310-321.)

On October 26, 1956, Imre Nagy—with threats of resigning—prevented action by the Defense Council aimed at annihilating the counterrevolutionary bandits of Corvin Alley. In the same way, he prevented the execution of the liquidation plan scheduled for October 28. (Statement of István Kovács, vol. 2, pp. 154-156; autograph notes of István Kovács, vol. 7, p. 20; statement of Károly Janza, vol. 3, pp. 171-177; statement of Lajos Tóth, vol. 3, pp. 151-170.)

The activities of Imre Nagy and his group were intended to camouflage the armed counterrevolution as a "democratic movement." They tried to underpin their hostile platform with a falsified "public opinion." It was Imre Nagy's group that organized the so-called delegation from Angyalföld, which voiced counterrevolutionary demands, and then Imre Nagy promised to carry out these demands. They organized the Writers' Association delegation with a similar purpose. (Statement of Miklós Gimes, vol. 17, pp. 290-292; statement of Sándor Herpai, vol. 2, pp. 131-135.)

Imre Nagy, as president of the Council of Ministers—dispensing with the communist majority in the order of state in violation of the constitution—used the cabinet[9] to make decisions in matters of nationwide significance. Subsequently,

Imre Nagy, terminating the communist-majority government operating to that time, with Tildy's concurrence, made changes which resulted in a government of reactionary, counterrevolutionary elements.

Imre Nagy organized a national guard which rallied all the counterrevolutionary groups in armed struggle against the people's rule. The declaration-cum-order signed by Imre Nagy concerning the organization of the so-called national guard contained, among other things, the following: "I recognize and confirm . . . the formation on this day . . . [of the body] composed of delegates of the units taking part in the revolutionary fighting, and of representatives of the army and the police."

Imre Nagy named Béla Király, formerly an officer in Horthy's army sentenced to life imprisonment for espionage, to be commander in chief of the counterrevolutionary armed forces. Béla Király, after escaping to the West on November 9, 1956, started a campaign of defamation against the Hungarian People's Republic and the Soviet Union on Radio Free Europe and on the Voice of America. Then, in the service of the American intelligence agencies, he set up an international counterrevolutionary organization, and has sent, and is sending, a whole series of spies into the country. (Imre Nagy's written directive, vol. 8, p. 53; statement of Sándor Kopácsi, vol. 28, pp. 154-158.)

Imre Nagy and Géza Losonczy, as members of the cabinet—in keeping with their treasonous plans—deliberately took no measures to stop the fascist terror raging in Budapest and in a number of other places within the country. In giving her evidence, Mrs. József Balogh, Imre Nagy's former secretary, has testified as follows: "One day they sent over from the Party information with some horrible reports about atrocities against functionaries. I took the information in to Imre Nagy, who, upon my asking him twice, looked into the reports and then set them aside, saying that they were exaggerated. He told me not to bother submitting such things. After that, I was the only one who read such reports, and put them in the cupboard." (Statement of Mrs. József Balogh, vol. 3, pp. 78-86; statement of Sándor Kopácsi, vol. 28, p. 226.)

The lawlessness of the counterrevolutionaries and the conspicuous appearance on the scene of the most extreme reactionaries were sanctioned by Imre Nagy's illegal measure which—with Géza Losonczy and Zoltán Tildy's concurrence—pronounced the rehabilitation of the most pertinacious enemy of the people's democratic system, József Mindszenty.[10] [Nagy] reinstated Mindszenty in his "rights," and with Zoltán Tildy's cooperation, provided him with the opportunity to speak on the radio on November 3, and hold his subversive address with its explicit call for a capitalist restoration. (Rehabilitation document, vol. 8, p. 51.)

At Imre Nagy's initiative and with Zoltán Tildy's support, on November 2, 1956, the cabinet passed a resolution to enlarge the order of state with the inclusion of counterrevolutionaries. The text of the resolution reads: "Since the issue of restructuring the government is acquiring increasing urgency, the cabinet has resolved it should take place not by appointing new ministers but by adding new forces to the cabinet, including the insurgents." (Minutes of the cabinet session of November 2, vol. 8, pp. 58-59.)

Likewise at the November 2 session, as one of the measures aimed at obliterating the Communist Party, the cabinet, led by Imre Nagy, passed a resolution that "the cabinet declares the monetary funds of the MDP deposited with the National Bank to belong to the government, and shall see to its use by distributing it among the coalition parties this very day." (Minutes of the cabinet session of November 2, vol. 8, p. 59.)

Imre Nagy and the traitorous group, in alliance with the reactionaries, then carried out their earlier objective: the country's secession from the socialist camp. As early as his speech in front of the Parliament, on October 31, Imre Nagy announced the untrue fact that they had started negotiating the withdrawal of Soviet troops from Hungary's entire territory and discussions on "repudiating the obligations that accrue to us [as members of] the Warsaw Pact." Imre Nagy presented the cabinet that met on November 1 with another *fait accompli* by having had the declaration of neutrality drafted prior to the cabinet session. At the session itself, he simply read out two previously drafted, printed resolutions. It was upon this that the resolutions declaring the country's neutrality and its withdrawal from the Warsaw Pact were passed. The proposed design of the street placard announcing the [country's] neutrality was also passed around at this cabinet session. (As reported in the newspaper *Magyar Szabadság*, November 1, 1956, and registered in the minutes of the cabinet session of November 1, vol. 8, p. 32; statement of Géza Losonczy, vol. 9, pp. 143-148; statement of Zoltán Tildy, vol. 19, pp. 22-23; statement of Zoltán Szántó, vol. 3, pp. 110-130.)

Imre Nagy's November 2 telegraphic instructions to the United Nations delegation in New York was at the center of the efforts to have the country join the capitalist camp. The essence of the telegram was that the Hungarian delegation speak up before the United Nations "on behalf of the revolution." The text of the telegraphed speech contained, among other things, the following "It is not the first time in history that the Hungarian people have risen in defense of its independence and freedom, but our freedom-fighters have always died forsaken. The Hungarian people are counting on the sober and considered assistance of the great powers and on their active support." In connection with this, Imre Nagy addressed several verbal statements to the Soviet ambassador. He forwarded copies of these to all embassies accredited to Budapest. In his circular, he further incited anti-Soviet sentiment with his statements slandering and abusing the Soviet Union. (Original telegraphic texts, vol. 8, pp. 18-50.)

Along with their political and military activities against the Soviet Union, the members of the traitorous faction were in the vanguard of the nationalistic, chauvinistic, and anti-Soviet agitation designed to strengthen the reactionary forces. Imre Nagy personally called upon Kopácsi to hit an anti-Soviet note at the meeting of the so-called Police Committee, which Kopácsi did. (Statement of Sándor Kopácsi, vol. 28, pp. 228-230.)

When Imre Nagy learned, at dawn of November 4, that the internal socialist forces and the Soviet troops they had called in to help them had begun their military action to put down the counterrevolution, in a statement prepared with the help of Donáth and Zoltán Tildy and broadcast over the radio, he called upon the inhabitants of the country to fight against the Soviet troops. (Nagy's broadcast in Radio Budapest, November 4, 1956.)

To avoid being held accountable and to be able to carry on their hostile activities, Imre Nagy and several members of the traitorous group took refuge in a foreign embassy. From there they conducted an active campaign to prevent the functioning of the Revolutionary Workers' and Peasants' government and the implementation of the measures taken in the interest of consolidation. The members of the group, under the leadership of Imre Nagy, calling themselves the "Administrative Committee," passed a "resolution" to maintain [the country's] neutrality, and resolved, further, that they did not recognize the legality of November 4, 1956; that the Soviet troops [ought to] withdraw to their positions of prior to October 23; and that they "hereby inform world opinion that [they] disavow the Revolutionary Workers' and Peasants' government, and will engage in no negotiations with it." They forwarded this resolution, as a message, to Radio Free Europe, which broadcast its text. (Statement of Ferenc Donáth, vol. 13, p. 228; statement of György Fazekas, vol. 2, pp. 251-273; statement of Zoltán Vas, vol. 3, pp. 92-109; statement of Zoltán Szántó, vol. 3, pp. 110-140; Géza Losonczy's signed confessions.)

Dr. Ferenc Donáth played an active role in the organization of the faction's activities and in planning the takeover of power. He adopted the hostile views of Imre Nagy and his associates. He took part in spreading the faction's hostile views at the debates of the Petőfi Circle, and led the debates dealing with economics and market gardening in Hungary. (Statement of István Márkus, vol. 14, p. 26; statement of Sándor Haraszti, vol. 14, p. 32.)

Donáth, along with Géza Losonczy and Sándor Haraszti, participated in the illegal meetings at which the requisite methods of taking over power were developed. At the October 23 meeting, where they discussed preparing an illegal government program aimed at the takeover of power, Donáth undertook to work out the program's agricultural section. (Statement of Sándor Haraszti, vol. 14, pp. 32-33; statement of Zoltán Vas, vol. 14, pp. 48-49; statement of Szilárd Ujhelyi, vol. 14, p. 57.)

From October 24, 1956, Donáth—together with Géza Losonczy—took an open stand for the mobilization of the counterrevolutionary forces and for the activation of the armed struggle. Donáth and Losonczy's activities were directed at changing the composition of the top leadership to the benefit of their faction and forcing the reevaluation of the counterrevolutionary events. Donáth and Losonczy ostentatiously refused the party functions offered to them, and demanded that their actions be publicized. Upholding their renunciation, they attended the October 25-26 session of the Central Leading Body, and insisted that the events be evaluated as a "democratic movement." In order to achieve their goal, they made use of the demands of the Writers' Association "delegation" organized by Ferenc Jánosi. Donáth and Losonczy agreed in advance that at the Central Leading Body session, Losonczy would introduce the demands and Donáth would provide the reason why it was "imperative" that they be met. Accordingly, at the October 26 Central Leading Body session, they made counterrevolutionary demands; that is, they demanded, among other things, an immediate, general amnesty for the counterrevolutionaries conducting an armed offensive against the order of state of the Hungarian People's Republic, the immediate withdrawal of Soviet troops from Budapest, and the incorporation of the armed counter-revolutionaries into the armed forces. As they were unable to get the Central Leading Body to accede to their demands, they reiterated their renunciation. After leaving the session, they informed the delegations of the armed insurgents of what had taken place at the Central Leading Body session and of the failure of their attempts; and they repeatedly expressed their support for the counterrevolution to the counterrevolutionary delegations. (Recollections of Ferenc Donáth, vol. 15, p. 15; documents, vol. 15, pp. 10-11.)

In a statement published in the November 2 issue of the *Magyar Honvéd*, Ferenc Donáth praised the armed struggle of the "revolutionaries." (*Magyar Honvéd*, November 2, 1956, vol. 15, p. 13.)

On November 4, he took part in the composition of the hostile radio appeal which Imre Nagy read at dawn over the radio. (Statement of Imre Nagy, vol. 1, p. 245; statement of Zoltán Tildy, vol. 19, p. 31.)

After November 4, as a member of the so-called Administrative Committee, he took part in the continuing hostile activities of the group led by Imre Nagy. They decided to emigrate and establish contacts with the leaders of the so-called coalition parties who had escaped to the West earlier, in order to develop a unified platform against the Revolutionary Workers' and Peasants' government. Géza Losonczy contacted Tivadar Pártay, one of the leaders of the FKP, and tried to persuade him to escape to the West, along with several bourgeois politicians. (Statement of Géza Losonczy, vol. 9, pp. 244-247; statement of Tivadar Pártay, vol. 10, pp. 279-280.)

Miklós Gimes played a leading role in the group's hostile activities and in planning the group's power takeover. Once the counterrevolution had been put down, he was one of the initiators in establishing an illegal organization, and composed and circulated counterrevolutionary leaflets.

Gimes drew persons of a reactionary mentality into the coterie around Imre Nagy: Pál Löcsei and György Fazekas. He was one of the initiators of the hostile operations aimed at discrediting the policies of the party and of the order of state.

In the summer of 1956, at one of the group's meetings, he suggested that an illegal "committee" be set up to coordinate the activities of the persons belonging to the group, and to work out the methods and concrete forms of the group's hostile activities. (Statement of Sándor Haraszti, vol. 18, pp. 218-219; statement of Zoltán Vas.)

Gimes attended the group's October 22-23 illegal meetings. He undertook to work out the section of the illegal government program pertaining to external affairs. From October 23, he participated, on an ongoing basis, in the activities of the counterrevolutionary center established in the Budapest Police Headquarters building. He influenced Chief of Police Sándor Kopácsi in his appraising the events as a "democratic revolution." He was one of the organizers of the so-called workers' delegation of Angyalföld. The "delegation" had only two Angyalföld workers, two youngsters who had come to Budapest to procure provisions, and who, at the group's persuasion, took part as passive bystanders in the "delegation" organized by the group. These were the "workers" in whose name Gimes and his associates listed and made their counterrevolutionary demands. (Statement of Sándor Kopácsi, vol. 28, pp. 205-210; statement of György Fazekas, vol. 18, p. 205; statement of Sándor Herpai, vol. 18, pp. 192-200.)

From October 30, Gimes published the *Magyar Szabadság*, a daily glorifying the counterrevolution. In an article published in the first issue of the daily, he made incendiary statements violating the interests of the Hungarian people. He praised the armed insurgents as "the nation's heroes." (Editorial of vol. 1, no. 1 of the *Magyar Szabadság*, vol. 18, p. 291.)

After the counterrevolution was put down, between November 6 and 8, he wrote counterrevolutionary leaflets, of which four hundred copies were circulated. (Statement of István Márkus, vol. 18, p. 136.)

As of November 13, 1956, Gimes—along with György Ádám—was the moving spirit behind the "Hungarian Democratic Independence Movement," an illegal conspiracy. Gimes took part in the secret meetings of the group, formed against the Revolutionary Workers' and Peasants' government, and edited the leaflets entitled "October 23rd" put out by the group on ten occasions in several hundred copies. The aforementioned counterrevolutionary leaflet called for continued fight against the state and for resistance to the order of state's measures. The message of the Imre Nagy group, forwarded to György Ádám via Gábor Tánczos in the name of the "Administrative Committee," played a role in the formation of the illegal organization initiated by Gimes. (Copies of the leaflets, vol. 18, pp. 303-320; statement of György Ádám, vol. 17, pp. 346-347.)

Gimes carried on incendiary activities at the meeting of the Journalists' Association and at the assembly at the student hostel in Hess András Square. At the latter, in a speech of November 13, 1956, he praised the hostile activities of the counter-revolutionaries and of Imre Nagy's group, and incited to continued resistance.

Zoltán Tildy, in his capacity as counterrevolutionary minister of state in October and November 1956, and as an old-time bourgeois politician, helped activate the reactionary forces. He supported Imre Nagy and his faction in their treasonous political activities. As an overt advocate of bourgeois democracy, through his own actions and through the measures he introduced, he promoted the efforts to overthrow the dictatorship of the proletariat and to launch the nation on the road to a capitalist restoration.

As early as October 28, at a meeting held in the Parliament, and again on October 30, at a cabinet session, he called for the abolition of one-party rule and the inclusion of the coalition parties' representatives in the government. By Tildy's own admission, this action resulted in forcing the communists out of the government and in individuals opposed to the people's democracy taking their place. It was partly at his insistence that three Smallholders' Party, two Peasants' Party, and three Social Democratic Party representatives sat alongside Imre Nagy and Géza Losonczy already at the November 2 cabinet session.

After the October 30, 1956, cabinet session, Tildy, in a radio address, arbitrarily announced that Hungary's representatives to the United Nations were being recalled. He called on the one-time membership of the FKP to lose no time organizing the party, for they were to take part in the work of the government. (Text of the October 30 radio address, vol. 21, p. 17; press release on the enlargement of the cabinet.)

As a result of Tildy's radio address, the FKP was rapidly re-formed, and it elected a leadership of reactionaries who had earlier been ousted from the political arena by their own party because of their stand against the people's democracy. People such as István B. Szabó, Ferenc Kövágó—who subsequently escaped to the West—Sándor Kiss, and József Adorján, among others, got into positions of leadership. In an effort to completely destroy the dictatorship of the proletariat, these rightist FKP leaders demanded the abolition of the Presidium and the distribution of ministerial portfolios according to their allocation at the time of the 1945 coalition government. (Statement of Tivadar Pártay, vol. 20, pp. 25-26.)

On November 3, Tildy made a telephone call from the Parliament building to Ferenc Nagy in Vienna, who offered his services. Tildy told him not to come back to Hungary for the time being, but instructed him to take steps to have Radio Free Europe temper the tone it used in speaking of the government of Imre Nagy.

As minister of state from October 30, Tildy staffed his secretariat with reactionaries headed by his personal secretary, one-time newspaperman Dr. Zoltán Hámori. Hámori, acting on Tildy's behalf, appointed reactionaries to various government posts.

Tildy authorized the rightist leaders of the Smallholders' Party to withdraw 300,000 forints from the current account of the former MDP to finance the organization of their activities against the people's democracy. (Statement of Tivadar Pártay, vol. 20, pp. 17-18.)

In a press conference on November 2, 1956, Tildy stated that "we wish to live as a neutral country. To this end, we have announced our withdrawal from the Warsaw Pact." (Newspaper article of November 2, vol. 21, p. 24.)

Tildy issued orders for the illegally freed József Mindszenty to be brought to Budapest and accommodated in the castle, and decided, in agreement with Imre Nagy and Géza Losonczy, to reinstate Mindszenty in his "rights" and arrange for him to deliver a radio broadcast. Tildy took part in the preparation of the document ordering Mindszenty's illegal rehabilitation. (Press release, vol. 21, pp. 117-118, and statement of Pál Maléter.)

Tildy conferred with Mindszenty on two occasions on the subject of the radio broadcast. Subsequently, Mindszenty delivered—without prerecording—his subversive radio address, openly calling for a capitalist restoration.

In the course of the meetings with members of the executive committee of the newly formed FKP, Tildy stated, that "if necessary he would go as far as military dictatorship, and Pál Maléter would assist him." With regard to the matter of the Warsaw Pact, he said at one of the meetings that if the withdrawal should result in military action, "we will resist." (Statement of Tivadar Pártay, vol. 20, pp. 7-15.)

On October 30, Tildy, editing an announcement to be broadcast on the radio, corrected "people's republic" to "republic," "people's democracy" to "democracy," "socialist objective" to "our great objective," and deleted the word "socialist" from "for an independent, sovereign, socialist Hungary." (Statement of Ferenc Almásy, vol. 21, p. 168.)

In the early dawn of November 4, he took part in the composition of Imre Nagy's radio address, and personally ordered that the text be delivered to the secretary general of the United Nations. (Statement of Ferenc Donáth, vol. 13, p. 227.)

It was at this same time that he authorized Gyula Háy to broadcast his appeal to Western writers, in which he protested, in the name of Hungary's authors, against the intervention of the Soviet troops, and asked for "help." (Final verdict in the criminal action against Tibor Déry et al.)

Pál Maléter, colonel in the Hungarian army in the period between October 25 and 28, disobeyed the orders of the minister of defense, and breaking his oath, together with his unit, went over to the side of the counterrevolution, reported this to the minister of defense at 1:15 p.m. on October 28, 1956, and subsequently became the commander of the insurgent forces. On the merits of his counterrevolutionary activities as the "heroic defender" of the Kilián barracks, Imre Nagy made him a member of his government. As deputy minister, and later, as minister of defense, he played a coordinating and leading role in establishing the military dictatorship of the counterrevolution. (*Magyar Honvéd*, November 2, 1956, vol. 25, p. 92; statement of Vilmos Koltai, vol. 23, p. 155; statement of Lajos Józsa, vol. 24, p. 252; statement of János Tari, vol. 24, p. 174; statement of József Szanati, vol. 24, p. 90; statement of Lajos Tóth, vol. 23, p. 58.)

From October 28, he maintained close contact with the leaders of the Corvin Alley counterrevolutionary command, that is, with László Iván Kovács, who has since been sentenced and executed, and Gergely Pongrácz, who has since escaped to the West.

On October 29, the Ministry of Defense sent Brigadier General Gyula Várady to the insurgents at Corvin Alley to discuss their surrender. Maléter, who was also invited to the meeting, prevented their unconditional surrender, and spoke up in the interest of the insurgents. In concurrence with the Corvin Alley insurgents, he put into writing the counterrevolutionary demands which emerged in the course of the negotiations. He demanded the withdrawal of the Soviet troops by December 15, 1956, the total disarmament and abolition of the ÁVH, and that people who fought in the insurgent forces [be able to] keep their arms and be recruited into either the police force or the regular army, with the youngsters being admitted to the Military Academy. Maléter's treasonous behavior completely vitiated the surrender negotiations. (Statement of Gyula Várady, vol. 24, p. 228.)

From October 29, Maléter had a personal bodyguard consisting of a group of six of the Corvin Alley insurgents. On October 30, one of the group commanders of the Corvin Alley insurgents sent a report to Maléter on the armed attack on the Party headquarters at Köztársaság Square, and on the acts of terrorism that ensued. Maléter praised the reporting terrorists. (Statement of Gyula Uszta, vol. 23, p. 223; and statement of Mihály Horváth, vol. 23, p. 261.)

From October 30, the Corvin Alley counterrevolutionaries began arresting and dragging off from their homes party functionaries, communists, and ÁVH personnel, and with Maléter's approval, kept them under arrest in the Kilián barracks. Maléter gave personal instructions to the Corvin Alley insurgents as to how to conduct the fight. On one occasion, he sent a message to János Virágh, known to him as one of the commanders of the Corvin Alley insurgents, ordering him to fight against the Soviet troops called in to help defeat the insurgents. Through his subordinates, Maléter drilled the Corvin Alley insurgents in the use of tanks and armored vehicles. He arbitrarily "promoted" several members of the armed group to officer's rank. For instance, he rewarded Gábor Dilinkó, a convicted criminal, with the rank of major on the merit of his counterrevolutionary activities. (Statement of János Virágh, vol. 23, p. 209; Maléter's orders to János Virágh, vol. 25, p. 79.)

Maléter, as a member of Imre Nagy's government, established his own military headquarters in the Kilián barracks, with a view to concentrating a significant force of armed units around himself to help him establish a military dictatorship and to prepare the armed forces to fight the socialist forces and against the Soviet troops. To this end, he concentrated a number of large units under his personal command, and gave them their military assignments. (Statement of János Mecséry, vol. 23, p. 176; statement of László Egervári, vol. 24, p. 58.)

On November 1, 1956, the British Embassy in Budapest decided to get in touch with Maléter. On November 2, Military Attaché Cowley went to see Maléter in the Kilián barracks. There, Maléter supplied Cowley with classified information on Hungary's armed forces and on the strength and the movements of the Soviet troops. He authorized Cowley to study various Soviet weapons and tanks. During his meeting with Cowley, Maléter asked for the Western powers' moral support. Cowley advised Maléter on door-to-door fighting, and suggested that he concentrate the individual armed units under a unified command, for that was the only way they could hold on to what they had already gained. Among other things, Cowley stated that "what is needed is strong central leadership, a military dictatorship, whose primary goal is to ensure the withdrawal of the Soviet troops." (Statement of József Molnár, vol. 23, p. 106.)

Maléter conducted similar conversations with members of the Western press who had turned up at the Kilián barracks as early as November 1. On November 3, following a meeting with the Soviet delegation in the Parliament building, Maléter wanted to show a map of Soviet troop movements to Western reporters but was stopped by the intervention of an officer of the general staff. (*Magyar Honvéd*, November 2, 1956, vol. 25, p. 92; statement of Miklós Szücs, vol. 23, p. 126; statement of István Kovács, vol. 23, p. 245.)

On November 2, Maléter ordered Brigadier General István Kovács to make preparations for a meeting of high-ranking military commanders to be called for November 4. One of the tasks he was assigned was to draw up "defense" plans against the Soviet troops in the event that they did not withdraw. (Statement of János Mecséry, vol. 23, p. 178; statement of István Kovács, vol. 23, p. 245; document pertaining to the preparation for the November 4 meeting, vol. 25, p. 75.)

Sándor Kopácsi, as Budapest's police commissioner, played a leading role in the shaping of the counterrevolutionary events, in the disorganization and demoralization of the police force, and following his openly going over to their side, in the arming of the insurgents.

Prior to the counterrevolutionary attack of October 23, 1956, he had joined the coterie around Imre Nagy. He was in personal contact with Imre Nagy, György Fazekas, Miklós Gimes, and József Szilágyi, and under their influence, became a believer in, and follower of, the political views of the hostile grouping. (Statement of György Fazekas, vol. 30, p. 166.)

On October 23, Kopácsi assured the students coordinating the demonstration that the Budapest police would not interfere with the demonstration. In the course of the counterrevolutionary events, with Kopácsi's cooperation, various intellectual and petty bourgeois individuals established a counterrevolutionary center at police headquarters. With Kopácsi's blessings, and totally without authorization, people such as Tamás Aczél, Tibor Mérai, György Fazekas, Miklós Gimes, Pál Lőcsei, József Szilágyi, and others belonging to Imre Nagy's hostile group took an active part in the running of the police headquarters, and prevailed upon Kopácsi to issue orders which disorganized the police force, and which were aimed at obstructing the liquidation of the counterrevolution. From October 25, with the orders he issued to district police stations, Kopácsi prevented their working out a defense strategy against the attacks of the counterrevolutionary groups and mounting effective counterattacks. As a result of Kopácsi's orders, a significant part of the police force capitulated, and handed over their arms and buildings to the insurgents. (Statement of Tivadar Végh, vol. 29, pp. 88-89; written record of telephone messages, vol. 32, p. 20.)

On October 29, Imre Nagy commissioned Kopácsi with organizing the "new" police force, that is, the national guard. Kopácsi, who concurred with the notion that the core of the national guard should be composed of the armed insurgents who had taken part in the counterrevolutionary fighting and other counterrevolutionaries yet to be armed, issued some twenty thousand weapons, ammunition, and national guard identification certificates mostly to criminal, hooligan, and counterrevolutionary elements. (Documents, vol. 31, pp. 212, 214; vol. 31, p. 16.)

On November 1, in a statement published both in the *Kis Ujság* and the *Magyar Világ*, he declared that on his orders the police force had gone over to the insurgents' side. (Newspaper articles, vol. 32, pp. 104-105.)

Beginning on November 1, units under his command made illegal arrests and took over two hundred individuals into custody. (List of detainées, vol. 32, p. 80.)

On November 3, at the meeting of the so-called Revolutionary Police Committee in the Police Headquarters building, he made an anti-Soviet statement.

On November 4, at Imre Nagy's request, he went to the Parliament to organize the Parliament's "defense" against the Soviet troops. On November 5, he attempted to flee to one of the foreign embassies, so as not to have to answer for his actions.

Béla Király took the initiative and played a leading role in militarily organizing the armed counterrevolution, in the disorganization of the armed forces, and in the execution of plans aimed at the destruction of the people's rule.

Király, as an officer of the Horthy regime, had belonged to Gyula Gömbös's immediate circle; then, during the Szálasi era, he had cooperated with the Arrow Cross minister of defense, Beregfy. In 1951, he was convicted of espionage and other criminal acts, and sentenced to death; later his sentence was commuted to life imprisonment. His sentence was interrupted in the summer of 1956.

On October 26, he offered his services to the Imre Nagy faction. Imre Nagy appointed him to be commander in chief of the national guard. He used his position of power to isolate and demoralize the military units loyal to the people's rule, and to plan the armed attack against the socialist forces and the Soviet troops that they had called upon for help. (Statement of Ferenc Jánosi, vol. 26, p. 34; letter to Jánosi, vol. 26, p. 265.)

On October 30, at the first meeting of the "Revolutionary Police Committee," held at the Budapest Police Headquarters, he demanded that the armed counterrevolutionary groups be incorporated into the national guard. In accordance with other demands made by Király, it was resolved that the Soviet troops be withdrawn, the ÁVH be disbanded, and the "operative arms" of the Counterrevolutionary Committee be elected. At the same time, they formed a parliamentary delegation which included Király and Kopácsi and which was charged with reporting to Imre Nagy on the formation of the "Revolutionary Police Committee." (Documents, vol. 26, p. 267.)

On October 31, Imre Nagy appointed Király Budapest's military commander; he thus had jurisdiction over all the armed forces stationed in Budapest. Király considered securing power for the armed counterrevolutionaries his primary objective. Concurrently with organizing the national guard, he established his own headquarters in the Ministry of Defense. He ordered his staff officers to gather intelligence on Soviet units and troop movements, and to devise the so-called defense plan. He appointed Colonel László Zólomy, a one-time Horthyist officer, his second in command. (Statement of István Kovács, vol. 26, p. 57; his own notes, vol. 26, p. 286.)

On November 1, Király secured the Timót Street armory for the national guard. On his orders, the not yet "sufficiently" armed counterrevolutionary groups were outfitted with weapons from the military armory. (Statement of István Kovács, vol. 26, p. 57.)

On November 3, with the leaders of the counterrevolutionary groups and representatives of the police and military units which had joined the counterrevolution in attendance, and with Király presiding, the "Permanent Revolutionary Police Committee" was elected in the Budapest Police Headquarters building. Béla Király was elected its chairman, and Sándor Kopácsi its vice-chairman. (Minutes, vol. 26, p. 312.)

On November 9, Király and his associates escaped to the West. Since then, he has been carrying on his activities against the Hungarian People's Republic and against the socialist camp through Radio Free Europe, the Voice of America, and in the service of the American intelligence agencies. He has appeared before the United Nations with a series of lies as the "émigré military commander," and has established a large-scale émigré organization with traitors, murderers, Horthy-fascists and other criminals among its members. From his residence in New York, he has sent circular to fascist émigrés in different countries, instructing them on how to expand the counterrevolutionary organization with a view to attacking the Hungarian People's Republic. One of the organizers of the West German émigrés is Gábor Rédey, a one-time SS soldier and former prisonmate of Béla Király, who was the chairman of the "Revolutionary Alliance of Political Prisoners" during the counterrevolution. Király has prepared a draft constitution for the counterrevolutionary organization, and calls the organization the "Alliance of Hungarian Freedom Fighters (National Guard)." In the service of American intelligence agencies, Király and his associates are sending spies into the territory of the Hungarian People's Republic. (Király's letter to Lajos Steiner, *Life*, February 18, 1957, vol. 21, p. 354; draft constitution of the MSZSZ, vol. 26, p. 379.)

József Szilágyi, as a member of the group headed by Imre Nagy, played an initiating and commanding role in organizing the demonstration that prepared the ground for the October 23, 1956, armed insurrection and in establishing the counterrevolutionary center in the Budapest Police Headquarters building.

Szilágyi made contact with Imre Nagy in 1955 through Miklós Vásárhelyi;

then, in the spring of 1956, he brought Sándor Kopácsi into the coterie around Imre Nagy and got Kopácsi in touch with Imre Nagy. (Statement of Sándor Kopácsi, vol. 33, p. 80; statement of Miklós Vásárhelyi, vol. 36, p. 211.)

In the first part of October 1956, immediately preceding the counterrevolutionary events, he set up a select, confidential meeting in Kecskemét for some officials of the county council, openly called upon the participants to overthrow the government, and demanded that power be vested in the faction headed by Imre Nagy. (Statement of Károly Mohácsi, vol. 33, p. 188.)

On October 22, 1956, at the mass meeting of the students of the Budapest University of Technology, his hostile attitude contributed, to a large extent, to the eruption of the demonstration. In the incendiary, nationalistic address he delivered to the youth rally, he emphasized that he was acting as Imre Nagy's confidant. His provocatively worded speech, calculated to stir up the feelings of his audience, contained, among other things, the claim that "Soviet troops had surrounded Warsaw, and they wanted to drown the movement in a sea of blood." He delivered his inflammatory speech at the meeting at a time when a relatively sober attitude had started to gain the upper hand, but his performance had the effect of turning the mood of the assembled into one of hostility. He declared, among other things, that "there are forces in this country, too, capable of seeing a fight to its conclusion." A number of expressly counterrevolutionary demands got included in the points of the rally as a result of his speech. His words were followed by a multitude of overtly reactionary and nationalistic manifestos, which directly set the stage for the demonstration inaugurating the armed counterrevolutionary attack. (Statement of István Marián, vol. 33, pp. 205-207; the resolutions of the meeting, vol. 33, p. 399.)

On October 22, prior to his hostile performance at the university rally, and again on October 23, Szilágyi conferred with Sándor Kopácsi, and they agreed that the police would not block the demonstration; on the contrary, they would ensure that it would run its course undisturbed. (Statement of Sándor Kopácsi, vol. 33, p. 80.)

Szilágyi, in cooperation with Sándor Kopácsi, helped bring about and took part in the activities of the counterrevolutionary group that installed itself in the Police Headquarters building. Szilágyi had a significant part in Kopácsi's giving orders that precluded the quashing of the counterrevolution, and helped to disorganize the police detachments, which, as a result, capitulated to the insurgents. (Statement of József Vári, vol. 33, pp. 304-306; statement of Sándor Kopácsi, vol. 33, pp. 83-86; statement of József Balogh, vol. 33, pp. 296-300.)

Imre Nagy had plans for appointing Szilágyi minister of the interior.

Szilágyi had been the one to initiate organizing the so-called workers' delegation from Angyalföld of October 27, whose arrival gave him the opportunity to voice radical counterrevolutionary demands. (Statement of Sándor Kopácsi, vol. 28, pp. 205-210; statement of György Fazekas, vol. 18, p. 205; statement of Sándor Herpai, vol. 18, pp. 192-200.)

On October 29, Imre Nagy appointed Szilágyi to head the secretariat of the prime minister's office. In this capacity, as part of Imre Nagy's entourage, he maintained contact with the leaders of the insurgent groups, and conducted several meetings with them. (Statement of Mrs. József Balogh, vol. 3, pp. 80-85.)

Ferenc Jánosi took part in the group's hostile activities and in planning the takeover of power. He was a liaison between Imre Nagy and the other members of the group. He organized the illegal meetings where they discussed ways of carrying out their hostile plans. He acted as liaison also between Imre Nagy and the Petőfi Circle, and between the Writers' Association and the leaders of other reactionary organizations used by the group. He took part in the illegal distribution of Imre Nagy's studies. He was an active participant in the illegal meetings of October 23, 1956. (Statement of Miklós Gimes, vol. 17, pp. 285-286; statement of Sándor Haraszti, vol. 35, p. 74; statement of Miklós Vásárhelyi, vol. 36, pp. 73, 94; testimonies of Szilárd Ujhelyi and Géza Losonczy; Géza Losonczy's notes, no. 8.)

On October 25, Jánosi notified the reactionary writers belonging to the Imre Nagy circle that "Imre Nagy is engaged in a grave struggle within the Party leadership" and called upon them to form a delegation. (Statement of Sándor Haraszti, vol. 35, p. 74.)

Jánosi relayed to unauthorized persons confidential information obtained from Imre Nagy about action contemplated against the counterrevolution. (Statement of Ernő Havas, vol. 35, p. 97.)

On October 25, Jánosi was notified by telephone that counterrevolutionary bandits in Csepel had attacked Comrade Kalamár. Jánosi was asked to intervene but refused. (Statement of Pál Ipper, vol. 35, p. 17.)

Jánosi personally requested of Imre Nagy that he appoint Béla Király commander in chief of the national guard. (Letter of Béla Király, vol. 35, p. 213.)

Jánosi took part in preparing the radio message which announced Hungary's neutrality.

Miklós Vásárhelyi, as a member of the group, played an active part in the group's taking over power. During the counterrevolutionary events, as press secretary, he allowed reactionary forces to spread their propaganda against the people's democracy through the press as well.

Prior to the counterrevolutionary events, he took part in enlarging the group led by Imre Nagy. He introduced several people to Imre Nagy. He took part in the illegal distribution of Imre Nagy's studies. He regularly attended the meetings of the group. (Statement of Ferenc Jánosi, vol. 35, pp. 26-36; statement of Sándor Haraszti, vol. 37, pp. 12-14.)

On October 23, he attended the illegal meeting held in Losonczy's home. (Statement of Ferenc Jánosi, vol. 35, p. 36.)

During the counterrevolution, he took part in preparing the counterrevolutionary statement formulated at the October 28 meeting of the "Revolutionary Committee of Intellectuals." (Statement of the Revolutionary

Committee of Intellectuals, vol. 37, p. 198.)

As the press secretary appointed by Imre Nagy—with the concurrence of Géza Losonczy—he allowed the dissemination of publications propagating the counterrevolutionary aims of the parties and organizations of the extreme right. Among other things, he authorized the publication of the *Szív Ujság*. (Statement of Géza Losonczy, vol. 9, pp. 199-203, 210, 213-217, 238-239.)

IV

The facts, as set forth in the accusation, have been established on the basis of partial confession and admissions as to the guilt of the accused, the statements of the witnesses questioned in the course of the investigation, and original documents, material evidence, memoranda, official reports, registers, press and radio materials, and other evidence confiscated from the defendants and attached to the documentation of the criminal proceedings.

On the basis of the above, I ACCUSE

Imre Nagy, defendant no. 1, under preliminary detention since April 17, 1957 (born in Kaposvár; in 1896; mother's name, Rozália Szabó; of poor peasant parentage, doctor of economics, academician, married; president of the Council of Ministers of the Hungarian People's Republic from June 1953, then university professor, and from October 24, 1956, again president of the Council of Ministers, resident of Budapest, II, Orsó u. 43);

Dr. Ferenc Donáth, defendant no. 2, under preliminary detention since April 8, 1957 (born in Jászárokszállás, in 1903; mother's name, Ilona Vitál; of intellectual parentage, college-educated, lawyer, journalist with the *Szabad Szó* from 1940; deputy chairman of the National Land Reform Council after the liberation, then undersecretary of state for agriculture until 1948, deputy director of the Institute of Economics from 1954; married, resident of Budapest, XII, Szilágyi Erzsébet fasor 26);

Miklós Gimes, defendant no. 3, under preliminary detention since January 15, 1957 (born in Budapest, in 1917; mother's name, Dr. Livia Hajdú; of intellectual parentage, graduated from high school in 1935, had six semesters in medical school, in forced labor service from 1942, newspaper reporter with the *Szabad Nép* from 1950, expelled from the MDP in 1955; married, separated, resident of Budapest, II, Virágárok u. 10);

Zoltán Tildy, defendant no. 4, under preliminary detention since May 23, 1957 (born in Losonc, in 1889; mother's name, Emma Fabriczky; of intellectual parentage, theologian, Presbyterian minister, cofounder of the FKP before the liberation, prime minister after the liberation, then president of the republic until 1948; his son-in-law, Victor Csolnoky, was sentenced to death and executed for espionage; minister of state in Imre Nagy's order of state from October 27 to November 4, 1956; married, resident of Budapest, XII, Budakeszi ut 46);

Pál Maléter, defendant no. 5, under preliminary detention since November 4, 1956 (born in Eperjes, in 1917; mother's name, Margit Lakner; of noble parentage, his ancestors were landowners; graduated from the Ludovika Academy in 1942; as a professional officer with the rank of lieutenant took part in the war as intelligence platoon commander in the Soviet theater of war; he served as a commanding officer with the rank of colonel in the people's army after the liberation, then was appointed minister of defense by Imre Nagy; married, resident of Budapest, XII, Orbánhegyi u. 29);

Sándor Kopácsi, defendant no. 6, under preliminary detention since November 5, 1956 (born in Miskolc, in 1922; mother's name, Ilona Simon; of working-class parentage; finished law school, police superintendent, attached to the police force after the liberation, of late as chief of the Budapest Police Headquarters; married, resident of Budapest, XII, György Aladár u. 8);

Béla Király, defendant no. 7, escaped to the West on November 9, 1956 (born in Kaposvár, in 1912; mother's name, Etel Lotz; father, senior official at the MÁV; graduated from the Ludovika Academy in 1935, then from the War Academy in 1942; saw active service in the Soviet theater of war, then served in the Ministry of Defense; from 1946 to 1951, he served in the People's Army as commander of the Army Academy; on December 21, 1951, was sentenced to life imprisonment for disloyalty, which sentence is still in effect; on October 30, 1956, Imre Nagy reinstated him to the rank of brigadier general, and appointed him to be the commander in chief of the national guard; married, resident of New York);

Dr. József Szilágyi, defendant no. 8, under preliminary detention since March 27, 1957 (born in Debrecen, in 1917; mother's name, Julianna Szilágyi; of peasant parentage; propertyless, married, graduated from law school, one-time police superintendent, then head of the TEMERT Company's planning department; resident of Budapest, XII, Dániel u. 28);

Ferenc Jánosi, defendant no. 9, under preliminary detention since April 14, 1957 (born in Sárospatak, in 1916; mother's name, Erzsébet Szueta; father, craftsman; graduated from the Academy of Theology in 1938, Presbyterian minister; received a teacher's diploma in 1941; served as army chaplain in Ukraine from 1943, was captured in February 1944; after the liberation, he served in the Education Department of the Ministry of Defense; until 1951, he was assistant department head of the Political Command Department with the rank of colonel, then was promoted to reserve brigadier general; he was first deputy to the minister of education from 1951 to 1954; from 1954 to May 1955, was first secretary of the People's Patriotic Front, then director general of the Petőfi Museum; in June 1956, was expelled from the Party; on November 2, 1956, Imre Nagy reinstated him as brigadier general and appointed him to head the Ministry of Defense's Education Department; married, resident of Budapest, II, Orsó u. 4); and

Miklós Vásárhelyi, defendant no. 10, under preliminary detention since April 14, 1957 (born in Fiume, in 1917; mother's name, Irén Róth; father, a bank employee; graduated from high school and completed four semesters at law

school; did forced labor service from 1942 to 1944; after the liberation, worked as a reporter for the *Szabad Nép* until 1950; head of the Ministry of Education's Information Department in 1950-1951; editor in chief of the *Müvelt Nép* from May 1951; editor of the *Vengria* from 1952 to 1954; and deputy director of the Information Bureau of the Council of Ministers in 1954-1955; he was expelled from the Party in January 1956; in early November 1956, Imre Nagy appointed him to be the head of the Council of Ministers' Press Department; married, resident of Budapest, II, Hankóczy Jenö u. 15)
as follows:

Imre Nagy, defendant no. 1, of the crime of initiating and leading a conspiracy aimed at subverting the people's democratic order of state, as entered in section 1, paragraph /1/ of the BHÖ; and of the crime of treason, as entered in section 35, paragraph /1/ of the BHÖ;

Dr. Ferenc Donáth, defendant no. 2, of the crime of initiating and leading a conspiracy aimed at subverting the people's democratic order of state, as entered in section 1, paragraph /1/ of the BHÖ;

Miklós Gimes, defendant no. 3, of the crime of initiating and leading a conspiracy aimed at subverting the people's democratic order of state, as entered in section 1, paragraph /1/ of the BHÖ;

Zoltán Tildy, defendant no. 4, of the crime of abetting a conspiracy aimed at subverting the people's democratic order of state, as entered in section 1, paragraph /2/ of the BHÖ;

Pál Maléter, defendant no. 5, of the crime of leading a conspiracy aimed at subverting the people's democratic order of state, as entered in section 1, paragraph /1/ of the BHÖ; of the crime of mutiny in violation of section 29 of the KTBTK, and upgraded as such in section 30, paragraph /2/ of the KTBTK; and of the crime of treachery, as entered in section 37, paragraph /1/, item b/ of the BHÖ, and upgraded as such in section 38, paragraph /1/, regulation 3 of the BHÖ;

Sándor Kopácsi, defendant no. 6, of the crime of leading a conspiracy aimed at subverting the people's democratic order of state, as entered in section 1, paragraph /1/ of the BHÖ; and of the crime of mutiny, in violation of section 29 of the KTBTK, and upgraded as such in section 30, paragraph /2/ of the KTBTK;

the absent Béla Király, defendant no. 7, of the crime of leading a conspiracy aimed at subverting the people's democratic order of state, as entered in section 1, paragraph /1/ of the BHÖ; and of the crime of treason, as entered in section 35, paragraph /1/ of the BHÖ;

Dr. József Szilágyi, defendant no. 8, of the crime of initiating and leading a conspiracy aimed at subverting the people's democratic order of state, as entered in section 1, paragraph /1/ of the BHÖ;

Ferenc Jánosi, defendant no. 9, of the crime of actively participating in a conspiracy aimed at subverting the people's democratic order of state, as entered in section 1, paragraph /2/ of the BHÖ; and

Miklós Vásárhelyi, defendant no. 10, of the crime of actively participating in a conspiracy aimed at subverting the people's democratic order of state, as entered in section 1, paragraph /2/ of the BHÖ.

For:

In the period prior to October 23, 1956, defendants nos. 1, 2, 3, and 8 formed a hostile group and through destructive activity in various social organizations launched an assault against the people's democratic system; then, following the outbreak of the counterrevolution, assumed its leadership, and made a direct attempt at disrupting the alliance of socialist states and at overthrowing the people's democratic order of state.

Defendant no. 4, as the Imre Nagy government's minister of state between October 28 and November 4, 1956, intentionally promoted the government's shift to the right and the development of a foreign policy contrary to the interest of the state, with a view to achieving a bourgeois restoration, and with the aim of overthrowing the people's democratic order of state.

Defendants nos. 5, 6, and 7, as the military leaders appointed by Imre Nagy, disorganized the armed forces loyal to the people's rule, and organized and carried out the arming of the counterrevolutionary forces in an effort to prevent the armed liquidation of the counterrevolution and with the aim of overthrowing the people's democratic order of state.

Defendants nos. 9 and 10, in the period prior to October 23, 1956, engaged in coordinating activity with a view to establishing the hostile group, then actively participated in the attack on the people's democratic order of state and in the achievement of the treasonous aims of the group, which had assumed the leadership of the counterrevolution.

Furthermore:

Defendant no. 1 urged the intervention and interference of foreign powers hostile to the Hungarian People's Republic in the interest of preventing the annihilation of the counterrevolution; then, in his radio address of November 4, he called for actions hostile to the Hungarian state.

Defendant no. 3, after November 4, 1956, participated in the leadership of the illegal organization called "Hungarian Democratic Independence Movement" by the fact that under his editorship an illegal paper called *Október Huszonharmadik*a was established and distributed, which set out, in the form of a program, the task of the illegal organization, with the aim of overthrowing the people's democratic order of state.

Defendant no. 5, a professional soldier with the rank of army colonel, between October 25 and 28, 1956, defying the orders of the minister of defense, went over to the side of the counterrevolution with the military unit under his command; on

November 2, 1956, he gave upgraded military information to the British military attaché, Cowley, and allowed him to study military weaponry and tanks.

Defendant no. 6, as the chief of the Budapest Police Headquarters, in the course of the October 1956 events, went over to the side of the counterrevolution with the police units under his command.

Defendant no. 7, following his November 9, 1956, escape abroad, entered into the service of Radio Free Europe, and then took part in forming, on foreign soil, the "Alliance of Hungarian Freedom Fighters (National Guard)," a diversionary espionage organization directed against the Hungarian People's Republic.

The first instance jurisdiction and competence of the People's Court Division of the Supreme Court is based on section 5, paragraph /1/ of Law Decree No. 34 of 1957; on the basis of section 8, paragraph /1/ of the same, I hereby move for accelerated proceedings.

In view of the fact that this case involves both military and civilian defendants, on the basis of section 5, paragraph /2/ of Law Decree No. 34 of 1957, I move that the competent court division be appointed.

I move for maintaining the preliminary detention of the defendants.

The following are to be summoned before the court: defendants nos. 1 to 6, and nos. 8 to 10, as accused, through the procurator general.

As witnesses:

István Kovács	Sándor Herpai
István Márkus	Péter Józsa
Tivadar Pártay	János Virágh
György Ádám	György Fazekas
Miklós Szűcs	Gyula Háy
József Vári	Gyula Várady
László Regéczy Nagy	János Mecséry
Sándor Haraszti	István Marián

Through the procurator general:

Lajos Tóth	Ernő Havas
Károly Janza	Jenő Hazai
Mrs. József Balogh	Szilárd Ujhelyi
Zoltán Vas	Zoltán Szántó
József Szanati	Ferenc Almásy
Vilmos Koltai	Lajos Józsa
Gyula Uszta	Mihály Horváth
László Egervári	József Molnár
Tivadar Végh	Károly Mohácsi
János Tari	Pál Ipper
József Balogh	

Budapest residents.

Budapest, January 28, 1958.
Dr. Géza Szénási
Procurator General of the Hungarian People's Republic

To authenticate this copy:

NOTES

1. Communist Order of State—Communist Regime.
2. There were absolutely no anti-Semitic demonstrations anywhere, let alone pogroms.
3. The arrested communists were to be put on trial; there is absolutely no evidence that executions were being planned.
4. There never was any such training activity, and no such units ever entered the country.
5. On October 18, 1955, fifty-nine communist writers and artists signed a memorandum addressed to the Central Committee of the MDP, demanding an end to administrative interference in cultural affairs. The memorandum was framed by Miklós Gimes, Sándor Haraszti, Géza Losonczy and Miklós Vásárhelyi.
6. On March 25, 1955, young reform communists supporting Imre Nagy organized the DISZ Petőfi Circle, which for the next eighteen months was the forum of regular open discussions on issues of current political interest. These discussions did a great deal to mobilize public opinion.
7. The titles of the twelve albums that formed part of the "evidence" submitted in connection with the investigation contained thematically arranged newspaper articles and other written documents pertaining to the events of the revolution.
8. This writing of Imre Nagy's was taken abroad after the revolution was put down.
9. On October 30, 1956, a cabinet consisting of Imre Nagy, Zoltán Tildy, Béla Kovács, Ferenc Erdei, János Kádár, Géza Losonczy, and persons to be delegated by the Social Democratic Party was formed within the order of state.
10. The Roman Catholic József Cardinal Mindszenty was condemned to life imprisonment for political reasons in 1948; a few years later, he was placed under house arrest, whence he was freed on October 30, 1956.

Judgment Against József Szilágyi
April 22, 1958

Top-secret!
The People's Court Division of the Supreme Court of
the Hungarian People's Republic
TB. NB. No. 14/1958/12

IN THE NAME OF THE PEOPLE'S REPUBLIC!

The People's Court Division of the Supreme Court of the Hungarian People's Republic, on the basis of the closed first instance trial held in Budapest, on April 16, 17, and 18, 1958, brought, and on April 22, 1958, pronounced, the following **judgement**:

Dr. József Szilágyi, defendant, born in Debrecen, in 1917; father, József (deceased); mother, Julianna Szilágyi; resident of Budapest, XII, Dániel u. 28; married to Gabriella Gömbös, has three children; company department head with a monthly income of 2,300 Ft; education, doctor of law; propertyless; and regarded as having no criminal record, is **guilty** of the crime of leading a conspiracy aimed at subverting the people's democratic order of state, and is, therefore, hereby sentenced to **death**, and confiscation of all his property.

The costs associated with the criminal proceedings are to be borne by the defendant.

GROUNDS

—— I ——

The procurator general filed the written act of accusation (No. 07092/1957) with the People's Court Division of the Supreme Court against the accused as co-defendant no. 8 in the criminal action against Imre Nagy and his associates. The People's Court Division of the Supreme Court determined it had competence under sections 5 and 8 of Law Decree No. 30 of 1957, and ordered a supplementary investigation to be conducted in the case of the other defendants. In a communication dated March 29, 1958, the procurator general moved that the action against the defendant be separately tried. The People's Court Division of the Supreme Court, in accordance with section 36 of the Code of Criminal Procedure, separated the defendant's case from the others'.

On the basis of evidence presented during the trial, the Court has established the following **facts:**

II

The forty-one-year-old defendant is of poor peasant parentage. As a law student at the University of Debrecen, he joined the Turul Fraternal Society, then the left wing of the student movement (the "March Front"), and later, the young workers' movement. There he took part in the underground activity; for this, he was sentenced to three years' imprisonment during World War II. From the time of his release in October 1944 until the liberation, he hid out on isolated farmsteads around Debrecen; after the liberation, he was given the task, as a communist, of organizing the national police force. Following a lengthy illness, he became the head of the MKP (Hungarian Communist Party) Central Committee's department in charge of police matters. When this department was abolished in April 1949, he was transferred to the export-import trade; then in August 1950, he went to work for the Terményforgalmi Vállalat (Produce Marketing Company) as head of their planning department. From that time on, in his dealings with the Party he projected the air of one offended. He even voiced his feelings at two separate Party meetings, and as a consequence, in 1955 he was expelled from the Party. At the end of 1955, when those who disagreed with the Party's policies grouped around Imre Nagy, he also found a way through Miklós Vásárhelyi to establish direct contact with Imre Nagy. At this point in time, the defendant's behavior was relatively passive. (Statement of Miklós Vásárhelyi.)

In mid-1956, the Party's internal problems were given a highly public airing at the meetings of the "Petőfi Circle," where, with demagogy and the gross exaggeration of the actual problems, as well as through stifling the mention of positive results and discrediting the achievements of the working class, they tried to turn people, especially the intelligentsia and the young people, against the Party and the political system. The Imre Nagy group took part in this incitement, and József Szilágyi also wanted to do so with a speech at one of the meetings. He prepared a speech and had his wife take it to Imre Nagy for his comments: whether he thought it too harsh, or its message proper from a tactical point of view. When Imre Nagy sent back the speech along with an article of his own entitled "Fighting for Lenin's Ideals" to be incorporated into the speech, he [the defendant] complied. The speech was never delivered, due to circumstances beyond his control.

In 1956, when he learned that Sándor Kopácsi disagreed with the Party in the matter of György Fazekas's expulsion, he looked him up, and using the influence he had acquired over Kopácsi at the time of heading the Party's department for police matters, when the latter was already a member of the police force, prevailed upon him to adopt the Imre Nagy group's political views. After this, he met with Sándor Kopácsi a number of times, and when, following the Twentieth Congress of the Communist Party of the Soviet Union, Sándor Kopácsi's views started to come closer to their [the group's] own, he attempted to extend his influence over him and to allay his anxieties. Just before the journalists' debate was held at the Petőfi Circle, he stated in Kopácsi's presence that he could hardly wait to march at the head of a demonstration and shout, "Down with Rákosi." Finally, in October 1956, he managed to bring together Sándor Kopácsi and Imre Nagy at a social gathering. (Statement of Sándor Kopácsi.)

On the morning of October 20, 1956, he made the abusive statement contained in Andor Komlósi's statement in regard to N. S. Khrushchev, secretary general of the SZKP. (Statement of Andor Komlósi.)

On the afternoon of October 20, 1956, he traveled to Kecskemét, where, drawing on his personal connections, he wished to take part—as a member of the Imre Nagy group—in organizing a meeting of intellectuals, and inform the county's leading state functionaries of the Imre Nagy group's evaluation of the situation. Commenting on the events taking place in Poland, he said that a similar removal of the "Stalinist members" of the Party and government leadership was needed [in Hungary, too] and that political demonstrations and the explosive mood of the masses were nothing to be afraid of. "I get a kick out of revolutionaries who get scared before anything's ever happened," he said. He consistently talked about "taking over power," even after one of those present corrected him twice in a row. (His own admission and the testimonies of witnesses Ferenc Dallos, Imre Szelepcsényi, and Károly Mohácsi.)

On October 22, he was present at the student rally at the University of Technology, where he attended night school, and spoke twice. Some 5,000-6,000 students had assembled to discuss the recommendations of the University of Szeged (the dissolution of the DISZ, the establishment of the MEFESZ and various university-related as well as economic and political demands). As the meeting progressed, there were more and more indications of a growing extremism. In his first address—which was the first explicitly and strictly political one—the defendant, analyzing the events in Poland, stated that the fight for democracy and against the "Stalinists" still went on and that the declaration denouncing the events in Poznan was null and void. He also stated that Soviet troops had surrounded Warsaw, that the Polish troops had taken up positions against the Soviets, and that these were the circumstances under which Khrushchev had arrived in Poland to negotiate. He drew a parallel between the Polish and the Hungarian events, and considered the university's meeting an important step in the fight. As a result of his speech, harsh anti-Soviet shouts could be heard for the first time at the meeting; his comments added fuel to the already-explosive atmosphere, and were an incitement to mass demonstration. His second speech came a few hours later, when Dean Csolnoky cautioned the students to be circumspect, and proposed that he would deliver their demands to Imre Nagy. At that time, the defendant said that he, as a member of the Imre Nagy group, was against their sending their demands to Imre Nagy instead of demonstrating, for Imre Nagy was not in power at the moment, and therefore could play no part in getting their demands met. (Statements of witnesses István Marián, Károly Herczeg, Kálmán Gernyei and Ferenc Reichart, and the admission of the defendant.)

That same evening he telephoned Imre Nagy, reporting to him on how the meeting went and on the role he personally played in it. He also telephoned Sándor Kopácsi, informing him of the meeting and the demonstration the students were organizing for the following day. The next morning he went to see Kopácsi in person, and asked that the police not interfere with the demonstration. In the course of the discussion, when Kopácsi said that he had had negative experiences in connection with both the Miskolc (1946), and the Budapest (1954) demonstrations, that is, with this kind of political demonstration in general, he said: "That's the policeman in you; a communist is not afraid of the masses. . . . If we want something, we also have to want the means to get it." (Statement of Sándor Kopácsi, and the defendant's comments on the witness's statement.)

He then went over to the University of Technology, Imre Nagy having, in their conversation of the night before, disapproved of a member of his circle's calling for a demonstration and referring to his ties to himself to give weight to his words. Accordingly, Szilágyi went to tell people at the university that his emotions had got the better of him the previous day; he told them he thought that it was unwise to have urged the demonstration, but there was no way to undo what had been done. He offered to address the students again, to ask that the demonstration be a disciplined one. No such address, however, ever took place. (Statements of István Marián, and Károly Herczeg.)

On October 23, 1956, he took part in the demonstrations at the Bem memorial, at the Parliament and at the Stalin memorial, and then, once the "siege" of the Radio commenced, went to the police headquarters. On this occasion, as on October 25 and 27, he spent a considerable length of time in the Budapest Police Headquarters building with members of the Imre Nagy group, with various writers, newspapermen, and so forth. (Tamás Aczél, Tibor Méray, Pál Löcsei, Miklós Gimes, György Fazekas, etc.) They entrenched themselves in the Budapest Police Headquarters, and prevailed upon Sándor Kopácsi and the high-ranking officers at headquarters to consider the events a revolutionary move on the part of the working people and to forestall the use of arms against the "insurgents." The defendant had a major role in the success of this persuasion. (Statement of Sándor Kopácsi, and admission of the defendant.)

The defendant and his companions thought that Imre Nagy was not consistent enough in representing their common political ideas. On October 27, together with two persons claiming they came from Angyalföld, they went to see Imre Nagy at Party Headquarters, and tried to persuade him to dissociate himself from the MDP's Central Leading Body and lead the fight for the counterrevolutionaries' political demands. On October 29, when he already knew from police headquarters that they had received orders to arm a national guard for protection against the counterrevolution and that these orders had been carried out in the form of arming the very people taking part in the demonstrations, and so forth, he still felt that the Imre Nagy government was not representing their political ideas consistently enough. With a view to persuade Imre Nagy to be more consistent in implementing their ideas, he went to see him in the Parliament, and offered to operate in his close proximity. Until November 4, he did just that. One morning, when, in Imre Nagy's outer office, the behavior and criminal activities of József Dudás and his gang were discussed, the defendant took the position that they should talk to Dudás and involve him in reestablishing law and order. (Statement of Mrs. Ferenc Molnár.) (Imre Nagy did, in fact, take steps to involve Dudás that very day; yet, there is no evidence that the defendant initiated these steps.)

On November 2, Andor Komlósi and his wife visited the defendant, and he kept telling them that this was not a counterrevolution but a fight for independence. He said that while he was aware that there were also some hooligans and counterrevolutionaries in the national guard, in his opinion, at least for the time being, the primary threat was the Russian threat, for the Russian armored "hordes" were advancing, and it was they that had to be fought. He said that he, too, had "kids," but he would still fight to the last bullet. He said that it was not the communists, only the ÁVH people who were getting murdered. (Statement of Andor Komlósi.)

On November 4, at dawn, he and his family fled to one of the foreign embassies along with Imre Nagy and his associates.

III

By and large, the defendant has admitted to the [above] facts. He has denied having made certain statements, which the People's Court has, nevertheless, established on the basis of the assertive and convincing statements of disinterested witnesses, supported—unbeknown to the witnesses—by the defendant's behavior in front of others. As to his guilt, the defendant has, however, presented an extensive defense:

1.) He has claimed, first of all, that the Court must acquit him, for he left the premises of one of the foreign embassies where he had been given asylum in the belief that the Hungarian government had granted him impunity in connection with his earlier actions. Defendant's reasoning in this matter is marked by confusion. A foreign state can grant asylum only on its own territory. In such cases, if the necessary conditions obtain, extradition proceedings can be initiated (Bp sections 235-237), in the course of which the two states may reach an agreement as to the procedure to be followed in connection with the accused in question. The fact that the defendant, after committing the crimes, took refuge in one of the foreign embassies, thereby precluding his actually being taken into detention, does not create such a situation. Furthermore, international agreements reached on matters other than the law of extradition can be modified at any time and in any way upon mutual understanding without the knowledge and consent of the perpetrator.

2.) The defendant also stated as part of his defense that when they were taken into preliminary detention, the rules of procedure were repeatedly violated in connection with him, his associates, and their families. The People's Court examined these complaints from the point of view of whether, if true, these violations could have influenced the establishment of the true facts concerning the actions which are the subject of the proceedings. The Court has come to the conclusion—which, by the way, the defendant has also recognized—that in that respect they were irrelevant. Investigation of the complaints was outside the sphere of the Court's inquest, and at most, the Court could call the matter to the attention of the procurator general for investigation, once the proceedings were concluded.

3.) In essence, the defendant's defense was geared to make it appear that these political proceedings were "ideological" proceedings conducted against him because of his "anti-Stalinist" theoretical stand. The People's Court Division of the Supreme Court hereby reiterates, as a matter of principle, that it has not convicted and cannot convict the defendant or anyone else for taking an ideological stand, for being either a revisionist or a sectarian Marxist. It has to examine, however, whether anybody's de facto political behavior constitutes a criminal act, and on the basis of equality before the law, has to punish the perpetrator if his actions constitute a criminal act, whether that person professes to be a Marxist or an adversary of Marxism, whether he belongs to the revisionist, to the sectarian, or to none of the Marxist wings.

Finally, in his address to the Court under the "right to the last word," the defendant argued that the Court must consider his ideological stand in the proceedings for the simple reason that was what motivated him in his actions. The People's Court so noted, and accepted the argument as an unrefuted line of defense. The fact, however, that his ideological stand was one of the motivating forces in the defendant's political actions, which were criminal in nature, no more mitigates than aggravates his actions.

4.) The defendant also stated in his defense that the people rallied around Imre Nagy did not form a structured unit in the sense that they could be considered a closed organization operating on the basis of a common political platform and under group discipline. The admitted fact, however, that the defendant, on October 25 and October 29—that is, on two different occasions—reproached Imre Nagy for not keeping consistently to their political platform proves beyond doubt that this political platform extended not only to general principles but to concrete political conduct as well. And the fact that he showed Imre Nagy the manuscript of his proposed address to the Petőfi Circle to see if it was not too harsh or if its message was proper from a tactical point of view, and that when Imre Nagy criticized his behavior at the October 22 meeting at the University of Technology, the following day—against his better judgment—he attempted to at least temper its impact, indicate that the group did, indeed, operate under a group discipline to which the members, the defendant included, submitted voluntarily.

The notion of "group" (faction) in a political sense is to be distinguished from the legal concept of an "organization or movement" aimed at subverting the people's democratic order of state. For one thing, "group" (faction) as a political notion does not necessarily entail that its aim be the subversion of the people's democratic order of state. For another, in the case of affiliations for this purpose [i.e., subversion], correct judicial practice based on Hungarian law does not require [evidence of] a high degree of organization but only of coordinated collective action based on the common platform of subverting (undermining) the order of state. Not even the defendant has denied the existence of this lesser degree of organization.

5.) He has denied, however, and made this denial an essential part of his defense, that their group's aim was the subversion of the people's democratic order of state. The defense counsel has also stated that it cannot be presumed that defendant's aim was to subvert the dictatorship of the proletariat. This, however, has been contradicted by the facts revealed in the course of the trial. Never during the proceedings has the defendant denied that his political activities between October 23 and November 4, 1956, were aimed at effectuating what he has called the demands of the "entire people," including the abolition of the "one-party system" and the establishment of a "multiparty system." In his written comments on the written act of accusation, he has added and has maintained throughout his statement at the trial that the reason he speaks of the abolition of the one-party system rather than of the dictatorship of the proletariat is that, in his opinion, the latter "was already overthrown by the Rákosi regime."

Given, however, that the matter of a socioeconomic system's being socialist or capitalist in nature is determined not by whether certain of its political leaders have committed grave and distortive mistakes but by property and class relations, including the matter of power, the defendant's allegation that there was no dictatorship of the proletariat in Hungary before October 23, 1956, is fundamentally false. It was precisely the distortion of the dictatorship of the proletariat by these grave mistakes and infractions of the law which, along with other factors—the defendant's actions included—led to the Hungarian working class's inability to defend its rule by itself and to the fact that, with various slogans, the counterrevolution was able to temporarily bring into its fold some of the backward elements of the working class.

The class character of the armed attack of October 23-November 4, 1956, is demonstrated by the fact that the target of this armed attack, led by the remnants of the one-time ruling classes—and the defendant, too, has acknowledged that they were the leaders—was precisely the temporarily weakened dictatorship of the proletariat, the rule of the working class. What obscured this fact and misled the workers was principally the fact that traitors calling themselves communists aligned themselves with the attackers, covered for them, and supported the aims of the imperialists. This is how individuals calling themselves communists came to share a common platform with those heading Radio Free Europe. And it is this that accounts for the tragic fact that in October 1956—as in every counterrevolution throughout history—the blood that was shed on both sides was not the blood of the exploiters but the blood of the sons of the working class.

Therefore, in view of the data gathered during the trial, the defendant's political activities between October 23 and November 4, 1956, can only be assessed as having been aimed directly and deliberately at subverting the people's democratic order of state.

The People's Court Division, however, has gone beyond this to examine how the defendant's political attitude and his activities within the group prior to October 23, 1956, should be evaluated. On the basis of the trial data, the Court has come to the conclusion that [these activities were] a travesty of his communist past: way before October 23, 1956, the defendant's purpose was not to remedy the shortcomings of the system but to eradicate the entire social order along with its faults. His stubborn and obsessive insistence that the Party's internal problems had to be solved by engaging an outside force, by "revolutionary means," and by "taking over power," precludes the possibility that a person with the defendant's political and police experience envisioned these changes within the framework of the existing political system. Furthermore, he was warned on October 20 and 23 as to where his ideas might lead. These warnings moved him as little as the events that took place between October 23 and November 4: the mass murder of communists; the white terror; the recapitulation of the bloodiest, the most brutal, and most inhumane crimes of fascism; the book burnings and the burning of red flags; the veritable orgy of gangsterism. He was unable to abandon his course, and considered the Soviet troops fulfilling their international obligation as the prime enemy, against whom one had to ally oneself with hooligans and class enemies. As far as he is concerned, the traitors are those who put an end to this interminable St. Bartholomew's Eve Massacre.

This type of behavior is in such sharp contrast with anything even remotely connected with socialism that it obviously has to stem from the defendant's hatred of the system, of socialism as a whole—his own past included—which clearly antedates October 23, 1956. Thus, his later actions are not only the logical extension of this earlier attitude but must also be attributed to the same motive. The validity of this conclusion is supported by the fact that even while the defendant and his associates tried to mislead the working class and the socialist public by claiming to be the sole Hungarian representatives of the Twentieth Congress of the SZKP and the only ones determined and able to act in the spirit of the Congress in Hungary, prior to October 23, 1956, he was making abusive statements about the author and executor of these congressional principles, as has been recorded in the statement of facts.

IV

After due consideration of the foregoing, the People's Court Division of the Supreme Court found the defendant guilty of a leading role in a conspiracy aimed at subverting the people's democratic order of state as entered in section 1, paragraph /1/ of the BHÖ. A "leading role" is any and all definitive leadership activity which influences the plot as a whole or a substantial part thereof. The defendant's actions at the rally at the University of Technology and at Budapest Police Headquarters, as set down in the statement of facts, can only be interpreted as such.

In view of the above, it would be redundant to elaborate on the fact that the defendant's actions constitute criminal behavior maximally dangerous to society. Given this high degree of danger to society, what are traditionally considered extenuating circumstances (first offense, etc.) carry so little weight that they cannot even enter into consideration. In passing sentence, the People's Court has had to determine whether there was any indication—at least in retrospect, during the course of the proceedings—that the defendant would, at some future time, realize that his actions were criminal and a betrayal of his class, and would attempt to rectify them. The People's Court found no such indication, and therefore had no reason to refrain from imposing the maximum penalty.

Sentence was based on section 11, paragraph /1/, and item 5 of the BHÖ.

Budapest, April 22, 1958.
Signatures:
Dr. Ferenc Vida, presiding judge.
Mrs. Péter Lakatos, people's judge.
Mihály Biró, people's judge.
Kálmán Fehér, people's judge.
György Sulyán, people's judge.

RULING

As per Bp section 187, paragraph /1/, there is no appeal.
The judgment is final.

Budapest, April 22, 1958.
Dr. Ferenc Vida, presiding judge
Prepared in five copies on nine pages.

Judgment Against Imre Nagy
June 15, 1958

The Supreme Court of the Hungarian People's Republic
TB. NB. No. 003/1958-18

IN THE NAME OF THE PEOPLE'S REPUBLIC!

The People's Court Division of the Supreme Court of the Hungarian People's Republic, on the basis of the closed trial of the first instance held in Budapest, on February 5 and 6, and on June 9-14, 1958, brought, and on June 15, 1958, pronounced the following **judgment:**

Imre Nagy, defendant no. 1, born in Kaposvár, in 1896; father, József Nagy; mother, Rozália Szabó; married to Mária Égetö, has one grown-up child; professor; has a monthly pension of 5,600 Ft.; propertyless, with no criminal record; a Hungarian citizen, and resident of Budapest (II, Orsó u. 43), is **guilty** of the crime of leading a conspiracy aimed at subverting the people's democratic order of state, and of treason; for this reason the People's Court Division sentences him to **death** and confiscation of all assets.

Dr. Ferenc Donáth, defendant no. 2, born in Jászárokszállás, in 1903; father, Lipót Donáth; mother, Ilona Vitál; married to Éva Bozóki, has three minor children; research fellow with a monthly income of 4,000 Ft.; propertyless, with no criminal record; a Hungarian citizen, and resident of Budapest (II, Szilágyi Erzsébet fasor 26), is **guilty** of the crime of leading a conspiracy aimed at subverting the people's democratic order of state; for this reason the People's Court Division sentences him to 12 (twelve) years of imprisonment, 10 (ten) years of prohibition from exercising certain rights as enumerated in the Criminal Code, and confiscation of all his property.

Miklós Gimes, defendant no. 3, born in Budapest, in 1917; father, Dr. Miklós Gimes; mother, Dr. Livia Hajdú; married, living separated from his wife, Alíz

Földes; has one minor child; newspaper reporter with a monthly income of 2,500 Ft.; propertyless, with no criminal record; a Hungarian citizen, and resident of Budapest (II, Virágárok u. 10), is **guilty** of the crime of leading a conspiracy aimed at subverting the people's democratic order of state; for this reason the People's Court Division sentences him to **death**, and confiscation of all his property.

Zoltán Tildy, defendant no. 4, born in Losonc, in 1889; father, László Tildy; mother, Emma Fabriczky; married to Erzsébet Gyenis; has three grown-up children; pensioner with a monthly income of 4,000 Ft.; registered owner of thirteen cadastral holds of land which he de facto gave to the state in 1945; no criminal record; a Hungarian citizen, and resident of Budapest (II, Budakeszi ut. 46), is **guilty** of the crime of abetting a conspiracy aimed at subverting the people's democratic order of state; for this reason the People's Court Division sentences him to 6 (six) years of imprisonment, 6 (six) years of prohibition from exercising certain rights as enumerated in the Criminal Code, and confiscation of all his property.

Pál Maléter, defendant no. 5, born in Eperjes, in 1917; father, Dr. István Maléter; mother, Margit Lakner; married to Judit Gyenes; has three minor children from his previous marriage; professional soldier with a monthly income of 3,600 Ft.; propertyless, with no criminal record; a Hungarian citizen, and resident of Budapest (II, Orbánhegyi u. 29), is **guilty** of the crime of mutiny committed through taking action, as a leader, aimed at subverting the people's democratic order of state; for this reason the People's Court Division sentences him to **death**, degradation and the loss of all medals and decorations, and confiscation of all his property.

Sándor Kopácsi, defendant no. 6, born in Miskolc, in 1922; father, József Kopácsi; mother, Ilona Simon; married to Ilona Fried, has one minor child; police superintendent with a monthly income of 3,600 Ft.; propertyless, with no criminal record; a Hungarian citizen and resident of Budapest (III, György Aladár u. 8), is **guilty** of the crime of leading a conspiracy aimed at subverting the people's democratic order of state, and as a leader, of mutiny; for this reason the People's Court Division sentences him to life imprisonment, removal from office, 10 (ten) years of prohibition from exercising certain rights enumerated in the penal laws, the loss of all medals and decorations, and confiscation of all his property.

Dr. Ferenc Jánosi, defendant no. 7, born in Sárospatak, in 1916; father, Ferenc Jánosi; mother, Erzsébet Szueta; married to Erzsébet Nagy; has two minor children; museum director with a monthly income of 3,200 Ft.; propertyless, with no criminal record; a Hungarian citizen, and resident of Budapest (II, Orsó u. 4), is **guilty** of the crime of actively participating in a conspiracy aimed at subverting the people's democratic order of state; for this reason the People's Court Division sentences him to 8 (eight) years of imprisonment, 10 (ten) years of prohibition from exercising certain rights enumerated in the criminal laws, and confiscation of all his property.

Miklós Vásárhelyi, defendant no. 8, born in Fiume, in 1917; father, András Vásárhelyi; mother, Irén Róth; married to Edit Poór, has three minor children; newspaper reporter with a monthly income of 2,000 Ft.; propertyless, with no criminal record; a Hungarian citizen, and resident of Budapest (II, Hankóczy Jenő u. 15), is **guilty** of the crime of actively participating in a conspiracy aimed at subverting the people's democratic order of state; for this reason the People's Court Division sentences him to 5 (five) years of imprisonment, 5 (five) years of prohibition from exercising certain rights enumerated in the criminal laws, and partial confiscation of his property in the amount of 1,000 (one thousand) Ft.

The preliminary detention of Dr. Ferenc Donáth, defendant no. 2, as of April 8, 1957; of Zoltán Tildy, defendant no. 4, as of May 23, 1957; of Sándor Kopácsi, defendant no. 6, as of November 5, 1956; and of Miklós Vásárhelyi, defendant no. 8, as of April 14, 1957, is to be deducted in full from their terms of imprisonment. The incurred costs of procedure are to be charged jointly and severally to defendants nos. 1-8.

GROUNDS

I

The procurator general brought indictment no. 07092/1957 at the People's Court Division of the Supreme Court against Imre Nagy and his nine associates. The People's Court Division of the Supreme Court, acting under section 5, paragraph /1/ of Law Decree No. 34 of 1957, established its own competence, and on February 6, 1958, in accordance with section 8, proceeding as court of first instance, ordered a supplementary investigation into the case against Imre Nagy, Ferenc Donáth, Miklós Gimes, Zoltán Tildy, Pál Maléter, Sándor Kopácsi, Ferenc Jánosi, and Miklós Vásárhelyi. Based on section 36 of the Bp, it ordered separate proceedings against József Szilágyi and Béla Király. At the conclusion of the supplementary investigation, and taking its findings and the evidence gathered in connection with the defendants into consideration, the Court established the following **facts**:

After 1945, once the wounds of war were healed and the fundamental prerequisites of democracy (land distribution, a republican form of government, etc.) were achieved, the Hungarian people, liberated from the yoke of fascism and led by the working class, with the help of the Soviet Union and under the guidance of the Party, established the rule of the working class, the dictatorship of the proletariat. They embarked on the building of socialism, and in a short while and in a relatively peaceful manner, changed the country from a backward agricultural state into an industrial country with a well-developed agriculture. As a result of their own immense and generous efforts, boundless prospects opened up for our working people. In the course of our liberated people's and nation's development—immense, considering the size of the country—the errors of some leaders of the party resulted in certain distortions which were out of keeping with the dictatorship of the proletariat and which not only hampered our progress but actually jeopardized our results (they weakened the relationship between the Party and the masses; led to a decline in the standard of living; violated the law, etc.). The Party recognized the problems, and decided to remedy the situation: the June 1953 resolution of the Central Leading Body identified the causes of the problems, and pointed out ways to eliminate them.

Imre Nagy, however, who was prime minister at the time, bent the Party's political direction to the revisionist right. This provoked a retrograde sectarian counterattack, which was no less of an impediment to the party implementing the appropriate policies. During the period of October 1954 to July 1956, these two factions—both distorting the Party's correct program—managed to destroy the unity of the Party and its already-undermined influence over the masses. Uncertainty and vacillation plagued the Party's leadership, and the hegemony of the working class fell into jeopardy.

But the Party found itself again: the Central Leading Body's resolution of July 1956 put an end to the retrograde sectarian faction without giving ground to the revisionist right wing, and clearly and unequivocally pointed out the way to remedy the mistakes and forge ahead in building socialism. The resolution was put into effect quickly and with determination. At the same time, however, the dictatorship of the proletariat did not take strong enough measures to subdue the ever more arrogant enemy, for it underestimated their strength. This is why it came as a surprise to the Party when, on October 23, 1956, with active imperialist support, the class enemies managed to turn the chauvinistic, reactionary demonstration "justified" in terms of the "events" in Poland into a nationwide, counterrevolutionary insurrection. Throughout the country, they "freed" tens of thousands of criminals, sworn enemies of the people's rule, who then came to set the tone of the insurgent troops. They began to "liquidate" communists and patriots true to the people's democracy: they brutally tortured and killed 234 communists and patriots; they carried out manhunts and lynching in broad daylight on the streets, planned to execute the three thousand patriots they had taken prisoner, and put tens of thousands of patriots on various "death lists." [1]

In the face of these events, the leaders of the government and the Party took twofold action. On the one hand, they took military action, calling for help on the Soviet troops stationed in the country in accordance with the terms of the Warsaw Pact; on the other, in an effort to isolate the attacking enemy from the masses, they made more and more concessions to the revisionists, believed, at the time, to be working for the Party. When these revisionists seized power within the Party and the government, they did not use it to save the people's rule but capitulated to the counterrevolution. They dismantled some of the forces fighting for the people's rule, and put others under the direct command of the insurgents. They eliminated opposition to the counterrevolution, and fully satisfied all counterrevolutionary demands: they switched to a coalition government, withdrew from the Warsaw Pact, declared the country's "neutrality," and so on.

When it seemed that the filthy flood of the counterrevolution would—for the second time in our nation's history—relentlessly lead to the restoration of bourgeois rule, the Soviet Union, with yet another instance of brotherly help in the spirit of the internationalism of the proletariat, complied with the requests of those communists who, in opposition to both factions, represented the Party and the basic class interests of the working class. The newly formed Revolutionary Workers' and Peasants' government took the situation in hand: it destroyed the armed forces of the counterrevolution, eliminated the counterrevolutionaries who had retreated to continue their rearguard action within "Workers' Councils" and "Revolutionary Committees," and with amazing speed, consolidated the dictatorship of the proletariat. This, too, proves that in Hungary, in 1956, the mass support of the counterrevolution was based on demagogy, on misleading the masses and defrauding the people.

In contradistinction to the requirement expressed by defendant no. 1 that every single detail of the above historical chain of events in all its historical, economic, and political ramifications, as well as all the actions of the principal players, be explored and considered before a verdict is reached, the People's Court Division of the Supreme Court, in establishing the facts of the case, had—by the nature of its office—to limit itself to establishing the facts concerning the following questions:

A. Does the political power group which formed around the person of Imre Nagy constitute "a conspiracy or movement aimed at overthrowing the order of state" as defined in section 1 of the BHÖ?
B. If it was, in fact, such a conspiracy (movement), what criminally relevant role did their collective activities play in:
   1.) the October 23, 1956, eruption of the counterrevolution;
   2.) the course the counterrevolution took between October 23 and November 4, 1956;
   3.) the fight to frustrate the consolidation of the dictatorship of the proletariat after November 4, 1956?
C. Were the individual defendants' activities part of the collective activities of the seditious conspiracy (movement), and if so, to what extent?

== A ==

1.) From the second half of 1955, a coterie of resentful bourgeois intellectuals gathered around the person of Imre Nagy, defendant no. 1, who coupled correcting the errors made in the course of building socialism with a rightist distortion of the dictatorship of the proletariat. This group, which, in the early stages, did not constitute a seditious conspiracy, was heterogeneous in respect to the political past and views, and so on, of its members. Some of them (Miklós Gimes, Pál Löcsei, etc.) wanted to erase the memory of their sectarian past and the political responsibility they personally bore for the mistakes referred to above by now following an extremely rightist ideology. Quite early on already, they suggested that the way to correct these mistakes was to return to bourgeois democracy. Others (Ferenc Donáth, Géza Losonczy, etc.) were driven by a thirst for vengeance, on account of the grave and unjustifiable injuries they had suffered in the course of the above-mentioned mistakes. They sought the solution in radical personal changes in the leadership of the Party and the government ("a changing of the guard"), and they gathered around the person of Imre Nagy because they thought he would facilitate these changes. In the final analysis, they, too, reached a point where they identified the injuries they had suffered with the dictatorship of the proletariat, and in order to prevent future mistakes of the kind, they acquiesced in its eradication. Closing ranks with these two types of individuals were people wavering in their socialist conviction, opportunists, and so forth. (Sándor Haraszti's statement as a witness; Szilárd Ujhelyi's statement made during the investigation and read at the trial on the basis of section 165, paragraph /2/, item b/ of the Bp; statements of the defendants Ferenc Donáth, Miklós Gimes, Ferenc Jánosi, and Miklós Vásárhelyi.)

At the end of 1955, this group planned to take collective action to block the possibility of Imre Nagy's expulsion from the MDP. When they were persuaded to drop the plan, they contemplated another collective action at the initiative of the defendants Miklós Gimes, Ferenc Jánosi, Miklós Vásárhelyi, and others, against the real and existing shortcomings in the MDP's cultural policies. Imre Nagy, defendant no. 1, had advance knowledge of the plan and agreed with it, but took exception to the fact that the action would not be extended to other issues, such as economic policy, and so on. (statement of Sándor Haraszti). The originators, however, went ahead with the initial plan, modifying it only in that they brought writers, artists, and so forth, into its execution rather than government functionaries involved in the cultural sphere. They drew up what later became known as the "writers' memorandum," and organized, in a conspiratorial manner, to have this document signed by persons engaged in the cultural, artistic, and scientific fields. The conspiratorial nature of this collective action—not even its staunch supporters knew whence the movement originated; signatures were gathered through indirect channels, often through a chain of two or three intermediaries, though the people involved were in close personal contact with each other; and so on—the fact that people working in a specific field were made to repudiate not only the shortcomings in that particular field but also to oppose the leadership of the Party and of the government, as well as the fact that for the first time (though later repeatedly), non-Party members were called upon to decide on matters that were strictly the Party's internal affairs, placed these activities beyond those of an "in-Party factional grouping," and lent them the complexion of a conspiracy to undermine the order of state. While the majority of the signatories—having been convinced of the impropriety of the action—did withdraw their signatures (something which Imre Nagy took strong exception to), they did not expose or dispense with either the powers behind it, or their methods, but allowed them to go on to convince others that "essentially" they had been right and their actions were objectionable from "only a formal" point of view.

With this collective action, therefore, the circle of persons supporting Imre Nagy was substantially expanded in various cultural organizations (the Journalists' Association, etc.), and the political influence of the action's organizers, Imre Nagy's "inner circle," greatly enhanced.

2.) During the same period of time (late 1955-early 1956), Imre Nagy, defendant no. 1, put his political ideas in writing, and secretly circulated them among his "inner circle"—as witness Sándor Haraszti noted, "He peddled his papers." The "circle" then began to spread the contents of these writings by word of mouth, as a political platform. (József Szilágyi, for example, copied long sections from one of the papers given to him by Imre Nagy for this purpose, to include them in a speech he planned to deliver at the Petőfi Circle.) From the contents of the original papers (mimeographed by Imre Nagy) contained on pp. 127-337 of vol. 7 of the documents of the investigation, the People's Court Division wishes to highlight the following:

a.) In his December 1955 essay of twenty typewritten pages, "Timely Moral and Ethical Issues in Hungarian Public Life" (hereafter referred to as "Morals and Ethics"), exaggerating the mistakes that were actually made, Imre Nagy claimed that prior to June 1953, the Party leadership had "bankrupted" the country; "It had compromised the ideal of socialism, and proved the untenability of the targeted aims and tasks." This statement was meant to prove that in 1955, and subsequently, the leadership of the Party and the government was a "degenerate Bonapartist power," which was itself jeopardizing the future of socialism and which warned against the dangers of capitalist restoration (not a real danger, as he saw it), only to thwart "the only solution": their removal by force, the "changing of the guard."

b.) In a study of October 1955, 172 typewritten pages (twenty-five chapters) long, written—according to the defendant—"to clear up some misunderstandings," he not only gossips about happenings within the ranks of the MDP's leadership, but in chapter 1 ("Some Timely Questions about the Application of the Theories of Marxism-Leninism") elaborates his notion that the people's democracy is a "democratic" transformation from capitalism to socialism, and not, therefore, the dictatorship of the proletariat. In the course of expounding this theory, he goes as far as to indirectly deny the leadership role of the working class and its Party, and talks about returning to a multiparty system, even about the idea of alliance with the forces opposing the people's democracy.

c.) In a nineteen-page composition of January 1956 called "The Five Basic Principles of International Relations, and the Timely Issue of Our Foreign Policy," he uses the term "power blocs," thereby equating the aggressive imperialist bloc with the defensive alliance formed to counterbalance it. The latter he refers to as "a Stalinist dogma that needs to be done away with." He goes on to say that participation in this alliance "violates" Hungary's independence and sovereignty; it is, thus, "an immediate and realistic task" of our people's democracy's foreign policy "to oppose all power blocs on the basis of either neutrality or active coexistence as the country's position on the international scene."

The People's Court Division hereby establishes the fact that the tenor and the content of these writings—though not fully illustrated by this admittedly short excerpt, or rather by the highlighting of some of the thoughts characteristic of the whole—is such that they are defamatory to the people's democratic order of state, and incite hatred against it. How far this is so is illustrated by the fact that one of the members of Imre Nagy's "inner circle"—who is not named as defendant in these proceedings—thought it appropriate to forward them to the Revolutionary Council of Strasbourg, to be used in their hostile campaign against Hungary. It was to this end that he contacted one of the employees of the British Embassy in the spring of 1957, who got the manuscript to the "West." The gang of traitors had it reproduced in tens of thousands of copies, and has tried to get them back into the country as the most effective weapon in their smear campaign against the Soviet Union and Hungary. (Statement of László Regéczy-Nagy; material evidence presented to defendant no. 1 at the trial.)

3.) As of the spring of 1956, Imre Nagy's "inner circle" began using its earlier-attained and growing political influence within the cultural mass organizations (writers', journalists', and artists' associations) to spread Imre Nagy's "ideas" among the intelligentsia in general, and the intellectual youth in particular, thereby to increase the number of Imre Nagy's "followers" and to sow the seeds of distrust and hostility toward the Party and the government. They infiltrated various other cultural fora as well (Petőfi Circle, TTIT, the people's college alumni reunions, etc.). At the Petőfi Circle's press debate, Tibor Tardos openly referred to "our growing troop" as he spoke up as the representative of the new party destined to rule.

The fact that Imre Nagy and his "inner circle" discussed and coordinated these activities at social and family gatherings (such as "birthday celebrations") was established on the basis of statements of witness Sándor Haraszti and the statements of the defendants Ferenc Jánosi and Miklós Vásárhelyi. Imre Nagy exerted his influence on the Petőfi Circle directly through Balázs Nagy, who subsequently fled to the West, and both he and his associates—primarily Géza Losonczy and Miklós Vásárhelyi—through Gábor Tánczos and László Kardos. Those leading the Petőfi Circle's debates were almost exclusively the members of this "inner circle" (Géza Losonczy, Szilárd Ujhelyi, and Ferenc Donáth).

The speeches that were planned to be given were discussed in advance. József Szilágyi, for instance, had his wife take the manuscript of his planned speech—which, incidentally, he never delivered—to Imre Nagy for his comments: did he think it too harsh, or its contents proper from a tactical point of view?

When Imre Nagy returned the composition along with his own article entitled "Fighting for Lenin's Ideals" to be incorporated in the speech, Szilágyi complied. (Judgment rendered in the criminal case against József Szilágyi, and Imre Nagy's partial confession.) Géza Losonczy, Sándor Haraszti, and other members of the group held a preliminary discussion on Tibor Déry's planned address at the Petőfi Circle's so-called press debate. They relayed the essence of the speech to Imre Nagy, who, also prior to its delivery, sent a message to Déry to make certain tactical changes in the text. (Judgment rendered in the proceedings against Tibor Déry and his associates; partial confession of Imre Nagy, defendant no. 1.) Immediately prior to delivering the speech, already at the meeting, with witness Sándor Haraszti as the intermediary, he showed the part of the text in question to Ferenc Donáth, defendant no. 2. The importance Imre Nagy, defendant no. 1, attached to strict adherence to his "tactical guidance" is well illustrated by the letter—introduced at the trial—that Tibor Déry wrote to him a few days after Déry delivered the speech without altering the text to comply with the message (Documents of the criminal investigation in the case against Tibor Déry and his associates, vol. 4, p. 237). In this letter, Déry stated that he was so deeply offended by Imre Nagy's sharp attack during their conversation a few days after the speech that he decided to terminate all his political activities.

4.) On the basis of defendant Sándor Kopácsi's defense confirmed by several parties and of the judgment rendered in the criminal proceedings against József Szilágyi, the People's Court Division also established as fact that it took József Szilágyi and György Fazekas—to all appearances working independently—a year to recruit Sándor Kopácsi, or to use defendant Sándor Kopácsi's term, to "ensnare" him. Szilágyi built on the influence he had gained over Kopácsi as his one-time superior and on the fact that Kopácsi disagreed with the expulsion from the MDP of his friend and relative, György Fazekas. Imre Nagy's study "Morals and Ethics," was also brought into the persuasion effort. When, as a result of the lengthy persuasion, defendant Sándor Kopácsi's political views began to approximate their own views, in early October 1956 Szilágyi introduced Kopácsi to Imre Nagy at a social gathering, so that the latter might finally allay the former's doubts.

5.) The People's Court Division of the Supreme Court established as fact the truth of that part of Imre Nagy's, defendant no. 1's, defense, whereby in the summer of 1956 he rejected Miklós Gimes's, defendant no. 3's, suggestion that the members of the ever-growing group form an illegal committee to coordinate, direct, and supervise their activities. In comparing the line of defense of Imre Nagy, defendant no. 1, as presented in the course of the proceedings, the self-damaging confession of Miklós Gimes, defendant no. 3, and the statements of Miklós Vásárhelyi, defendant no. 8, and of witness Sándor Haraszti, the People's Court Division was obliged to establish as facts, and draw conclusions from them concerning further facts as follows:

Miklós Gimes, defendant no. 3, first made his proposal to witness Sándor

Haraszti, who protested vehemently, and at the next chance he had, informed Imre Nagy of the proposal, terming it a deplorable thought. Miklós Gimes, defendant no. 3, presented his idea to Imre Nagy, defendant no. 1, as well. Imre Nagy, defendant no. 1, took the position that as long as they could carry on their activities within "legal" parameters (in reality, with the appearance of legality), no illegal means should be employed. On the one hand, Imre Nagy's position reflected his fear of being found out; that is why he disapproved of the usual conspiratorial means—when they were not needed. On the other hand, he was satisfied with the coordination his personal "guidance" created. Certainly, he never put his "guidelines" to a vote, but as the already-established facts also indicate (see section 3 above), he expected his followers to accept them as a measure of their behavior. Imre Nagy did not wish to transfer his personal power to any committee. The third point is that this direct, personal leadership gave Imre Nagy an opportunity to use his personal prestige and influence to involve people in their activities who would not have accepted the leadership and control of such a conspiratorial committee. (See Sándor Haraszti's reaction to the proposal.) This type of organizational structure would, therefore, have narrowed their sphere of influence.

6.) The validity of these conclusions is lent further support by another fact likewise established by the People's Court Division on the basis of the statements of Miklós Gimes, defendant no. 3, Ferenc Jánosi, defendant no. 7, and Miklós Vásárhelyi, defendant no. 8, namely, that Imre Nagy, defendant no. 1, rejected the use of conspiratorial means only when they were not expedient. At the same time, he commissioned the above-mentioned individuals to draw on their personal contacts with Georgievich, first secretary of the Yugoslav Embassy, and deliver to him, in a conspiratorial manner (see statement of facts above, section 2, paragraphs a and c), the written studies he was secretly circulating among his "followers" but kept carefully hidden from the leaders of the party and the government, with whom he was carrying on negotiations at that time.

7.) On the basis of the statement made during the investigation by the since-deceased Géza Losonczy presented at the trial and of the statement of witness Sándor Haraszti, the People's Court Division established as fact that in mid-October 1956 they arranged, at the residence of a third person (Dr. Lajos Hatvany), a likewise conspiratorial meeting with Anna Kéthly to discuss and find out what position the right-wing social democrats would take vis-à-vis a new Imre Nagy government which would realize the aforementioned goals. During the trial, Imre Nagy, defendant no. 1, in face-to-face confrontation with witness Sándor Haraszti, admitted that the above individuals reported to him on the meeting, and that he had objected to neither the means nor the subjects discussed.

Having collated all the above facts, the People's Court Division could only come to the conclusion that while the political power group forming around Imre Nagy started out as an "in-Party faction," with their collective action in connection with the "writers' memorandum," with their distribution of Imre Nagy's articles on his "views," with their recruiting of "followers" on the basis of the above writings, with their negotiations on collective action with parties of a different political conviction, and with their airing of the Party's internal problems in order to find solutions outside the Party, it took on the character of a conspiracy to undermine and overthrow the order of state. This conspiracy, exerting pressure on various mass organizations, youth groups, and associations, created a movement appropriate to the above objectives. The political activities of the members of the conspiracy were planned and coordinated, and were, in essence, directed by Imre Nagy, defendant no. 1.

== B ==

1.) In examining the correlations between this conspiracy and the movement it created, and the counterrevolution of October 23, 1956, the People's Court Division refers, first of all, to the above-stated facts. It has, furthermore, established the following:

a.) It was the propaganda activity carried on by the members of the conspiracy in the manner described above (part A, section 3) which gave political and ideological meaning to the writers' and journalists' campaign of "exposure," in which the "trendsetters" were Imre Nagy's "followers," the members of the movement. In their articles and writings, the participants in this offensive deliberately suppressed or belittled the advances made during the twelve years of building the socialist system, vilified the achievements of the working class, and magnifying the mistakes that were made, exploited them in a campaign of demagogic incitement. They tried to outdo one another in their particular campaign, hitting an ever more demagogic note; at best, they became indifferent to the dictatorship of the proletariat, to the issue of correcting past mistakes. With increasing frequency, they expressed in their writings the idea that correcting the mistakes of the past was possible only at the price of "basically changing the system." The possibility of solving the problems within the dictatorship of the proletariat came to be alien to their reasoning, and ever more openly and consistently, they declared the writers and the intelligentsia in general to be the ones destined to lead the nation. (Judgment in the criminal case against Tibor Déry and his associates.) As a result of the activities partly of the writers and partly of the people motivating them—the members of the conspiracy—the hysterical raging of this senseless destruction spread to the various intellectual youth organizations and fora (Petőfi Circle, TTIT, the people's college alumni reunions, etc.), where they began a concentrated attack to discredit the policies of the Party and the government, and against the hegemony of the working class.

With perfidious references to the spirit of the SZKP's Twentieth Congress and the claim that they and only they constituted its representatives in Hungary, and that without them, this spirit would never be realized in Hungary, they managed to forge a link between honest people legitimately worried by the circumstances slowing down our progress and the attack by forces hostile to the people's democracy. They made use of every means of demagogic incitement, including capitalizing on people's chauvinistic and even irredentist sentiments. With this, they cleared the way for the class enemies and imperialist agents who—by using the same "terminology"—managed to draw significant numbers of young people, intellectuals, white-collar workers, and even workers under their influence. This clouded the judgment of many decent people, preventing them from dealing with the enemy as enemy. All sorts of enemies of the people's democracy recognized the immense significance this movement held for them as a force destructive of our political order, and joined in confusing the parameters of the class struggle.

Not even this fact's becoming obvious, and the MDP's denouncing their machinations within the Petőfi Circle in a resolution of June 30, 1956, stopped [the group] in their downward slide. In the face of witness Sándor Haraszti's suggestion that they call a temporary retreat, it was specifically Imre Nagy, defendant no. 1, who charged the witness, as well as Ferenc Jánosi and Miklós Vásárhelyi, not to desist but rather to help accelerate and consolidate the attacks. (Statements of witness Sándor Haraszti, and statements of defendants Ferenc Jánosi and Miklós Vásárhelyi.) The fact that they took this stand partially lest their retreat be construed as an admission of the guilty nature of their earlier activities is irrelevant.

It was this stand that prevented them from being able to contain the movement they had created, or to reject even the most extremist of views. By September and October of 1956, it was the movement itself, the movement they had created—and the class enemies and imperialist agents (Radio Free Europe, etc.) which "supported" it—that forced Imre Nagy and the members of his conspiracy to draw practical conclusions from their proclaimed principles.

On the basis of the partial confession which Imre Nagy, defendant no. 1, made during a face-to-face confrontation at the trial, and on the self-damaging statement of Ferenc Donáth, defendant no. 2, the Court Division has established as fact that at the time the movement was turning into the kind of conspiracy it became, leaders of the Party and government gave several warnings—as, for example, through Ferenc Donáth, defendant no. 2—that Imre Nagy and his "inner circle" should dissociate themselves from the reactionary elements applauding them, lest they become the standard-bearers of reactionary views. (Not a direct quote.) Not only did Imre Nagy and his "inner circle" disregard the warning, but during the face-to-face confrontation at the trial, Imre Nagy stated that his reply had been that they should identify by name which reactionaries they had in mind.

b.) The People's Court Division has established as fact that prior to October 23, 1956, the group accelerated their destructive activities, and extended them to new areas as well. Gyula Háy and other writers held a "literary" conference at the Zrinyi Academy to determine if there were any "Kucsera"[2] in the army. They held and planned gatherings of intellectuals in the rural cities as well. They gave lectures in Győr, Debrecen, and in the cities of Hajdú county. (Statement of Ferenc Donáth, and the judgment delivered in the criminal case against Tibor Déry and his associates.) The rally held in Kaposvár by the Writers' Association to protest against the organization of agricultural cooperatives sent a telegraphic greeting to Imre Nagy. József Szilágyi wanted to organize a similar meeting in Kecskemét. He went to Kecskemét on October 20, 1956, and presented "the Imre Nagy group's evaluation of the political situation" to the leading functionaries of the county government. Commenting on the events taking place in Poland, he said that a similar removal of the "Stalinist members" of the Party and government leadership was needed [in Hungary, too], and that political demonstrations and the explosive mood of the masses were nothing to be afraid of. "I get a kick out of revolutionaries who get scared before anything's ever happened," he said in response to the anxiety expressed by his listeners. He consistently talked about "taking over power," even after one of those present corrected him twice in a row. (Judgment delivered in the criminal case against József Szilágyi.)

c.) In the judgment delivered in the criminal case against Tibor Déry and his associates and introduced at these proceedings, it was established that developing the consistent political platform against the MDP in the period immediately preceding, and in the initial stages of, the counterrevolution took the form of various groups condensing their political programs into "points" and circulating them as such. The common denominator was arrived at by the "Revolutionaries" subsequently through their adoption of some points and the deletion of others. It was this system which made total unity possible in matters of detail among parties with irreconcilable views. In addition to the aforesaid, the People's Court Division, in the light of part A, section 2 of the statement of facts, must establish the additional fact that all their differences notwithstanding, some of these "points" were even originally in agreement as concerns certain matters:

As is clear from the evidence submitted in the large number of counterrevolutionary criminal actions brought before the People's Court Division of the Supreme Court, practically all the "program declarations" (flyers) called for the following: a "changing of the guard" (statement of facts, part A, section 2, paragraph a); the "extension" of "democracy," a demand which, in essence, was aimed against the leading role of the working class and its Party (statement of facts, part A, section 2, paragraph b); the repudiation of the international solidarity of the proletariat, the declaration of the country's neutrality, and its withdrawal from the Warsaw Pact (statement of facts, part A, section 2, paragraph c). It was Imre Nagy who had first formulated these demands in his cited writings of 1955 and early 1956, and it was the members of the conspiracy who had disseminated them sometimes explicitly, sometimes in the form of oblique references.

d.) On the basis of the statement of witness Sándor Haraszti, of the statement made during the investigation by, and autograph notes of, the since-deceased Géza Losonczy presented during the trial, of Imre Nagy's partial confession, and of the confession of Ferenc Donáth, the People's Court Division has established as fact that a person not named as defendant in these proceedings looked up Sándor Haraszti, and offered to introduce at the following meeting of the Party's Central Leading Body a motion stressing the necessity of those radical changes within the highest leadership which the group was urging. He also offered to work out, or rather, to organize the drafting of an all-inclusive program for the future Imre Nagy government, and to present this, too, at the meeting. (The People's Court Division wishes to point out as characteristic [of the people involved] that in return for his "services," the individual in question "requested" membership in the political committee and the position of secretary to the Council of Ministers.) (Géza Losonczy's notes.) The individual informed Imre Nagy of his plan; then, on the evening of October 22 and 23, he arranged a meeting between Géza Losonczy, Ferenc Donáth, Miklós Gimes, and a number of careerists from outside the group (a total of some eight to ten people), who agreed to undertake the outlining of the program, and divided the work among themselves into four sections: domestic policy and people's front; foreign policy; economic policy; and party building and ideology.

e.) Likewise, on the basis of Géza Losonczy's statement during investigation and of his autograph notes, as well as on the basis of the statement by witness István Márkus, the Court has established as fact that the company gathered on the evening of October 23, 1956, at the home of László Kardos discussed how the "followers" of Imre Nagy were to take over the crucial functions within the DISZ and how this "changing of the guard" would improve the situation as far as "party positions" were concerned.

f.) The People's Court Division established as fact that in the evening of October 22, József Szilágyi appeared and spoke twice at the student rally at the University of Technology. Some 5,000-6,000 students had assembled to discuss the recommendations of the University of Szeged and the on-campus "auxiliary circles" of the Petőfi Circle (the dissolution of the DISZ, the establishment of the MEFESZ and various university-related as well as economic and political demands). As the meeting progressed, there were more and more indications of a growing extremism. In his first address—which was the first explicitly and strictly political one—the defendant, analyzing the events in Poland, stated that the fight for democracy and against the "Stalinists" still went on and that the declaration denouncing the events in Poznan was null and void. He also stated that Soviet troops had surrounded Warsaw, that the Polish troops had taken up positions against the Soviets, and that these were the circumstances under which the Soviet leaders had arrived in Poland to negotiate. He drew a parallel between the Polish and the Hungarian events, and considered the university's meeting an important step in the fight. As a result of his speech, harsh anti-Soviet shouts could be heard for the first time at the meeting. His comments added fuel to the already-explosive atmosphere, and were an incitement to mass demonstration. His second speech came a few hours later, when Dean Csolnoky cautioned the students to be circumspect. It seemed as if he would succeed in dissuading them from demonstrating in the streets, and in having them dispatch a delegation to Imre Nagy instead, when the defendant declared that he, as a member of Imre Nagy's "immediate circle," was against their sending their demands to Imre Nagy instead of demonstrating, for Imre Nagy was not in power, and turning to him was not the way to get their demands met. Again he urged the need for a demonstration. After leaving the student rally, József Szilágyi telephoned Imre Nagy, reporting to him on how the meeting went and on the role he personally had played in it. Imre Nagy told him it had been a tactical blunder to have taken a clearly pro-demonstration stand, and to have referred to his ties to himself to give weight to his words. After his conversation with Imre Nagy, József Szilágyi also telephoned Sándor Kopácsi, informing him of the rally at the University of Technology and the demonstration the students were organizing for the following day. The next morning he went to see Kopácsi in person, and again asked that the police not interfere with the demonstration. In the course of the discussion, when Kopácsi said that he had had negative experiences in connection with both the Miskolc (1946), and the Budapest (1954) demonstrations, Szilágyi told him: "That's the policeman in you; a communist is not afraid of the masses. . . . If we want something, we also have to want the means to get it." (Judgment delivered in the criminal case against József Szilágyi.)

g.) On the basis of autograph notes confiscated in the house search of the since-deceased Géza Losonczy and his statement in the course of the investigation, on the basis of the testimonies of witnesses Sándor Haraszti and Gábor Tánczos, of the statement made in the course of the investigation by Szilárd Ujhelyi and cited during the proceedings, as well as of the confessions of defendants Miklós Gimes, Ferenc Jánosi, and Miklós Vásárhelyi, the People's Court Division has also established as fact that on October 23, 1956, at 10:30 a.m., at Géza Losonczy's telephone request, there appeared at his residence Imre Nagy, Ferenc Jánosi, Miklós Gimes, Miklós Vásárhelyi, and several other members of the group not named as defendants in these proceedings. The individuals thus gathered were in constant telephone contact with Gábor Tánczos, one of the leaders of the Petőfi Circle organizing the demonstration, who kept them abreast of the developments of the demonstration, while they, in turn, provided him with "advice." It was on October 22 and 23 that the leadership of the Petőfi Circle extended its central direction and coordination to most universities and colleges, where demonstrations were initiated by the "auxiliary circles" of the Petőfi Circle. By this time, József Szilágyi had taken a stand at the University of Technology in support of the demonstrations, while Géza Losonczy and others not named as defendants in these proceedings had direct personal experience of just what was going on.

The above initiatives were enthusiastically welcomed by the members of the conspiracy as being a significant step toward their realizing their aims, though the developments did occasion a certain amount of anxiety. (See Kopácsi's opinion above.) The People's Court Division has established as fact that Imre Nagy, too, expressed concern during the discussions, and told his associates that "he was very much afraid of the demonstration, and if possible, it should be stopped." Nevertheless, when Miklós Gimes, Géza Losonczy, and Miklós Vásárhelyi replied that there was no way to stop the demonstration, Imre Nagy continued to actively participate in discussing the "advice" they would give the organizers of the demonstration. (Statement of Miklós Gimes, defendant no. 3, at the trial.)

At the same time, evaluating the information they were receiving and discussing the situation as it was developing, they came to the conclusion that the situation was ripe for the effectuation of "due changes": the Political Committee of the MDP would soon be forced to negotiate with them. They decided that at these negotiations they would make their participation in the leadership contingent on certain conditions; they also decided who was to be removed from the Political Committee, the Central Leading Body, and from certain government functions, and who would be co-opted in their place. "There was a brief discussion on whether Imre Nagy should become prime minister or first secretary of the party. Nagy was of the opinion that he should be prime minister, not first party secretary. That was how people remembered him, and they wanted him to be prime minister once again. The others eventually concurred. . . . It was understood that we would all consider this agreement a binding one. We would act in strict adherence to it. In light of the situation, we would meet on a daily basis." (Documents of the investigation, vol. 3, pp. 130-150; vol. 11, p. 481.) The issue of whether to return to a coalition government or to give their political theories—as outlined in the statement of facts, part A, section 1, paragraph d—some alternate, "people's front-type" form, was also discussed at this meeting. This question, however, remained unresolved. Defendant Ferenc Jánosi prepared some notes on the discussions, which contained primarily the names of those involved in the proposed changes, but at the end of the meeting, it occurred to them that the ÁVH could still catch them unawares, so they decided to destroy the notes.

h.) Thus, the members of the conspiracy—Imre Nagy, defendant no. 1, included—considered the October 23, 1956, demonstration as the irreversible result of the movement they had created, and looked upon it as the vehicle that would carry their "ideals" on to victory. The since-deceased Géza Losonczy's statement in the summer of 1956 to Elon Ámos, the Israeli journalist staying in Budapest at the time, bears this out. Géza Losonczy declared that he would not rule out the possibility of the people overthrowing the government in Hungary, and if it came to that, that would suit him fine. Losonczy added: "This is my personal opinion, and probably the opinion of my political friends as well." (Documents of the investigation, vol. 9, pp. 158-160.) Witness Gábor Tánczos, the Petőfi Circle's secretary, the one who, on October 23, 1956, had relayed to the demonstrators the "guidance" of the conspiracy's leadership (see paragraph g above), made the following statement in his radio address of October 24, 1956: "I am speaking to you in the name of the Petőfi Circle, in the name of the organization that has done so much in the past few months to attain true democracy, to abolish the Rákosi-type, disgraceful tyranny . . ." and "has called for the peaceful demonstration of all young people in support of the correct goals." On October 28, 1956, in a radio address full of pathos, Tibor Déry said: "When the first gunshot was heard, the blood rushed out of my head: 'You, too, are responsible for this. You talked, you agitated; how will you account for the dead?'" At the time, he had "gladly and proudly" accepted responsibility before the whole world. (Judgment delivered in the criminal case against Tibor Déry and his associates.)

On the basis of the statement of witness Zoltán Szántó, and despite denials by Imre Nagy, defendant no. 1, and Ferenc Jánosi, defendant no. 7, the People's Court Division of the Supreme Court has established as fact that in November 1956, at the Yugoslav Embassy, in the presence of the witness, defendants nos. 1 and 2, and others, Ferenc Jánosi, defendant no. 7, made the following statement: "We all have to realize that we were the ones who initiated, organized, and touched off the enormous popular movement which burst into flame on October 23, 1956." Those present accepted this statement, for no one objected. Similarly, no one objected to another statement made at another time by another member of the conspiracy (György Fazekas), when he said: "We shouldn't mind those who falter. Comrade Nagy remembers that when we told the Yugoslav comrades that we were heading for an uprising, they, too, were hesitant for a while." (Zoltán Szántó's statement at the trial.)

In collating the above facts, the People's Court Division had to arrive at the conclusion that, as a result of the destructive political agitation of Imre Nagy and the other members of the conspiracy, it was the movement they created, that is, the campus auxiliary circles of the "Petőfi Circle," that launched the October 23, 1956, demonstration, with the personal collaboration of some of the members of the conspiracy (Gábor Tánczos, József Szilágyi, etc.) with the purpose of carrying Imre Nagy's "ideals" on to victory, while subverting the existing order. Other members of the conspiracy (Géza Losonczy; Imre Nagy, defendant no. 1; Miklós Gimes, defendant no. 3; Ferenc Jánosi, defendant no. 7; Miklós Vásárhelyi, defendant no. 8; and others), themselves considering the demonstration the irrevocable result of their own activities, strove to define its direction and take "command" of it through Gábor Tánczos and the leadership of the "Petőfi Circle."

2.) Concerning those activities of the conspiracy, or rather, of the movement it created, which contributed to the development of the counterrevolution between October 23 and November 4, 1956, the People's Court Division of the Supreme Court hereby registers the following facts:

a.) Between October 23 and 28, 1956, certain members of the conspiracy and the movement they created concentrated around three different nuclei which maintained close contact with one another. They exchanged information, kept each other abreast of their activities, and coordinated them. One of the nuclei (consisting of the since-deceased Géza Losonczy; Ferenc Donáth, defendant no. 2; Ferenc Jánosi, defendant no. 7; and others) was established around the person of Imre Nagy, defendant no. 1, and was located in the MDP Central Leading Body building. Another nucleus, located in the Deák Square building of the Budapest Police Headquarters, was established around the person of Sándor Kopácsi, defendant no. 4. József Szilágyi, Tamás Aczél, Miklós Gimes, defendant no. 3, György Fazekas, Pál Löcsei, Tibor Méray, and others gathered there.

The third nucleus was located on the premises of the Writers' Association.

Between October 23 and 25, 1956, there was a certain degree of reluctance, uncertainty, and ambiguity in the behavior of some of the individuals within these nuclei, as noted in connection with the defendants by the People's Court Division in part C of the statement of facts. During this time as well, however, the initiatives and the directives came from the nucleus established around the person of Imre Nagy, although—especially after October 25—the Deák Square nucleus, and József Szilágyi in particular, showed an inclination to take over, in order to speed up developments. The People's Court Division here refers to the section of the verdict delivered in the criminal case against József Szilágyi, establishing the circumstances of the "workers' delegation from Angyalföld," as well as of József Szilágyi's "reporting" to Imre Nagy on October 30.

In the first part of this period—between October 23 and 25—insistence on the group's earlier political platform and adherence to its resolutions were specific mainly to the conduct of the since-deceased Géza Losonczy, Ferenc Donáth, defendant no. 2, and Ferenc Jánosi, defendant no. 7. Between October 25 and 27, however—due primarily to central directives and initiatives—those grouped around the three nuclei closed ranks. Through personal appearances by Géza Losonczy and Ferenc Donáth at various party fora, and through a variety of delegations organized under a multitude of names by József Szilágyi and sent to Imre Nagy, defendant no. 1, they demanded that the MDP leadership change its evaluation of the events, meet their demands, take over the leadership of the "revolution," trust itself to the armed forces of the "insurgents," and openly declare its agreement with their political platform. The most persuasive of the above delegations was the so-called workers' delegation from Angyalföld, through which members of the conspiracy (József Szilágyi, Miklós Gimes, etc.) obliged Imre Nagy to stand by their ideals, and introduced the thought of openly and demonstratively breaking with the party.

b.) On October 28, when, faced with this concerted and categorical action of the conspiracy, the MDP leadership was compelled to compromise, the group called together the members of the Petőfi Circle, the one-time students of the people's colleges, and the writers, in short, all the members, followers, and sympathizers of the conspiracy, or rather, the movement, and formed a new body, the Revolutionary Committee of Hungarian Intellectuals, hereafter MÉFB. The signatories to the "Declaration" (documents of the investigation, vol. 37, p. 198) issued at this constitutive meeting of the "Committee" were selected not to reflect the composition of the circle who had framed it but to imply that the MÉFB held a summit position within the network of "revolutionary committees" set up by the various intellectual groups and organizations (the University Revolutionary

Committee, and those of the Writers' Association, the Journalists' Association, the Artists' Association, the Musicians' Association, the university faculty members, NÉKOSZ members, the Petőfi Circle, the MEFESZ, etc.). The MÉFB, however, did not concern itself with any of these other committees. Instead, their debates centered around what party or movement to organize to take the place of the MDP, should it be dissolved. They arranged the negotiations between Imre Nagy and József Dudás, tried to mediate on József Mindszenty's behalf, and initiated the formation of the National Committee, which dispatched students all over the country to "rouse up" the rural population. As the members of the Imre Nagy conspiracy and movement saw the situation at the time, though they had managed to bend the MDP leadership to compromise, the "danger of a left-wing restoration" was growing. They had to be on the alert lest the "revolution" lose its élan, and the forces defending the dictatorship of the proletariat gain the upper hand as the armed confrontations dragged out, and the peasantry continued to be passive. (Statement of witness István Márkus.) This is how Géza Losonczy evaluated the situation to those gathering on October 29, and this is what motivated them to publish the "Declaration" simultaneously with issuing the "Government Proclamation."

The concurrent publication of the "Declaration," they felt, was necessary because they were not satisfied with the "Government Proclamation" in the form that had been accepted by the party fora and by the one and only meeting of the Council of Ministers of the Imre Nagy government, that is, in the form in which Imre Nagy was to announce it in his radio broadcast the following day. They found it inadequate despite the fact that the theses on which the "Proclamation" was based had been formulated by the most prominent members of the conspiracy (Ferenc Donáth, Géza Losonczy, Miklós Gimes, Tibor Déry, Sándor Haraszti, etc.), whom Nagy Imre had assembled at the Deák Square center for this purpose and who had made use also of the text proposed by Miklós Gimes, defendant no. 3. The group's stand notwithstanding, the "Proclamation" did not announce the "dissolution of the ÁVH" (as was falsely stated in the "Declaration") but touched on it only in connection with the forming of a new police force once order had been reestablished. Nor did it announce the withdrawal of the Soviet troops (also stated in the "Declaration"), only that negotiations to that effect would be initiated. The most serious discrepancy between the two stands, that is, between the two announcements, centered around the issue of the "national guard." The "Government Proclamation" called upon "all who have taken to arms to refrain from fighting, and surrender their arms without delay. A new police force will be established immediately from units of the military and the police, and from armed contingents of the workers and the young people."

The authentic interpretation of this passage of the "Proclamation" comes from a concurrent order issued by the Ministry of Internal Affairs (statement of Sándor Kopácsi), whereby 75 percent of the contingents attached to the police and military units were to be composed of factory workers who had taken up arms in defense of party buildings, and so on, and 25 percent of young people. The true intent of this government action, therefore, was to ensure the dominance of communist influence within every individual unit and to give the young people an opportunity to take part, under this influence, in safeguarding the government and in reestablishing order. Imre Nagy himself acknowledged that this was what he had discussed with the minister of internal affairs and other officials.

In direct contradiction of the above, the "Declaration" of the MÉFB called on the followers of Imre Nagy—on the members of the Petőfi Circle and the NÉKOSZ, and so on—as well as on "all valiant insurgents" and "all armed groups" to form the new police force "to safeguard the achievements of the revolution." The logical conclusion to be drawn from the full content of the "Declaration" was that the "achievement" [that the framers of the document had in mind] was an "independent," "neutral," "democratic" state that stood "above classes." [It was to be] a state led by the intelligentsia and built on "workers' councils" and "revolutionary committees," one with privatized commerce, free competition, and unlimited (!) freedom of speech. This political program is in keeping with the ideas which Imre Nagy put into writing in 1955 and early 1956. (Statement of facts, part A, section 2.)

c.) This sort of maneuver, when the members of a front organization express their disagreement with the radio address of the parent organization's leader by distorting its text in a public declaration to mean what they want it to mean ("as you know from the broadcast . . ."), goes beyond the everyday conspiratorial tactics of subversive organizations. Concurrently, they launched an unparalleled press campaign to popularize "the Imre Nagy of the future," and to slander the forces remaining loyal to the Party and the government. It was the MÉFB declaration that set the tone for this campaign as well: "In vain did Ernő Gerő's criminal clique scheme with all their might. In vain did they try to isolate Imre Nagy from the revolutionary masses. . . . The shameful times when a gang of criminals foreign to the people could usurp power and hold true patriots in fear are gone once and for all."

In essence, the same message was conveyed by Pál Löcsei's "Open Letter to Imre Nagy," Tibor Tardos's "We Are Behind Uncle Imre," and the Revolutionary Student Committee's "Our Trust Is in Imre Nagy" (documents of the investigation, vol. 37, p. 198), as well as by Zoltán Zelk's newspaper interview with Sándor Kopácsi, defendant no. 6, entitled: "Who Are Behind the Machine Guns?"

Common to all the above is that in them, the members of the conspiracy give false statements to the effect that to that point, Imre Nagy had been "a prisoner of the ÁVH," and had been "forced" to make his statements. Sándor Kopácsi even recounted the epic story of his "rescue." (Documents of the investigation, vol. 32, pp. 107-108.) The message of all of them is that in "captivity," Imre Nagy had fought "heroically" for his ideals, had won, and now that he was about to satisfy their aspirations, their confidence in "the Imre Nagy of the future" was unbroken.

On October 30, the day of the bloodbath at Köztársaság Square,[3] between 6:30 and 7 p.m., they made a statement later repeated in an "official broadcast" on radio: "We wish to place on the record of history, fully cognizant of the responsibility we assume in so doing, that Imre Nagy, president of the Council of Ministers, had no knowledge of the Soviet troops being called in, nor of martial law being declared. . . . These orders do not bear his signature."

d.) The Imre Nagy "of the future" did not disappoint his followers. He never again convened the Council of Ministers, not even to hear them out about the most crucial government decisions. He also disregarded the provisions in the government proclamation approved by the Council of Ministers as to the measures to be taken. In Budapest, and all over the country, thousands of criminals were let out of prisons. There were manhunts in the streets in broad daylight; communists, democrats, and patriots loyal to the dictatorship of the proletariat were murdered, hung by the feet on the trees lining the streets and in the squares, and their dead bodies desecrated. Tortured people, still alive, were tied by their feet behind trucks, and pulled along the streets of Miskolc. The lives of three thousand captured patriots were in the hands of the counterrevolutionaries. Meanwhile, Imre Nagy, defendant no. 1, and the members of his circle began organizing and arming the "national guard" from among these "valiant insurgents," from these "members of the armed groups." (At the Budapest Police Headquarters alone, following the orders of Imre Nagy, defendant no. 1, Sándor Kopácsi, defendant no. 6, distributed over twenty thousand arms among the counterrevolutionaries.) They hoped to neutralize, with their help, the forces still capable of saving the country—primarily the brotherly assistance [of the Soviet Union]—from the wholesale repetition of the disgrace of 1919, the bloody white terror. It was József Szilágyi who, on November 2, described the true nature of the "national guard" most candidly and most succinctly when he said to some acquaintances that he was aware that there were also some hooligans, staunch enemies of the people, and fascists in the "national guard," but that in his opinion, the principal threat, for the moment, was the Russian threat, for the Russian armored "hordes" were advancing, and it was they who had to be fought by all. (Judgment delivered in the criminal case against József Szilágyi.)

This was why Imre Nagy, the president of the Council of Ministers, conducted negotiations with Iván Kovács, whom he knew to be a villain, with the Pongrácz group, and so forth, and why, on the evening of October 30, the evening of the bloodbath at Republic Square, he issued a joint communiqué with József Dudás, one of the most vicious of the thugs, about their "successful" negotiations. This was why he appointed Béla Király, whose conduct left little to the imagination (statements of Sándor Kopácsi and Pál Maléter), to be the commander of the "national guard." This is what explains the fact that likewise on the evening of October 30, the day of the bloodbath at Köztársaság Square, contrary to the government proclamation but in accord with the MÉFB declaration, Imre Nagy, defendant no. 1, ordered Béla Király, in writing, to set up the Revolutionary

Special Police Committee, the general staff of the "national guard" to be composed primarily of the representatives of "those who had taken part in the revolutionary fighting, and so forth." (Documents of the investigation, vol. 8, p. 53.)

e.) Imre Nagy, defendant no. 1, as president of the Council of Ministers and as acting foreign minister, in one of his telegrams to the U.N. (documents of the investigation, vol. 8, p. 45), stated, "The government of the Hungarian People's Republic hereby confirms that all telegrams, letters, and messages, as well as the information they contain, which we are and will be sending to Your Excellency, represent the official stand of the entire Hungarian government"; and he rejected the suggestion that statements he sent on behalf of the government did not represent the unanimous stand of all members of the government. It has been established as fact, however, that after October 28, 1956, Imre Nagy totally ignored the lawfully appointed government, and did not convene the Council of Ministers. He looked upon his ministers as office managers with no say in the business of government, did not consult them even in the matter of whom he would appoint as deputies to their individual portfolios, and humiliated them by discussing their replacement with their own subordinates.

This is how he appointed Pál Maléter, defendant no. 5—after he openly went over to the side of the counterrevolutionaries—first deputy to the minister of defense. On November 1, when he still had an active interior minister, he conferred with Sándor Kopácsi on appointing him to the post of minister of the interior. On October 30, he issued his announcement concerning the establishment of the "national guard," directly contradicting the orders of the minister of the interior and without first consulting with, or even advising, the minister.

In place of the lawful government, he instituted a governmental organ based on the "coalition" principle and foreign to the constitution called the "cabinet," into which—personally assuming the competence of the Presidential Council[4]—he "co-opted" originally five, and later, as a "coalition" move, more and more individuals. Without seeking authority from either the Council of Ministers or from the Presidential Council, he transferred all decision-making power to this private body. Eventually, with further extensions of its competence, the "cabinet" took over for the Council of Ministers, the Presidential Council, and Parliament, and later began to exercise even judicial power. It was this private body which installed Pál Maléter as minister of defense "on behalf of the insurgents"; implemented the restructuring of the government; determined the withdrawal from the Warsaw Pact, the declaration of neutrality, and the "rehabilitation" of Mindszenty; and kept sending telegrams to the U.N. urging the great powers to "guarantee" the country's declared neutrality.

The People's Court Division of the Supreme Court has established as fact—coinciding with the statement of Imre Nagy, defendant no. 1—that the official statement to the effect that the Presidential Council had relieved the earlier members of the Council of Ministers at their own request and replaced them with individuals already participating in the meetings of the cabinet was a sheer lie, with not a word of truth in it. The People's Court Division has also established that—contrary to the denial of Imre Nagy, defendant no. 1—the above-mentioned official statement was totally in keeping with the decision reached at the cabinet's November 2 meeting. The defendant's denial notwithstanding, the People's Court Division has, moreover, accepted as factual the recorded minutes of the meeting, which are substantiated by contemporary radio announcements and by the statement of Mrs. József Balogh.

The People's Court Division also established as fact that the since-deceased Géza Losonczy, one of the leaders of the conspiracy and a member of the private body usurping government authority, established and maintained conspiratorial contacts—through another member of the group—with the staff of the Yugoslav Embassy in Budapest, who gave him advice while he supplied them with information.

Imre Nagy and the leaders of his seditious group, relying on the "cabinet" and operating behind the iron curtain of white terror, lost no time in implementing the political program spread by his followers which he had formulated already in late 1955 and early 1956.

In an anti-Soviet alliance with the mushrooming new parties of the forces hostile to the people's democracy (in a matter of days, over seventy reactionary, fascist, and counterrevolutionary parties and organizations reported their operation to the "cabinet"), in alliance with murderous counterrevolutionary bandits and the "revolutionary," "national," "workers'," and sundry other "committees" in the clutch of the class enemy, they destroyed the rule of the working class and the dictatorship of the proletariat. They steered the nation into such desperate straits that not only the lives of honest people but world peace itself was in jeopardy, and it was only the steadfastness of its most loyal communist sons that saved the country. These forces, supported by the Soviet Union's brotherly help extended in the spirit of proletarian internationalism, swept away the counterrevolutionary mafia, and put an end to their manifest treason and class betrayal.

At that time, Imre Nagy, defendant no. 1, in his radio appeal, protested against the reestablishment of order. "This is Imre Nagy speaking, president of the Hungarian Council of Ministers. Today at dawn, Soviet troops—obviously aiming to overthrow the lawful government—launched an attack on the nation's capital! Our troops are engaged in battle; the government is standing firm!"

When Imre Nagy, defendant no. 1, delivered this proclamation, as the People's Court Division has already established, the "lawful government" was not only not functioning but according to a press release by the "cabinet" usurping governmental authority, had been dissolved. Furthermore, not even the "cabinet" was standing firm: Imre Nagy and the majority of his conspiracy's leadership had, at the invitation of the ambassador, moved into premises of the Yugoslav Embassy enjoying extraterritoriality.

3.) The People's Court Division of the Supreme Court pronounces as fact that the group taking refuge on the premises of the Yugoslav Embassy did not concede that they had been unmasked before the entire nation and that they failed to accomplish their goals. Taking advantage of the privileges afforded to foreign embassies, they continued to conspire against the reestablishment of the government and public safety. Some of the group's members, declaring themselves the "Executive Committee of the MSZMP," established contact, and/or started negotiating with:

a.) leaders of the Yugoslav government and its representatives, on internal affairs which have no place in the relations of even friendly states (documents of the investigation, vol. 7, pp. 360-379);

b.) their "coalition partners" (the most reactionary leaders of the one-time Smallholders' Party), urging them to flee abroad, so as to be in a position to cooperate with the Western foes of the people's democracy (statement of Tivadar Pártay during the trial);

c.) Radio Free Europe—indirectly—to inform "world public opinion" behind the backs of their hosts (witness testimonies of Zoltán Szántó and György Fazekas); and

d.) their followers, the members of the conspiracy who had stayed outside the embassy, concerning the steps they were to take to prevent consolidation and the reestablishment of the dictatorship of the proletariat.

Around November 10, through Gábor Tánczos, who was also staying at the embassy, they polled Balázs Nagy, among others, for their opinion as to the future of the movement: should they continue their disruptive work from within the MSZMP, should they form a new party, or would a people's front type of movement be more in line with what they [their supporters] had in mind? This "opinion poll" was what provided the impetus to the establishment, on November 13, of the "Hungarian Democratic Independence Movement," which later published the gutter rag called *October 23rd.* (Witness testimonies of György Ádám, Róbert Bohó, and Gábor Tánczos.)

== C ==

With regard to the individual activities and responsibilities of the defendants within the above-described parameters of conspiracy against the state in these criminal proceedings, the People's Court Division has established the following facts:

1.) The sixty-two-year-old Imre Nagy, defendant no. 1, of poor peasant parentage, a doctor of economic sciences, academician, university professor, and one-time prime minister, served his apprenticeship as fitter, then finished commercial college. He did his military service on the Russian front, was taken prisoner, and from 1917, took part in the Red Army's military actions in Siberia and in leftist movements. In July 1918, he joined the SZKP. In 1921, he returned to his home in Kaposvár, and participated in the MSZMP movement headed by Vági; then, acting on party orders, he left the country. He lived in exile in the Soviet Union, working on agricultural problems, and was, for a while, head of the Lenin School's Hungarian Department. Later, he worked in the Central Statistical Bureau of the Soviet Union. Then, from 1939, he headed the [Soviet] radio's Hungarian Department. During World War II, he volunteered for military service, but in 1942, he was ordered back to the radio's Hungarian Department. After the liberation, he was, first, minister of agriculture; then, for a short time, was minister of internal affairs. He then worked at Party Headquarters. After 1947, he became the speaker of Parliament, while his primary occupation was that of a university professor. At the end of 1951, he became minister of food administration, then minister for the collection of surplus agricultural products and livestock, then deputy prime minister, and in June 1953, prime minister. On account of the above-described differences of opinion, an April 1955 decision of the MDP's Central Leading Body relieved him of all his offices, and on December 5, 1955, he was expelled from the Party.

When, after being stripped of his offices, the defendant realized that the above-described circle was forming around his person, he suggested to this group, without success, that they initiate collective action (the collection of signatures to obstruct his expulsion from the Party) as a "Party opposition." Soon after this, when members of this circle suggested that people in the cultural field take collective steps against the Party's cultural policies (the writers' memorandum), he criticized the fact that they did not include the Party's overall—economic, and soon—policies in their attack, and disapproved when some people—realizing the imprudence of collective action—withdrew their signatures.

Concurrently—and this, by the way, coincided with his expulsion from the Party—he worked out his political platform in writing (statement of facts, part A, section 2), and began distributing copies of the same among his "followers." On his orders, Miklós Gimes, Miklós Vásárhelyi, and Ferenc Jánosi established illegal contact with First Secretary Georgievich of the Yugoslav Embassy, and arranged for his writings—whose very existence he kept a closely guarded secret from the MDP's Central Leading Body—to be sent to the Yugoslav leaders. It was with his explicit knowledge and concurrence that members of his "inner circle" (Géza Losonczy, Sándor Haraszti, László Kardos, etc.) began to organize those in the various social groups (Writers' Association, Journalists' Association, Petőfi Circle, TTIT) who shared their views to launch an attack against the people's government and to spread the ideas laid down in the written platform. Whenever the above individuals needed some coaching, defendant no. 1 himself provided it (e.g., his message to Déry, concerning Déry's speech; his editing of Szilágyi's planned speech, etc.). He objected to using conspiratorial means where they were not expedient. He acknowledged, after the fact, that Losonczy and Haraszti discussed with Anna Kéthly the possibility of [the group's] cooperation with the right-wing social democrats. It has not been proven, however, that the discussion he held with István Erdei, at the latter's residence in 1956, was to the same effect. He acknowledged that, on October 22, a person not named as defendant in these proceedings, for a chance to attain certain positions, did, in effect, start to work out a government program, and offered to present it to the MDP's Central Leading Body, along with proposals for changes in the leadership.

On the morning of October 23, he was at the illegal discussion where, through Gábor Tánczos, they provided the leaders of the Petőfi Circle with "advice" on organizing the demonstration and where they decided on the tactical effectuation of the "due changes."

Regarding the defendant's behavior during this period of time, the People's Court Division was particularly careful in evaluating the line of defense to the effect that he had a moderating effect on his associates, and tried to restrain them.

In this connection, the People's Court Division refers to a fact established in part B, section 1, paragraph a of the statement of facts, which contradicts this line of defense. It was he himself who charged those named that they not check but rather intensify and concentrate their attack. The Court Division also refers to the facts and conclusions established in part A, section 5 of the statement of facts, and cannot, on that basis, conclude as a fact in the defendant's favor that he rejected the use of conspiratorial means.

The Court refers to the facts established in part A, section 3 of the statement of facts as concerns Tibor Déry's speech at the Petőfi Circle. In this respect, the People's Court Division has come to the conclusion that the tactical difference of opinion between the two of them does not mean that the views of Imre Nagy, defendant no. 1, were the more moderate ones. The People's Court Division also refers to a fact established in part B, section 1, paragraph f of the statement of facts, namely, that when, on the night of October 23, 1956, József Szilágyi talked to Imre Nagy on the telephone and reported on his "performance" at the University of Technology, Imre Nagy, defendant no. 1, objected to—or, to use the expression József Szilágyi used at his own trial, "gave him a good dressing down" for—his referring to their relationship while urging the demonstration. It must be added that on the basis of the unrefuted defense of Imre Nagy, defendant no. 1, the People's Court Division has also established as fact that the same night, a delegation from the University of Technology went to see him. They asked that he go with them, talk to the masses gathered [at the university], calm them down, and thereby forestall the demonstration, but he refused.

Collating these facts with the facts established in part B, section 1, paragraph g of the statement of facts, namely, that on the following morning the "general staff"—along with defendant no. 1, who had, by then, mastered his uneasiness—provided the leaders of the Petőfi Circle, through Gábor Tánczos, with "advice" on organizing the demonstration, one can only conclude the fact that this change in behavior was also a tactical one. Defendant no. 1 was much more careful and more circumspect in achieving his subversive aims than were some of his associates. He took the precaution of trying to erase the traces of his seditious conduct as far as possible. This defendant also stated in his own defense that after October 23, he, unlike his associates and "comrades," did not tailor his actions to the decisions reached on October 23 (statement of facts, part B, section 1, paragraph g), but abided fully by the decisions of the MDP's leadership. Responsibility for his actions, therefore, lies not with him but with those who made those decisions.

Examining the facts also from this point of view, the People's Court Division declares the following:

On October 23, 1956, Imre Nagy, defendant no. 1, did remain at home and declined all public appearances until the leadership of the MDP called upon him to appear in public. At that point, he and his associates went to the Parliament, and delivered a pacifying speech to the masses gathered in the square (for which he was hooted down), and then, likewise at the request of the MDP leadership, went to Party Headquarters. He was present when the measures for militarily crushing the counterrevolution—calling in the Soviet troops being one of them—were approved. His passive behavior gave no hint to the rest of those bringing these decisions that Imre Nagy, defendant no. 1, was not in complete agreement. He accepted without comment or condition his nomination for the position of prime minister, as well as being co-opted into the MDP's leading organs. In general, his behavior was passive. He offered no [dissenting] opinion on any of the measures being contemplated, and some of his comments and gestures even strongly suggested that he was in full agreement with the central leadership's evaluation of the situation and with the contemplated measures (calling for the help of the Soviet troops; martial law—which he himself signed; the curfew; the military annihilation of the counterrevolutionary centers, etc.). The defendant himself testified that he welcomed as heroes and embraced the defenders of the radio building who had survived the attack and later reported to the central leadership.

Even as far into the events as October 25, 1956, Imre Nagy, defendant no. 1, declared in a radio address: "A small number of counterrevolutionaries and agitators have launched an armed attack against the people's democratic order. . . . The Soviet troops' armed intervention has been necessitated by the vital interests of our socialist order." (Documents of the investigation, vol. 8, pp. 11-12.)

The People's Court Division has had to establish as fact, however, that in the meanwhile and at the same time, Imre Nagy, defendant no. 1, was obstructing the implementation of the above measures. At the suggestion of Ferenc Jánosi, defendant no. 7, he lifted the curfew imposed for October 24, 1956, which was to ensure and facilitate the eradication of the counterrevolutionary centers, so that "his tenure as prime minister should not start off with the imposition of a curfew." Similarly, he registered his opposition to the military action being planned for the annihilation of the Corvin Alley counterrevolutionary core, and so on. (Witness statement of István Kovács.)

It has also been established that a great many delegations went to see him within this period, and he tried to receive all of them personally. The People's Court Division wishes to cite as typical the delegation of the conspicuously hooligan gang which had occupied the army's printing facilities and called themselves "the antigovernment." He promised them impunity, and postponed the hour the curfew was to start in order to allow them safe passage. (Statement of witness János Virágh.)

Further, it has been established that some of the delegations Imre Nagy received on behalf of the central leadership did not simply turn up, spontaneously, but were advised of the MDP leadership's actions and intentions by those associates of Imre Nagy, defendant no. 1, who "operated" as his immediate assistants and obtained their information directly from him. To boot, the writers' delegation received on October 26 was organized by Ferenc Jánosi, defendant no. 7, with the prior knowledge of Imre Nagy, defendant no. 1, and an armored vehicle was supplied for the transportation of this group and the concurrently received "student delegation" (which had hardly a student among them). [Imre Nagy] asked his "followers" within the Writers' Association for their recommendations in connection with the redistribution of ministerial portfolios, recommendations which were diametrically opposed to the composition of the government being discussed at Party Headquarters.

These delegations' views (already familiar to Imre Nagy from earlier consultations) were presented by defendant no. 1 to the leadership of the MDP as "public opinion." It has been proven that Imre Nagy, defendant no. 1, was telling these delegations ever more bluntly that for his part, he agreed with them, and denied that he had been the one to issue the orders for the declaration of martial law. He was not even aware, he told them, of the Soviet troops having been called on for help, and disavowed solidarity with the MDP leadership and with the measures it was taking.

The behavior of Imre Nagy, defendant no. 1, was, at the time, equivocal. In collating the facts, the People's Court Division has had to arrive at the conclusion that what was behind this equivocation was not uncertainty and hesitation, nor his suddenly recoiling from carrying out his seditious plans, but treachery and double-dealing.

What supports this conclusion is the circumstance under which Imre Nagy, defendant no. 1, discontinued his equivocal behavior, to pursue frankly and straightforwardly and in full cooperation with his associates, the goals he himself had set in late 1955 and early 1956.

The change in his behavior coincided with his realization that the MDP leadership would not appoint his candidates for the ministerial portfolios (József Szilágyi for minister of internal affairs, László Kardos for minister of education, etc.). Secondly, he realized that he was losing the confidence of some of his associates, those who did not know what motivated his conduct. Thirdly, but most importantly, there was the group's evaluation of the situation of the moment: with the counterrevolution dragging on and the peasantry's continuing passivity, there was a growing danger of the movement's losing its élan, the forces defending the dictatorship of the proletariat getting the upper hand, and a left-wing restoration.

It was Imre Nagy, defendant no. 1, who put the finishing touches on the web of lies directed against the ÁVH, the most stable of the units defending the Party and the government (statement of facts, part B, section 2, paragraph c), as part of a campaign started by the members of the conspiracy to popularize "the Imre Nagy of the future." Not only did he not remonstrate with his "comrades" for their deliberate campaign of vilification with lies rotten to the core, but on October 31, the day of the bloodbath at Köztársaság Square, he said the following to the several hundred people gathered in front of the Parliament: "We are living the first days of our freedom and independence. We've got enormous obstacles out of our way. We have swept Rákosi and Gerő's gangs out of the country. The gravity of their crimes is inconceivable. . . . They have spread the lie that I was the one who called in the Russian troops," he continued. "That is a filthy lie. The Imre Nagy who has championed Hungarian sovereignty, Hungarian freedom, and Hungarian independence could not possibly have called in those troops." (Documents of the investigation, vol. 8, folder no. 18.) The defendant Imre Nagy, who made these statements when manhunts were raging in the city streets cannot say, at the moment of reckoning, that in reality, he was on the side of the communists.

The People's Court Division has had to reject as factually untrue the defendant's line of defense to the effect that as president of the Council of Ministers, he engaged in his above-described actions and behavior (statement of facts, part B, section 2, paragraph d) acting on the decisions of the leadership of the MDP, or rather, of the MSZMP, and of the "cabinet." (The People's Court Division will return to some of the other nonfactual aspects of this line of defense when examining the question of culpability.)

In connection with the factual aspects of this defense, the People's Court Division wishes to refer to a fact already established, that the part the defendant played in setting up the "national guard" had nothing to do with either the compromise within the party, or with the government proclamation. It was, however, in keeping with the stand taken in the MÉFB declaration. As concerns the changes in government, the withdrawal from the Warsaw Pact, and the declaration of neutrality, on the basis of the statements of Ferenc Donáth, defendant no. 2, and Zoltán Szántó, witness, as well as on the partial confession of Imre Nagy, defendant no. 1, during a personal confrontation at the trial, the People's Court Division has had to establish as fact that the reason the above individuals reproached Imre Nagy in the first days of November—but before November 4—was precisely that he would not submit decisive measures to the party leadership for preliminary approval even when Zoltán Tildy, defendant no. 4, declared at a meeting of the so-called "cabinet" that he could not decide on matters of such importance without first consulting with the leaders of his own party (the Smallholders' Party).

The People's Court Division would not be misled by Imre Nagy's using the terms "government of national unity" and "coalition government" as synonyms. This kind of ploy would not delude the People's Court Division: the former concept does not involve forsaking the dictatorship of the proletariat, while the term "coalition government" rules out the dictatorship of the proletariat by definition.

It has also been established as fact that Imre Nagy and the general staff of his movement presented to the "cabinet" the most important of these measures, the withdrawal from the Warsaw Pact and the declaration of neutrality, in the form of *faits accomplis*. The "cabinet" meeting was started with putting up posters in the streets. (Defense of Zoltán Tildy, defendant no. 4, supported by the statement of witness Mrs. József Balogh.)

This is also substantiated by the fact that though there was no mention of withdrawal from the Warsaw Pact at the cabinet meeting of October 31, 1956, Imre Nagy announced "the termination of our Warsaw Pact obligations" in his above-mentioned speech to the masses gathered in front of the Parliament.

There was insufficient evidence to prove that defendant no. 1 had any knowledge, prior to his flight to the Yugoslav Embassy, of the conspiratorial contact Géza Losonczy and another member of the group not named as defendant in these proceedings maintained with the members of the embassy.

He had full knowledge, however, as the leader of the group, of the events taking place at the embassy. It was at his express wish that a member of the organization not named as defendant in these proceedings got in touch with Radio Free Europe. He took part in the discussion that determined on the "opinion poll" (statement of facts, part B, section 3, paragraph d), and it was he who, on behalf of the group, carried on negotiations with the Yugoslav leaders.

2.) The forty-five-year-old Dr. Ferenc Donáth, defendant no. 2, of intellectual parentage, finished law school, participated in the activities of the illegal communist party after 1932, and started working as a newspaperman for the *Szabad Szó* in 1940. After the liberation, he was vice president of the Estate Reallocation Council, then undersecretary of agriculture until 1948. He was arrested without cause, and unjustly sentenced to a long term in prison. Rehabilitated in 1954, he was named assistant director of the Institute for Economics. He wanted to withdraw from politics altogether. At the urging of a number of people and giving in primarily to Sándor Haraszti's persistent influence, he abandoned this stand, and in the spring of 1956, joined the already-established subversive movement grouped around Imre Nagy. He took part in their discussions, became familiar with some of Imre Nagy's above-mentioned writings, and took part in the group's organizational and propaganda activities. He became the leader of the Petőfi Circle's debates on economics and market gardening in Hungary. In the days immediately preceding October 23, he spoke publicly in Debrecen.

On the basis of the unrefuted defense of the defendant, the People's Court Division has established that his tone at these public speaking engagements was much more moderate than that of his associates. But though he did not approve of the kind of incitement they engaged in, he did not act on his conclusions. He did not leave the organization, and did not even loosen his ties to it. At the so-called "market gardening in Hungary" debate, he did not take exception to the hostile comments or repudiate the hostile incitement.

In the summer of 1956, one of the leaders of the MDP asked him to deliver a message to Imre Nagy, defendant no. 1, warning him [and his followers] to dissociate themselves from the reactionary masses who applauded them, lest they become the standard-bearers of the reactionaries. Ferenc Donáth, defendant no. 2, delivered the message but remained loyal to [Imre Nagy] and to the conspiracy despite the cynical answer given by defendant no. 1.

In the evening of October 23, 1956, returning from Hajdú county and having already heard of the demonstration, he took part in a meeting at the SZÖVOSZ dealing with setting up a new program, and offered to work out the program's agricultural section. Moreover, he handed over some written material he had prepared earlier on the subject, the contents of which the People's Court Division has been unable to learn.

Between October 24 and 26, 1956, he and the since-deceased Géza Losonczy were the two members of the conspiracy who fought most consistently for the decisions reached at the home of Losonczy on October 23. The Central Leading Body had co-opted the defendant to be a member as secretary; Géza Losonczy, too, became a member of the central leadership and an associate member of the Political Committee. On October 24, by joint decision, they both resigned from their respective functions, stating that they considered the turn of events to be solely the fault of the previous leadership. The changes initiated by the new leadership, they maintained, were inadequate. What they wanted was "decisive and fundamental change." Géza Losonczy told the defendant that a decision to that effect had been made at his residence on October 23, and criticized the conduct of Imre Nagy, defendant no. 1, who had taken part in making it but did not abide by the decision. They demanded that their action be made public. Upholding their resignation, they attended the October 25-26 meetings of the MDP's central leadership, and made their further participation in that leadership subject to certain conditions. They demanded that the counterrevolution be evaluated as a "democratic movement," that general amnesty be given to the armed insurgents, that the Soviet troops immediately withdraw from Budapest, that the armed counterrevolutionaries be consolidated into the armed forces, and so forth. To substantiate their demands, they, too, referred to the "writers' delegation" organized by Ferenc Jánosi, defendant no. 7, as one reflecting public opinion. Since their demands were not met, they reiterated their resignation, informed the counterrevolutionary delegations of what had happened, and put their resignation into writing. (Documents of the investigation, vol. 15, p. 11.)

They left the Party Headquarters together, and along the way, defendant no. 2 suffered some minor injuries. Still, he was present at, although he did not actively participate in, the meeting called by Imre Nagy, where the general staff of the movement drafted the "Government Proclamation." Along with Géza Losonczy, he also attended the informatory meeting of the MÉFB, and was present at the meeting with József Dudás.

Between November 1 and 4, he and witness Zoltán Szántó reproached Imre Nagy for his scornful treatment of the executive committee of the MSZMP, and objected to the manner in which the matter of the withdrawal from the Warsaw Pact had been handled.

On November 4, at dawn, however, he did take part in drafting Imre Nagy's radio address, and he, too, took refuge with his family at the Yugoslav Embassy. Here, he was a member of the conspiracy's leading organ, the so-called Executive Committee, and took part in the decisions specified in part B, section 3 of the statement of facts.

This defendant has stated that at the Yugoslav Embassy and subsequently, he began to realize that they had taken the wrong path, and had stood by Imre Nagy only because he felt that the latter was under the wrong influence and wanted to steer him in the right direction. The People's Court Division has established that it was, rather, Imre Nagy, defendant no. 1, who had managed to influence Ferenc Donáth.

3.) The forty-one-year-old Miklós Gimes, of intellectual parentage, had studied, before the liberation, to be a doctor of medicine, but did not complete his studies. He has been taking part in the workers' movement since 1942. After the liberation, he became a newspaper reporter. He was expelled from the party in 1955, but was reinstated in 1956. He was one of the first, in 1955, to join the group forming around the person of Imre Nagy. He was one of those who wanted to remedy the sectarian errors that had been made by returning to the multiparty system and doing away with the dictatorship of the proletariat. His friends (Pál Löcsei, György Fazekas, etc.) encouraged him to join the group. Imre Nagy gave him copies of his own writings, which he studied, and then he participated in the meetings of the conspiracy with full knowledge of their content. He began spreading the same ideas through his own articles, for example, "Two Kinds of Justice," "Let There Be Light." (Documents of the investigation, vol. 18, pp. 287-288.) It was he who proposed that they form an illegal committee for leading and coordinating the activities of the members of the conspiracy. As established earlier by the People's Court Division, Imre Nagy, defendant no. 1, rejected this proposal.

On October 22, 1956, he took part in the meeting called at the SZÖVOSZ to draft the new program, and undertook to work out the section pertaining to foreign affairs.

On October 23, 1956, he took part in the meeting held at the residence of Géza Losonczy, where they discussed the action to be taken.

Between October 23 and 27, he stayed at the editorial offices of the *Szabad Nép*, where, in the absence of the leading editors, he himself assumed editorship. On October 27, he went to the Budapest Police Headquarters building, where he took part in the meetings of that nucleus of the conspiracy and in the decision that the "workers' delegation from Angyalföld" go to see Imre Nagy, defendant no. 1, and urge him to openly stand by his own ideals. He was a member and one of the spokesmen of the delegation. As a result of his performance, Imre Nagy, defendant no. 1, asked him right away to help draft the text of his radio address in the event they won. He spent the night at the Deák Square Police Headquarters, where he was informed first by Ferenc Jánosi, defendant no. 7, and later by witness Sándor Haraszti, that "they'd won." He composed the text as promised, and on the morning of the 28th, he and his associates took it to Imre Nagy, defendant no. 1, where the most influential members of the conspiracy had assembled to discuss the proposed address. He, too, participated in the discussions, and several points of his proposed text got included in Imre Nagy's final version. (Imre Nagy took the proposed text to the leaders of the Party and to the Council of Ministers for their approval, and made certain changes, as already established by the People's Court Division.)

On October 29, 1956, with Pál Löcsei, Péter Kende, and other right-wing associates of the *Szabad Nép*, they started a new daily, the *Magyar Szabadság*. Miklós Gimes, defendant no. 3, wrote the editorial for the first issue, specifying the paper's program. In his article, he took a stand for a return to a "neutral" democracy "representing the people," and attributed the fact that there were some reactionary, antidemocratic, and antiprogressive "tendencies"—though only a few—present in "our glorious revolution" to "the cliques of Rákosi and Gerő having so criminally abused the patience of the Hungarian people." The People's Court Division has also established as fact, however, that immediately following the appearance of the first issue of the *Magyar Szabadság*, Miklós Gimes, defendant no. 3, gave up his editorship because in the interim, József Dudás and his bandits had occupied the *Szabad Nép* building, and were torturing and killing people there. Under the circumstances, defendant no. 3 saw no assurance that he would be able to continue to have the paper reflect his own political convictions. He got into a conflict with his associates over this issue.

This notwithstanding, he was moved to ponder neither his political stand nor his association with the conspiracy. Immediately after November 4, when he alone of the general staff remained outside the embassy compound, he accelerated the pace of his activities. On around November 6-8, with persons not named as defendants in these proceedings, he reproduced and distributed some four hundred copies of the leaflets composed by Miklós Gimes, defendant no. 3. The message of these handbills was that Imre Nagy was alive and in safety and that the Hungarian people should put up such a fight as to force the Soviet officials and government to negotiate with Imre Nagy. On November 13, at 11 a.m., he went to the meeting of the Journalists' Association held at the offices of the Writers'

Association. Then, in the afternoon, he went to the Hess András Square college of the University of Technology to attend a student rally. At both places, the gist of his speech was that "the legal government was Imre Nagy's government." The fight had to go on until such time as the Soviet authorities and government recognized this fact and started to negotiate with Imre Nagy.

He had been invited to this latter meeting by witness Sándor Herpai, who, the day before, had got the impression that the students might consider recognizing the Revolutionary Workers' and Peasants' government and be willing to cooperate with it in the interest of consolidation.

Upon succeeding in his incitement, again at the invitation of witness Sándor Herpai, Miklós Gimes, defendant no. 3, also appeared at the residence of witness Róbert Bohó, where they discussed the political situation with several comrades not named as defendants in these proceedings. It was to this meeting that the runaway Balázs Nagy, now abroad, delivered the message of the "Executive Committee" headquartered at the Yugoslav Embassy, the message transmitted through witness Gábor Tánczos. For the contents of this message, the People's Court Division refers to part B, section 3, paragraph d of the statement of facts.

The People's Court Division has established as fact that the thought that "something should be done" to prevent consolidation had occurred to some of the participants independently of the message. This, in fact, was why the meeting had been called. The results of the debate can be summed up as follows:

They established the "Hungarian Democratic Independence Movement," an illegal, subversive organization (the name came from Miklós Gimes, defendant no. 3). They decided that the leadership of this organization would be made up of the people present, and allocated their respective spheres of activity. They accepted as their political platform the MÉFB's already-known declaration, with the proviso that the corrections necessitated by the changed circumstances would be made by György Ádám and Miklós Gimes. (No data have come to light during the trial as to whether this was actually done.) They set as the movement's primary task the loose, not really organized, people's front-type coordination and leadership of all the forces standing on the platform of November 1, that is, those opposing the MSZMP, and the Revolutionary Workers' and Peasants' government. They decided to use the newly reorganized Revolutionary Council of Hungarian Intellectuals, established by the most distinguished scientists, writers, and artists, as their vehicle for exerting their influence, effectuating their leadership, and swaying public opinion, and hoped to get the Council to represent their views to the government. (No clarification was made during the trial as to what actually happened in this regard.) They also decided to start an "organization" paper under the name *October 23rd*, an illegal leaflet, whose technical production and distribution was undertaken by persons not named as defendants in these proceedings.

Miklós Gimes, as the editor of *Október Huszonharmadika*, invited his journalist comrades to his office and called upon them to participate in bringing out the paper. Péter Kende, who has since escaped to the West, and other persons not named as defendants in these proceedings volunteered to do so. They completed four issues under the editorship of Miklós Gimes, defendant no. 3, prior to his arrest, and another six to eight issues with Péter Kende as editor, and on November 13, with the help of some designated persons, they reproduced and distributed them in some three hundred to five hundred copies. As for the contents of this illegal gutter rag, other than referring to the copies on file and introduced in the course of the proceedings (documents of the investigation, vol. 18, pp. 303-320, 348-354), the People's Court Division goes on record in stating that in this collection of third-rate, filthy articles of contemptible tenor, the Party, the Revolutionary Workers' and Peasants' government, the Soviet Union, and the Soviet troops were abused, and the workers were called upon to resist, in a fascist tone which is without parallel in the history of even this conspiracy. Defendant himself saw the indefensibility of all this when, under the right to the last word, he noted: "After what has been said during this trial, I have very little to say. To fight facts with words would make no sense."

The People's Court Division establishes as fact that between November 4 and 25, 1956, Miklós Gimes, defendant no. 3, took part in several discussions held at the residences of various members and sympathizers of the Imre Nagy conspiracy. At these meetings, the defendant represented the most die-hard point of view. He declared that "if the Hungarian people does not want socialism, it cannot be forced upon them." He noted repeatedly that Marxism was "obsolete," and urged his associates to completely dissociate themselves from the MSZMP, the Revolutionary Workers' and Peasants' government, to stay away from the Party, to refuse any office they might be offered, and so forth.

4.) The sixty-nine-year-old Zoltán Tildy, of intellectual parentage, was originally a Presbyterian minister. Even prior to the liberation, he was one of the organizers and leaders of the Independent Smallholders' Party. After the liberation, he became prime minister, then held the office of the president of the republic until 1948. While he was in office, his son-in-law, Viktor Csolnoky, was caught spying against the republic, was sentenced to death, and executed. Following this, from 1948 to 1954, the defendant himself was under so-called house arrest and stayed away from all political activity. After October 23, 1956, at the request of the Party leadership, he delivered a calming radio broadcast, then became minister of state in the Imre Nagy government. As minister of state, he staffed his secretariat with reactionary elements (such as Dr. Zoltán Hámori, etc.), who acted in his name, appointed reactionary extremists to government posts, and so on. It could not be established in the course of the trial whether the defendant had ordered some of these measures, or had prior or subsequent knowledge of others. The People's Court Division has, thus, established only that he afforded the individuals concerned the opportunity to take these measures.

Zoltán Tildy, defendant no. 4, was quick to evaluate the political situation. He recognized Imre Nagy and his movement's tendency to hostility toward the dictatorship of the proletariat, and since this coincided with his own political views, he promoted them. At the October 28 discussion in the Parliament, and as a member of the "cabinet" at the October 30 meeting, he called for the abolition of the one-party system and the inclusion of the coalition parties in the business of government. With his active assistance and participation, by November 2, Imre Nagy had succeeded in having the private body that had usurped power consist of—besides himself and Géza Losonczy—three Smallholders' Party, three Social Democratic Party, and two Peasants' Party representatives, thereby ousting from the government the communist ministers appointed by the Presidential Council. In his October 30 radio address, he emphasized the need for the Independent Smallholders' Party to be established without delay, for they needed to take part in government. The People's Court Division wishes to point out as a characteristic fact that Zoltán Tildy was so convinced of the success of the line he was promoting that as he edited the draft of the radio address, he changed "People's Republic" to "Republic," crossed out the word "socialism," and so forth.

Zoltán Tildy, defendant no. 4, played a very active and instigative part in freeing József Mindszenty, in bringing him to Budapest, and in "reinstating him in his rights." He took part in the preparation of the so-called "rehabilitation announcement," he conferred with Mindszenty on two occasions, and it was, in essence, he who arranged for Mindszenty to deliver his memorable "address" in a direct, uncontrolled broadcast.

The People's Court Division has established as fact that as early as in his above-mentioned radio broadcast of October 30, and without even discussing it with Imre Nagy, the defendant unilaterally announced the recall of Hungary's representatives to the United Nations. On November 2, in an interview with the press (documents of the investigation, vol. 21, p. 24), he stated that "we want to live as a neutral country; therefore, we have withdrawn from the Warsaw Pact as well." At a later meeting, he added that in case of war over our withdrawal from the Warsaw Pact, we would "resist." (Witness statement of Tibor Pártay.) That is why, in establishing his responsibility, the People's Court Division has disregarded the otherwise factual line of defense that in the matters of the withdrawal from the Warsaw Pact and the declaration of neutrality, the members of the "cabinet"—including Tildy—were faced with a *fait accompli*.

The People's Court Division has, however, excluded from the statement of the facts serving as the basis of establishing guilt his having contacted Ferenc Nagy on the telephone on November 3. For while it is true that the telephone conversation did take place, the only fact that could be established as to its subject is that Zoltán Tildy, defendant no. 4, told Ferenc Nagy not to come home, for he was not needed, and that if he wanted to help, he could see to it that Radio Free Europe moderated its tone toward the Imre Nagy government.

The most pronounced differences in the accounts Imre Nagy, defendant no. 1, Ferenc Donáth, defendant no. 2, and Zoltán Tildy, defendant no. 4, gave of the facts appeared when it came to the matter of the preparation of Imre Nagy's

November 4 "radio appeal." Imre Nagy, defendant no. 1, wanted desperately to shift the responsibility for the radio address he himself delivered onto his associates. He claimed that while he was busy on the telephone making arrangements in various other matters, defendants 2 and 4 prepared the text. He had hardly had time to look at it before he read it on the air. The People's Court Division has found no evidence that Zoltán Tildy, defendant no. 4, took part in the wording of the text, but did establish as fact that it was he who gave orders following the broadcast to have the text forwarded to the secretary general of the United Nations, just as it was he who gave permission to Gyula Háy to broadcast the Writers' Association's memorable statement, which was also an appeal for help.

Lastly, the People's Court Division has also established as fact that after he gave the above-mentioned permission and during the almost half a year he was at large, he did nothing to impede the consolidation or the reestablishment of the dictatorship of the proletariat.

5.) The forty-one-year-old Pál Maléter, defendant no. 5, of gentry parentage, graduated from the Ludovika[5] in 1942. As a professional soldier with the rank of lieutenant, he was commander of an intelligence platoon. He then went over to the Soviet side, and fought along with the Soviet troops as a parachuter partisan. He remained a professional soldier after the liberation as well, always in a position of command, with the rank of colonel. He was a member of the MKP and the MDP. He married twice, and has three minor children from his first marriage. No evidence was found in the course of the trial that he had any connection with Imre Nagy's seditious conspiracy prior to October 23, 1956. On the contrary, according to data gathered in the course of the proceedings, at the time in question, he was opposed to all subversive tendencies. On October 25, 1956, however, while carrying out his orders to clear the Kilián barracks, he faltered. When, in the midst of battle, he allegedly received orders that the barracks were to be decorated with flags from which the national emblem had been cut out—the symbol of the counterrevolution—he construed this as capitulation before the insurgents and as grounds for rapprochement and negotiations, and he got in touch with the counterrevolutionary group at Corvin Alley.[6] The People's Court Division has also established, in support of the defendant's line of defense, that at that time he had not yet become the leader of the insurgents. His conduct reflected elements of duplicity and ambivalence: he conducted negotiations with the Corvin Alley group, even while he had his units carry out armed action in an attempt to clear the Kilián barracks. It was due to this ambiguity and the interception of certain telephone messages that news of his "changing sides" became widespread, to which defendant objected at the time. When he learned that the policies of the government and the Party were about to undergo a basic change, that is, that the reevaluation of the counterrevolutionary events was imminent, he jumped the gun and informed the duty officer at the Ministry of Defense that he would no longer obey the minister's orders; he and his unit went over to the "insurgents," the counterrevolutionaries. At the surrender negotiations with the Corvin Alley group, he presented himself to witness Várady and stipulated his conditions already in the capacity of the commander of one of the insurgent units. The defendant has, basically, admitted to all this, arguing only that his announcement to the minister of defense took place on October 28, at 1:15 p.m. However, according to the statements of witnesses József Szanati and Miklós Szűcs, corroborated by the statement of witness István Kovács, this took place probably on the afternoon of the day before, but in any case, prior to the cease-fire order. The People's Court Division has established the facts on the basis of the statements of the witnesses and despite the defendant's claim, for by 1:20 p.m. on October 28, the radio had announced the cease-fire order. It is hardly conceivable that in the light of this order, a logical person—such as the defendant certainly is—would refuse to follow the orders of the minister of defense, unless he was not prepared to join forces with the counterrevolutionaries, but was determined to continue the armed struggle against them. (Not even the defendant has made that claim, however.)

This was when the press began to popularize him as the "commander of the armed insurgent forces" and the "heroic defender" of the Kilián barracks. (See, for example, the November 2 issue of the *Magyar Honvéd* in the documents of the investigation, vol. 25, p. 92.) At the same time, Imre Nagy, defendant no. 1, appointed him, *qua* the representative of the "insurgents," to be first deputy minister, and later, minister of defense. By this time, his brotherhood in arms with the Corvin Alley group against the Soviet troops was common knowledge, thanks to the press. So much so, that several individuals warned Imre Nagy that in the light of Maléter's anti-Soviet statement, reported also in the press, the Soviet Union might consider his appointment a provocation. (According to the concordant statements of Imre Nagy, defendant no. 1, and Pál Maléter, defendant no.5, Maléter was appointed not to satisfy the "insurgents," but at the recommendation of the MSZMP. This line of defense has been refuted not only by the above-mentioned press communiqué but also by the statement of Ferenc Donáth, defendant no. 2.)

The People's Court Division has, further, established as fact that Pál Maléter, in his capacity as the leader of the insurgents and commander of the "armed insurgent forces," repeatedly declared that he was on the side of Imre Nagy and supported his aims.

On the basis of evidence introduced in the course of the trial and taking into consideration also the defendant's confession during a personal confrontation at the trial, the People's Court Division has also established that Pál Maléter, defendant no. 5, who went over to the side of the counterrevolutionaries, did, in the early morning hours of October 30, 1956, take charge of a prisoner (János Virágh) of the Corvin Alley group, whom they accused of being a plant of the Ministry of Defense and likely to expose their despicable plan (the attack on the Party Headquarters building). Pál Maléter, defendant no. 5, kept the prisoner locked up in the guardhouse of the Kilián barracks until three individuals ("insurgents") reported to him in the evening that "the order had been executed, and the resistance at Party Headquarters eliminated." At that point, he set the prisoner free.

On the basis of the above facts, the People's Court Division has come to the conclusion that Pál Maléter, as "commander of the armed insurgent forces," had prior knowledge of the siege of the Party building, and contributed to its success. The defendant's passionate anti-Soviet conviction was reflected in more than just his statements to the press and in his close alliance with the Corvin Alley group. As the People's Court Division has established, he consolidated various armed units under his own command to fight against the Soviet troops, issued written orders to the Corvin Alley group (documents of the investigation, vol. 25, p. 79) to attack the Soviet troops, and made preparations to hold the Kilián barracks "to the end" against the Soviet troops. (Testimonies of witnesses László Egervári and Miklós Szűcs.) He ordered plans of operations to be drawn up for the eventuality that the Soviet troops would not leave the country (his own confession), and gave orders to witness Mecséry to seal off the roads leading into Budapest (this order was partially carried out). Finally, he sank so low that on November 1, he accepted military advice on how to deal with the allied Soviet army from British military attaché Cowley, when the latter visited him in his capacity as deputy minister of defense. On the basis of the statement of witness József Molnár, the People's Court Division has also established as fact that the defendant gave permission for Cowley to study the destroyed Soviet tanks, but under the circumstances, this permission was not needed. The same morning he received six foreign journalists, and showed them some bottles of gasoline, saying that these were the weapons that had helped drive out the Soviet troops.

6.) The thirty-six-year-old Sándor Kopácsi, defendant no. 6, of working-class parentage, participated in the workers' movement, as did his father, mother, and entire family, starting in 1937. Toward the end of World War II, he carried on partisan activity. After the liberation, he went to work for the police department, became a police colonel, and of late, was in charge of the Budapest Police Headquarters. The People's Court Division, in accord with the defendant's line of defense substantiated by several quarters, established as fact that the defendant came to accept the conspiracy's program only after having been subjected to lengthy persuasion. To use his own term, he had been "ensnared." It was only immediately prior to the October 23, 1956, demonstration that he yielded to the repeated requests of József Szilágyi, and promised to disobey the orders of his superiors and not fire at the demonstrators.

Between October 23 and 26, his behavior, too, was somewhat equivocal. On the one hand, he opened the Police Headquarters premises to outsiders (members of the conspiracy), provided them with an office, allowed them to influence his subordinates, permitted the establishment of a counterrevolutionary nucleus on the premises (no data have come to light during the trial to suggest that he initiated this), and carried on negotiations with various counterrevolutionary groups. On the other hand, during this time, he was still fighting against the counterrevolutionaries, and ordered his subordinates to do the same. He abandoned this equivocal line of conduct when, on October 26, 1956, he ordered the district headquarters not to engage in armed confrontation with the counterrevolutionaries and retreat if they were attacked. Following this, it was in his office, and with his participation, that in direct defiance of the already-discussed orders from the minister of internal affairs, preparations were made for setting up the "national guard" in accordance with the conspiracy's aims. In the evening of October 30, Béla Király and Sándor Kopácsi, defendant no. 6, reported to Imre Nagy, defendant no. 1, on how far preparations had progressed. Imre Nagy approved and confirmed the results of this effort, appointed Béla Király to be the commander and Sándor Kopácsi the deputy commander of the "national guard," and ordered the latter to arm the new unit. As a result, over twenty thousand arms got distributed among counterrevolutionaries, hooligans, and so on, without even a minimum of supervision and control.

With the two interviews he gave, he took part in the incitement campaign carried out by the members of the conspiracy in an effort to popularize Imre Nagy. (Statement of facts, part B, section 2, paragraph c.)

After this, the defendant was pushed into the background behind Béla Király and Pál Maléter, and when, on November 5, he and his wife wanted to follow his associates to the Yugoslav Embassy, he was arrested. On the basis of his unrefuted line of defense, the People's Court Division has established as fact that József Szilágyi had already taken Kopácsi's little daughter to the embassy, and this also had influenced the defendant in his decision in this regard.

7.) The forty-two-year-old Ferenc Jánosi, defendant no. 7, of small craftsman parentage, suffering from lung disease, was originally a Presbyterian minister with a teacher's diploma. In 1943, he served in Ukraine as army chaplain. He was captured in February 1944. After the liberation, he was attached to the Ministry of Defense's Education Department; then, with the rank of colonel, he became the deputy head of the Political Department. In 1951, he was promoted to reserve brigadier general, and made first deputy to the minister of defense. From 1954 to May 1955, he was first secretary of the People's Patriotic Front,[7] and after his dismissal from this post, became the director general of the Petőfi Museum. In June 1956, he was expelled from the Party—of which he had been a member since after the liberation—and stripped of his military rank. He is the son-in-law of Imre Nagy, defendant no. 1. Because of this relationship, he has supported his father-in-law's political course and ideas. After Imre Nagy was stripped of his functions, the defendant worked for him as secretary and coordinator. His opportunities and importance grew in direct proportion with the growth of the conspiracy. He was the liaison between Imre Nagy and the members of the conspiracy, was the one maintaining close contact with the Writers' Association. He was the one whom Miklós Gimes conspiratorially put in touch with

Georgievich when Imre Nagy decided to send his articles to the Yugoslav leaders (statement of facts, part A, section 6). He took part in most discussions attended by Imre Nagy. At the October 23 meeting held at Losonczy's residence and repeatedly mentioned above, he was the one assigned to take notes of the decisions regarding the proposed changes in the leadership. (These notes, as the People's Court Division has established earlier, were subsequently burned.)

After October 23, 1956, too, it was as Imre Nagy's "associate" that he got into Party Headquarters, which he left on October 25 to go organize a delegation from the Writers' Association. When he returned to Party Headquarters, he arranged for an armored vehicle to pick up the delegation. The People's Court Division has established as fact that it was the defendant, along with other persons not named as defendants in these proceedings, who forwarded information from Imre Nagy on proposed measures, on matters of party policy, and so forth, to other members of the conspiracy and to the counterrevolutionaries. It was also he who, on October 27, on Imre Nagy's direct orders, informed the Deák Square nucleus that "they had won." It was also through him that Béla Király had originally offered his "services" to the Imre Nagy group, but by the time Ferenc Jánosi, defendant no. 7, received the letter, Béla Király had already been appointed. On November 2, his father-in-law appointed him, once again, to head the Ministry of Defense's Education Department with the rank of brigadier general. On November 4, he and his family joined his father-in-law in taking refuge at the Yugoslav Embassy, where, in the presence of the other members of the conspiracy, he declared: "We all have to realize that we are the ones who initiated, organized, and touched off the enormous popular movement which burst into flame on October 23, 1956."

8.) The forty-one-year-old Miklós Vásárhelyi, defendant no. 8, of lower-middle-class parentage, completed four years of studies, but never graduated from law school. He, too, participated in the workers' movement. After the liberation, he went to work as a journalist at the *Szabad Nép*; then, in 1950-1951, he was the head of the Ministry of Education and Culture's Publicity Department. In 1951, he became the editor of the *Müvelt Nép*, and between 1952 and 1954, he edited the paper *Vengria*. In 1954-1955, he was the vice president of the Council of Ministers' Publicity Department. In January 1956, he was expelled from the Party.

Miklós Vásárhelyi, defendant no. 8, was also one of the first to join the group forming around the person of Imre Nagy. He took part in transforming the group into a conspiracy ("writers' memorandum"), and continued to work to expand the conspiracy and propagate its aims.

On orders from Imre Nagy, defendant no. 1, he and Miklós Gimes, defendant no. 3, and Ferenc Jánosi, defendant no. 7, used their connection to the first secretary of the Yugoslav Embassy to conspiratorially hand him Imre Nagy's articles intended for the Yugoslav leaders (statement of facts, part A, section 6). He took part in the regular meetings of the members of the conspiracy, including the one held on October 23 at the residence of Géza Losonczy, as described in detail in part B, section 1, paragraph g of the statement of facts.

As to his behavior after October 23, 1956, the only fact that could be established was that on October 26, he helped to prepare the text of Géza Losonczy's and Ferenc Donáth's second resignation, and had a vital role in the debate over the text of the MÉFB "Declaration": he was the one who informed the people discussing the issue of the conspiracy's stand and the "Government Proclamation" in the making.

Later, he acted as "public relations chief" for Imre Nagy and Géza Losonczy. On November 4, like his associates, he tried to flee to the Yugoslav Embassy, but could not cross the Danube from the Buda side, and took refuge at the residence of one of the embassy employees. He, too, received the "Executive Committee's" polling questionnaire (statement of facts, part B, section 3, paragraph d), and his answer was that in his opinion, they should stop fighting the consolidation. Still, he never severed his ties with the conspiracy, although Imre Nagy, defendant no. 1, had called him an opportunist.

II

Of the defendants, only Imre Nagy, defendant no. 1, has claimed procedural violation. He has primarily objected to the fact that it was only forty-eight hours after his apprehension (on April 14, 1957) that he was shown the procurator general's order that he be placed under preliminary detention. This objection, however, is without foundation. In accordance with section 99, paragraph /1/ of the Bp as modified on February 1, 1957, by Act 8 of 1957, section 11, paragraph /1/, the police may hold a person for seventy-two hours before being required to produce an order for preliminary detention issued or approved by a procurator. (Prior to the modification, Act 5 of 1954, enacted on June 29, 1954, stated that an arrest made by the investigating authority may be extended over the initial twenty-four hours by an additional forty-eight hours. Thus, even prior to the modification, an order for preliminary detention had to be produced only after seventy-two hours of detention.)

He also took exception to the fact that he only learned from the written act of accusation what the charges were against him, rather than being told at the outset of the investigation. The People's Court Division has established that the document ordering the investigation (section 91 of the Bp) contains the reasons for the investigation. Discovering and providing the details given in the written act of accusation was precisely what the investigation was all about.

Another of his unfounded objections was that he did not have free access to all the evidence. By the terms of section 47, paragraph /2/ of the Bp, the accused is allowed to study the documents of the case in the course of an investigation only if that does not jeopardize the success of the proceedings. The People's

Court Division has established that the investigative authority did not take undue advantage of this restriction. On the contrary, at the appropriate stages of the investigation, the accused was given ample opportunity to study and comment on all of the documents. Nor was he restricted in his study of the documents after the written act of accusation had been presented, nor when the supplementary investigation was completed. He took advantage of these opportunities, and made notes on his findings. The Court has had opportunity to ascertain in the course of the trial that he knows the documents well, for he kept referring to them at the appropriate times. His motion that the proceedings should be postponed to give him more time to study the documents, therefore, had to be denied. The People's Court Division also disregarded the spurious argument the defendant presented on behalf of his retained defense counsel, namely, that the defense counsel, too, had insufficient time to study the documents and that was another reason for continuance. Upon receipt of the written act of accusation, the defendant did not wish to name his own defense counsel. Accordingly, at the hearings of February 5 and 6, he was represented by a court-appointed defense counsel. The defendant was dissatisfied with him, and named a defense counsel of his own choosing, who, however, on studying the documents, did not approach the Court to give him more time for preparation, and usually it is the defense counsel who submits requests on behalf of his client and not the other way around.

Lastly, the defendant took exception to the fact that during the investigation, one of the investigating officers offended him by calling him a "pig." While this kind of behavior on the part of a member of the investigating authority is certainly to be censured, in light of the fact that Imre Nagy, defendant no. 1, took outrageously undue advantage of the fact that a defendant cannot be compelled to tell the truth throughout the rest of the investigation, the People's Court Division has concluded that this procedural transgression in no way hampered the defendant in presenting his case.

Beyond this, the People's Court Division ex officio examined the entire procedure preceding the hearing also from this aspect, and found that the procedural rules had been strictly adhered to in that procedural phase as well.

Imre Nagy, defendant no. 1, also objected to the fact that the proceedings were conducted in closed trial. The reason that the People's Court Division had to insist on closed trial was precisely so that the defendants could present their defense freely, so that they would not be intimidated in their presentation of the facts by the public nature of the proceedings, and so that the Court would be in a position to examine certain facts and state secrets whose public disclosure in their intranational ramifications might have influenced public opinion in the wrong direction and excited unduly intense sentiments.

III

Summarizing the facts as detailed in Part I, the People's Court Division has established that at the end of 1955, the political power group forming around the person of Imre Nagy started out as an in-Party faction. However, in the course of their activities—their joint action in connection with the "writers' memorandum," the spreading of the political views Imre Nagy set down in writing, their recruiting of Imre Nagy "followers" through the distribution of the above material, the negotiations they carried on with political groups of differing views, their disclosure of the Party's inner problems to elements outside the Party for solution—the faction took on the aspect of a conspiracy aiming to undermine and subvert the order of state, and exerted its influence on various mass organizations (Writers' Association, Journalists' Association, etc.) and youth groups (Petőfi Circle, etc.) with a view to establishing a movement suited for promoting its goals. It was as a result of the planned and coordinated destructive political agitation and intellectual influence of the members of the conspiracy that the "Petőfi Circle" and its "auxiliary circles," with the participation of some of the members of the conspiracy (Gábor Tánczos, József Szilágyi, etc.), organized a reactionary and chauvinistic demonstration for October 23, 1956. The other members of the conspiracy—who themselves looked upon the demonstration as the irreversible result of their own activities—tried, through Gábor Tánczos and the leadership of the "Petőfi Circle," to steer the course of the demonstration and become its "leaders."

Between October 23 and November 4, the most active members of the conspiracy and the movement established three nuclei. Following an initial period of indecision and tactical maneuvering, as soon as they thought that the protracted and fragmented counterrevolutionary fighting and the peasantry's continuing passivity might lead to the forces loyal to the people's democracy gaining the upper hand, dashing their hopes of bringing their political views to victory riding the crest of the counterrevolution, they decided to take command of the counterrevolution themselves: on October 28, 1956, they established their front organization, the Revolutionary Committee of Hungarian Intellectuals. Operating through this committee, as well as through direct action, they stabbed the Party in the back. Behind the iron curtain of the white terror, and with incredible speed, they achieved their aims: the termination of the leading role of the working class and its Party, the return to coalition government, the separation of the country from the socialist community of nations, and so on, all goals set by Imre Nagy in his writings of late 1955 and early 1956, and subsequently propagated by members of the conspiracy.

When, with the brotherly help of the Soviet Union, the communists annihilated the counterrevolutionary forces and reestablished the rule of the working class, some members of the conspiracy, taking advantage of the extraterritorial privileges enjoyed by the Yugoslav Embassy, formed another organization, the Hungarian Democratic Independence Movement, and went on inciting against consolidation in a vulgar fascist fashion.

The leader of this conspiracy was Imre Nagy, defendant no. 1; it was Ferenc Donáth, defendant no. 2, who ensured its consistent functioning between October 23 and 26, as did Miklós Gimes, defendant no. 3, after November 4. Sándor Kopácsi, defendant no. 6, turned from an active member into one of the prominent leaders of the conspiracy when he put the Budapest Police Headquarters at the service of the counterrevolutionaries. Ferenc Jánosi, defendant no. 7, and Miklós Vásárhelyi, defendant no. 8, were organizers and active participants in the conspiracy. Zoltán Tildy, defendant no. 4, and Pál Maléter, defendant no. 5, were in political agreement with the conspiracy, and joined upon seeing its "success." With his changing sides, defendant no. 5 also had a significant role in the shaping of events.

The People's Court Division of the Supreme Court established the guilt of the defendants on the basis of the above facts. In establishing guilt, it took as its basis the stand reflected in the decisions of the Supreme Court in the years 1954-1956, namely, that as long as his ideological grounds are those of socialism, a person cannot be charged with the crime of subversion merely because he disagrees with certain methods used in the building of socialism, however erroneous the theoretical basis of his attack be. While the members of the People's Court Division might deplore such gross distortions of socialist theory as revisionism, they did not find the defendants guilty because they are revisionists. In determining the facts, the People's Court Division did not examine whether the defendants had any mistaken political views, or whether these views were to be condemned. It looked at these views only as they related to their movement and its nucleus: the conspiracy. In this light, the line of defense recurrently presented by Imre Nagy, defendant no. 1, that persons outside the conspiracy or movement, through imprudence, negligence, misguidedness, or sheer political error, or for other reasons, inadvertently perhaps, but nonetheless, might, objectively speaking, have helped further the defendants' conspiratory aims without even realizing what they were is totally irrelevant. It is not up to a criminal court of law to evaluate such behavior. The Court has examined with particular care the line of defense put forth by almost all of the defendants, that is, that they did not intend to subvert the people's democracy and the dictatorship of the proletariat, although admittedly, "objectively speaking," their activities did have that effect. The People's Court Division found that this line of defense was discredited in all of the cases, and wishes to point out the misapprehension under which defense counsel, too, labors, namely that section 1 of Act 7 of 1946 was to protect our social order only against a Horthy-fascist restoration. This is a total misconstruction of the law. The wording of the law leaves no doubt that this protection extends against all attacks aimed at undermining and subverting the government. Those who advocate fundamental changes in the class structure of our social order cannot claim "good intentions." A question that needed to be examined was whether or not failure to realize at the outset the full implications of joining a subversive organization, that is, finding oneself through one's own or through collective action sinking deeper and deeper into the dirt and mire of a treacherous road not seen at the outset, can constitute extenuating circumstances. The consideration, however, has no bearing on the issue of guilt or innocence; at most, it might be taken into account in determining the severity of the punishment.

In due consideration of all of the above and in the absence of any circumstance barring or suspending punishability, the People's Court Division found all the defendants guilty, and classified their crimes as follows:

Classifying the activities of Imre Nagy, defendant no. 1, as the crime of leading a conspiracy as defined in section 1, paragraph /1/ of the BHÖ requires an explanation only to the extent that some of his actions could be classified also as the initiation and leading of a movement; others, the withdrawal from the Warsaw Pact, the declaration of neutrality, and his radio address of November 4 could be interpreted as an action aimed at subverting the order of state, as defined within the same provision of law. In accordance with standard judicial practice, however, the unity of state order precludes the cumulation of those offences. Still, from the point of view of the external security of the Hungarian People's Republic as a national interest protected by law, this second group of his actions has required separate assessment by the law, since his having contacted foreign powers was not only an attempt to commit them to taking some action, but created the imminent danger of their doing so. The People's Court Division therefore classified these of his acts, too, as treason, as defined in section 35, paragraph /1/ of the BHÖ. The activities which Ferenc Donáth, defendant no. 2, engaged in between October 24 and 26 along with the since-deceased Géza Losonczy were of such importance to the conspiracy and to the movement, and had such a decisive impact on the fate of the conspiracy, that his crime, according to the standard practice of the courts, has had to be classified as the crime of leading a conspiracy as defined by section 1, paragraph /1/ of the BHÖ, and his prior and subsequent active participation was evaluated on the same basis.

In the case of Miklós Gimes, defendant no. 3, it is his criminal behavior after November 13, his illegal actions bearing on the future of the conspiracy as a whole, which puts his crime into the category of leading a conspiracy as defined by section 1, paragraph /1/ of the BHÖ. The People's Court Division does not wish to minimize the objective weight of his earlier behavior; that, too, particularly in the period prior to October 23, 1956, came close to meeting the criteria of this crime.

Zoltán Tildy, defendant no. 4, having recognized the seditious aims of the movement created by the conspiracy, and having found that they coincided with his own political views, joined and actively participated in it. Therefore, the People's Court Division has classified his criminal behavior as the crime of abetting a movement as defined in section 1, paragraph /2/ of the BHÖ.

Pál Maléter, defendant no. 5, when he declared that he would no longer follow the orders of the minister of defense, committed the crime of mutiny (section 29 of the KTBTK) in his capacity as a commanding officer; it is, therefore, section 30, paragraph /2/ that applies. This announcement, and the defendant's subsequent behavior, was a knife in the back of working-class rule and of its protectors, the armed forces. He also ordered military actions against them, which were carried out. The defendant's behavior goes beyond joining the conspiracy. It had a decisive influence on the entire progress of the counterrevolution as a historical process. Therefore, its proper classification is an action aimed at the subversion of the order of state, as defined in section 1, paragraph /1/ of the BHÖ. The People's Court Division, however, did not find the defendant guilty of the crime of espionage as accused, for although the suspicion of espionage was, essentially, substantiated (as recorded in the statement of facts), this criminal act was an organic part of the activity aimed at subverting the order of state, and in essence, was not aimed at the country's external security, as an interest protected by law. However, since it is only the legal classification of the written act of accusation that the Court has rejected, acquittal on these charges would have been out of order.

Sándor Kopácsi, defendant no. 6, as the head of Budapest Police Headquarters, held such a key position from the standpoint of the subversive movement, that his joining in the collective activities of the conspiracy was definitive for the functioning of the conspiracy as a whole, especially in the light of the armed insurrection which took place. His actions therefore qualify as the crime of leading a conspiracy as defined by section 1, paragraph /1/ of the BHÖ. In addition, since his actions included open defiance of the service regulations, an offense against another interest protected by law, the military discipline of the armed forces, he also committed the crime of mutiny by a commanding officer as defined in section 29, and graded in section 30, paragraph /2/ of the KTBTK.

Qualifying the criminal offenses of Ferenc Jánosi, defendant no. 7, and Miklós Vásárhelyi, defendant no. 8, as the crime of actively participating in a conspiracy as specified in section 1, paragraph /2/ of the BHÖ does not require special explanation.

IV

It is with a view to ensuring uniform sentencing consistent with the interests of the working population that the Presidential Council of the Hungarian People's Republic established the People's Court Division of the Supreme Court to deal with criminal cases prosecuted for counterrevolutionary crimes, and crimes against the order of state and public safety. In the present criminal proceedings, too, what has determined the severity of the punishment for the crimes committed by the defendants were considerations like the protection of the working people, the fundamental interests of the working class, the incredible suffering and destruction brought upon the nation by this conspiracy, as well as the danger of war that it had conjured up for the entire human race. Another aggravating factor is that had it not been for the defendants' betraying their class, the class enemies, the imperialist agents, would never, under any circumstance, have achieved the kind of successes they had during the October 1956 counterrevolution. The gravity of this class betrayal is by no means mitigated by consideration of the very real and grievous mistakes which the communist leaders of the earlier period had made, for the conspiracy used these past mistakes only as a pretext, their aim being not to correct the mistakes but to achieve their goals, enumerated in part A, section 2 of the statement of facts. Lastly, the People's Court Division had to bear in mind the severity of the punishment inflicted in connection with other counterrevolutionary activities, as well as the degree of danger each of the defendants constitutes to society and the punishment that would motivate the individual defendants to change their attitudes. Thus, after an in-depth analysis, the People's Court Division reached the following decision:

In the case of Imre Nagy, defendant no. 1, his stubborn impenitence, his double-dealing treachery, and his undying hatred rooted in excessive ambition precluded the possibility of the People's Court Division giving weight to his forty years in the workers' movement, to all the distinctions he gained throughout his life, and to his ill health, on the basis of which it could have foregone inflicting the most severe punishment befitting his crime of treason and class betrayal, determined in accordance with section 11, paragraph /1/ of the BHÖ.

In the case of Ferenc Donáth, defendant no. 2, on the other hand, his pacifying influence on his associates, the fact that he was motivated in his actions by the severe and unjust mistreatment he had suffered through the mistakes of the past, and his sincere and informative confession, which reflected an attitude of deep regret, all made it possible for the People's Court Division to inflict upon him a punishment that is not in keeping with the objective weight of his crime, but is a much lighter one: a term of imprisonment slightly longer than the medium-range sentence in accordance with section 11, paragraph /1/ of the BHÖ.

Miklós Gimes, defendant no. 3, manifested such a degree of impenitence that he intensified his criminal activities at a time when he was already in a position to see, and indeed saw, the terrible consequences of his earlier behavior. At that point, the defendant renounced his earlier ideals and went still further. In his illegal gutter sheet *Október Huszonharmadika*, he launched a vulgar and fascist campaign against those fighting for the reestablishment of order, and attempted to paralyze efforts to start productive work and the consolidation of the dictatorship of the proletariat. His repentance has been insincere, and the People's Court Division has found no reason to reduce his punishment from the maximum penalty befitting the objective weight of his crime, as defined by section 11, paragraph /1/ of the BHÖ.

In the case of Zoltán Tildy, defendant no. 4, the People's Court Division took into consideration his sincere and penitent full confession, the fact that initially, he was swept away, so to speak, by the events—though later he consciously participated in them. His earlier distinctions, the injustices he suffered, his advanced age, and his ill health have reduced his punishment from that befitting the objective weight of his actions to one approximating the lowest penalty as defined by section 11, paragraph /2/ of the BHÖ.

Pál Maléter, defendant no. 5, turned against the dictatorship of the proletariat, abusing both the boundless trust of the working class and its order of state and his high military rank, and breaking his oath as an officer. The protection of our people's democracy calls for the most severe punishment as defined by section 11, paragraph /1/, clause 1 of the BHÖ, as well as by section 30, paragraph /2/ of the KTBTK. The sentence could not be reduced either in consideration of his family, or of the fact that in the latter part of the proceedings, he came to realize the gravity of his criminal behavior and expressed remorse.

In the case of Sándor Kopácsi, defendant no. 6, while the objective weight of his class betrayal and his violation of his oath as an officer are not mitigated by his honest, informative, and remorseful confession, or by his like behavior during the entire proceedings, or by the fact that he was practically ensnared by people he respected as communists into joining the conspiracy, these circumstances made it possible for the People's Court Division to forgo the most severe punishment prescribed by section 30, paragraph /2/ of the KTBTK, and applying section 51, paragraph /2/, item a of the Btá, inflict upon him a much lighter sentence of imprisonment of unspecified duration in accordance with section 11, paragraph /1/, item 2 of the BHÖ.

Ferenc Jánosi, defendant no. 7, was influenced to a great extent by his family relations in committing his criminal acts. Both he and Miklós Vásárhelyi, defendant no. 8, have expressed remorse in the course of their honest and informative confession. The People's Division gave serious consideration to the above circumstances, as well as to the facts that both these defendants have families and both are in poor health, and inflicted sentences upon them far below the medium-level punishment prescribed by section 11, paragraph /2/ of the BHÖ, in the hope that an imprisonment of the lawful minimum duration will be sufficient for their rehabilitation.

Their criminal actions have rendered the defendants undeserving of the rights defined in section 40, paragraph 2, items a-d of the Btá. Therefore, the People's Court Division, in accordance with the modified section 41, paragraph /1/ of the Btá, and for the duration therein prescribed, has prohibited defendants nos. 2, 4, and 6-8 from exercising these rights.

In addition, defendants nos. 5 and 6 are to be subjected to secondary penalties in accordance with section 13, paragraph /1/, items 1 and 4 of the KTBTK. Lastly, in accordance with section 11, paragraph 5 of the BHÖ, defendants nos. 1-7 are subject to confiscation of all property, and defendant no. 8 to partial confiscation of property in consideration of his family circumstances.

Budapest, June 15, 1958.
Dr. Ferenc Vida, presiding judge;
Mrs. Péter Lakatos, people's judge;
György Sulyán, people's judge;
Kálmán Fehér, people's judge;
Mihály Biró, people's judge.

RULING

In accordance with section 187, paragraph /1/ of the Bp, there is no possibility of appeal against this judgment. It is final, and the principal imprisonment and subsidiary sentences of all defendants may be carried out.

Budapest, June 15, 1958.
Dr. Ferenc Vida, presiding judge.
TB. NB. No. 003/1958-19

WRIT

The above final judgment's principal sentences of death against Imre Nagy, defendant no. 1, Miklós Gimes, defendant no. 3, and Pál Maléter, defendant no. 5, may also be carried out.

Budapest, June 15, 1958.
Dr. Ferenc Vida, presiding judge.

To authenticate the copy: clerk's office.

NOTES

1. The majority of the confirmed 234 casualties on the order of state's side died in the street battles. There is no evidence of there having been any "death lists."
2. Author Gyula Háy had parodied all that was contemptible in the typical Party functionary in a notorious article entitled "Why I Don't Like Comrade Kucsera."
3. Location of the MDP headquarters, believed to be the center of Party resistance to the revolution, and the stronghold of the ÁVH; was besieged by the angry mob. Twenty-eight of the defenders, members of the ÁVH; were lynched.
4. Formally, the Presidential Council exercised the functions of head of state. In fact, it implemented Party directives indiscriminately.
5. Military Academy.

6. As of October 23, Corvin Alley and the Kilián barracks were the two major pockets of armed resistance, which only intensified their activities after the Soviet intervention of November 4.
7. The Patriotic People's Front was formed for the purpose of wooing non-Party members to support the Party's policies.

Remedial Petition of the Procurator General June 6, 1989

Emblem—The Procurator General
Bfl. 21. 206/1989
To the Presidential Division of the Supreme Court, Budapest

The People's Court Division of the Supreme Court, in a final judgment, no. TB. NB. 003/1958-18, dated June 15, 1958, pronounced Imre Nagy (born in Kaposvár, on June 7, 1896; mother: Rozália Szabó); Dr. Ferenc Donáth (born in Jászárokszállás, on September 5, 1913; mother: Ilona Vitál); Miklós Gimes (born in Budapest, on December 22, 1917; mother: Dr. Livia Hajdú); Zoltán Tildy (born in Losonc, on November 18, 1889; mother: Emma Fabriczky); Pál Maléter (born in Eperjes, on September 4, 1917; mother: Margit Lakner); Sándor Kopácsi (born in Miskolc, on March 5, 1922; mother: Ilona Simon); Dr. Ferenc Jánosi (born in Sárospatak, on January 13, 1916; mother: Erzsébet Szueta); and Miklós Vásárhelyi (born in Fiume, on October 9, 1917; mother: Irén Róth) guilty; and further, in a final judgment, no. TB. NB. 003/1958-12, dated April 22, 1958, pronounced Dr. József Szilágyi (born in Debrecen, on June 20, 1917; mother: Julianna Szilágyi) guilty, as follows: Imre Nagy, Dr. Ferenc Donáth, Miklós Gimes, Sándor Kopácsi, and Dr. József Szilágyi of the crime of leading a conspiracy aimed at subverting the people's democratic order of state, as entered in section 1, paragraph /1/ of the BHÖ; Zoltán Tildy of the crime of abetting a conspiracy aimed at subverting the people's democratic order of state, as entered in section 1, paragraph /2/ of the BHÖ; Pál Maléter of the crime of taking action aimed at subverting the people's democratic order of state, as entered in section 1, paragraph /1/ of the BHÖ; Dr. Ferenc Jánosi and Miklós Vásárhelyi of the crime of taking an active part in a conspiracy aimed at subverting the people's democratic order of state, as entered in section 1, paragraph /2/ of the BHÖ; furthermore, Imre Nagy of the crime of treason, as entered in section 35, paragraph /1/ of the BHÖ; Pál Maléter and Sándor Kopácsi of the crime of mutiny in a leadership capacity, in violation of section 29 and as graded in section 30, paragraph /2/ of the KTBTK.

Therefore it sentenced Imre Nagy, Miklós Gimes, Pál Maléter, and Dr. József Szilágyi to death as principal punishment, with confiscation of all their property as supplementary punishment, and the loss of all medals and decorations as additional supplementary punishment in the case of Pál Maléter; Dr. Ferenc Donáth to twelve years of imprisonment as principal punishment, with ten years of prohibition from exercising of certain rights as enumerated in the Criminal Code, and confiscation of all property as supplementary punishment; Zoltán Tildy to six years of imprisonment as principal punishment, with six years of prohibition from exercising of certain rights as enumerated in the Criminal Code, and confiscation of all property as supplementary punishment; Sándor Kopácsi to life imprisonment as principal punishment, with dismissal from office, ten years of prohibition from exercising of certain rights as enumerated in the Criminal Code, the loss of all medals and decorations, and confiscation of all property as supplementary punishment; Dr. Ferenc Jánosi to eight years of imprisonment as principal punishment, with ten years of prohibition from exercising of certain rights as enumerated in the Criminal Code, and confiscation of all property as supplementary punishment; Miklós Vásárhelyi to five years of imprisonment as principal punishment, and to five years of prohibition from exercising of certain rights as enumerated in the Criminal Code, and partial confiscation of property in the amount of 1,000 Ft.

The death sentences of Imre Nagy, Miklós Gimes, and Pál Maléter were carried out on June 16, 1958, and the death sentence of Dr. József Szilágyi on April 24, 1958.

The imprisoned Dr. Ferenc Donáth, Dr. Ferenc Jánosi, and Miklós Vásárhelyi were released on the basis of individual clemency on April 1, 1960; Zoltán Tildy was released on probation on April 3, 1959; while Sándor Kopácsi, who was serving a life sentence, fell under general amnesty in accordance with paragraph /1/, subparagraph c of Act 4 of 1963, and was released on March 25, 1963.

Dr. Ferenc Donáth, Zoltán Tildy, and Dr. Ferenc Jánosi passed away subsequent to their release.

The following is a verbatim quote of the statement of facts as established by the People's Court Division of the Supreme Court, in its judgment no. TB. NB. 003/1958-18:

(See Judgment Against Imre Nagy—June 15, 1958, pp. 69-109)

On April 16, 1958, the People's Court Division of the Supreme Court separated the case of Dr. József Szilágyi from the principal trial. The following is a verbatim quote of the statement of facts as established in judgment no. TB. NB. 003/1958-12 brought against Dr. József Szilágyi on April 22, 1958:

(See Judgment Against József Szilágyi—April 22, 1958, section II, pp. 58-61)

My official position is that both final judgments of the People's Court

Division of the Supreme Court are unlawful owing to the following violations of procedural and substantive law:

A

The criminal proceedings were conducted in accordance with the provisions of a repeatedly modified Act 3 of 1951 (Bp), and with Law Decree No. 34 of 1957 on the People's Court divisions in force at the time. Several fundamental provisions of these procedural rules were seriously violated during the investigation by the investigating authority and by the procuracy, and later, during the judicial phase, by the People's Court Division of the Supreme Court. These violations determined the entire course of the proceedings, and were, in part, the cause of the violations of substantive law.

1.) The procedural status of the persons against whom the criminal proceedings were being instituted remained unclarified up until January 20, 1958. In the investigation, the persons proceeded against were declared to be such just prior to the conclusion of the investigation on January 20, 1958. According to section 91/B, paragraph /1/ of the Bp, if the investigating authority possessed sufficient data to determine who committed the criminal act, it was obliged to bring a reasoned decision to declare that person charged. The decision had to contain a brief description of the criminal act as well. The investigating authority did not fulfill this obligation prescribed by law. As a result of this omission,

a.) There was no possibility of defense during the investigation, as the facts which formed the basis of the proceedings were not disclosed.

b.) The persons proceeded against were deprived of the opportunity of engaging their defense counsels, although paragraph /1/ of section 48 of the Bp stipulates that counsel may act on behalf of the accused in any phase of the proceedings. The opportunity to engage counsel was given only at the time of the declaration of the charge, that is, January 20, 1958.

c.) Declaring a person charged was a procedural prerequisite of ordering his preliminary detention. In its absence, preliminary detention should never have been ordered.

2.) On January 24, 1957, the preliminary detention of Pál Maléter and Sándor Kopácsi was ordered. As the Supreme Court's records no. Katf. I. 125/1957 show, the procurator general presented his written act of accusation against Pál Maléter and Sándor Kopácsi to the Military College of the Supreme Court on February 28, 1957. Pál Maléter and Sándor Kopácsi had been in captivity since November 3, 1956, under undisclosed circumstances. In this connection I wish to note that on February 28, the court held a preparatory session, set March 8 as the trial date, then postponed it. Subsequently, on August 29, 1957—without passing judgment on the contents of the written act of accusation admitted at the preparatory session—it had the case filed in the archives (the whereabouts of the records of the investigation are unknown).

3.) Section 3 of the Bp specified the ascertainment of both the incriminating and the extenuating circumstances [of a particular case] to be a fundamental principle of criminal proceedings. Although the People's Court was to abide by the rules of the Bp (section 7 of Law Decree No. 34 of 1957), it did not meet this requirement of the rules of procedure. Imre Nagy and his associates proceeded against made a number of references to circumstances and evidence which were not followed up, and, consequently, were not taken into consideration by the People's Court. As a result of this procedural violation, the evidence taken was one-sided, concentrating as it did only on the incriminating circumstances. Consequently, some of the "facts" established in the judgment of the People's Court—especially those to the effect that violations of substantive criminal law had actually taken place—are fallacious, and without foundation.

4.) The manner in which the proceedings as a whole—especially the interrogation of Imre Nagy—were conducted (audiotapes of the trial) makes perfectly clear that the People's Court restricted the defense of Imre Nagy and of all of his associates in the course of the proceedings. The trial was conducted in a manner which resulted in limiting the evidence taken to the actuality of the facts constituting the subject of the proceedings. As the records of the trial (minutes and tapes) indicate, no opportunity was given to present a de facto defense; the People's Court put this off to "after the facts have been established," but, in fact, never made time for it. Thus, there was no opportunity to present a defense as related to the background or the international aspects of some of the events, or to the actions and roles of other people in connection with certain other events. This is particularly true as concerns the statement of facts given in the judgment pertaining to the period from November 1 to November 4.

5.) Under section 160, paragraph /2/ of the Bp, the People's Court should have interrogated Imre Nagy and his associates in detail, in accordance with section 94, paragraph /2/ of the Bp. What this means is that each and every one of them should have been given the opportunity to present a comprehensive and uninterrupted defense. This, however, as is proven by the minutes and audiotapes of the trial, was never done.

6.) Part B, section 1, paragraph h of Judgment No. 18 of the People's Court (Judgment Against Imre Nagy—June 15, 1958, pp. 67-116) establishes as fact that it was the movement created by Imre Nagy and his associates which sparked the events which began on October 23, 1956. Elsewhere in the text, the judgment states: "They began to 'liquidate' communists and patriots true to the people's democracy: they brutally tortured and killed 234 communists and patriots. . . ." What we see here is that in its judgment, the People's Court blames the Imre Nagy group for the actions of the movement they created. In connection with Pál Maléter, for instance, the People's Court establishes as fact that he "had prior knowledge of the siege of the party building, and contributed to its success."

One of the victims of the events at Köztársaság Square was Péter Lakatos. His wife, Mrs. Péter Lakatos, acted in the capacity of people's judge on the People's Court in both proceedings (transcript no. IM. 34.274/1989. IM.III/2.). According to section 13, item c/ of the Bp, any person who is related, as specified in section 29 of the Btá, to an injured party is excluded from and may not participate as judge in the proceedings. A spouse is one of the specified relations.

7.) Section 2, paragraph /3/ of Law Decree No. 34 of 1957, [the procedural rule] which applied to the conduct of the proceedings, specified that the presiding judge of the People's Court Division be appointed by the president of the Supreme Court. Although formally this was done, "recommendations" were made by the Ministry of the Interior as to the person of the presiding judge, of the people's judges, of the prosecuting attorney, and even of the court clerk (vol. V-150.000/16). The makeup of the court and the identity of the people conducting the proceedings coincided with these recommendations. This and other facts concerning the proceedings indicate that the principles and regulations of the constitution relating to the independence of judges set out in section 50, paragraph /2/ were violated. In this connection, I note the fact that employees of the Ministry of the Interior evaluated all of what happened in the courtroom on a daily basis, and reported in writing to the minister.

8.) According to section 153, paragraph /2/ of the Bp, a postponed trial may be continued anytime within a two-month period simply by having the minutes of the previous session read, provided that there are no changes in the makeup of the court. Otherwise the proceedings have to start all over again. The People's Court Division of the Supreme Court held its first hearings of the case on February 5 and 6, 1958. On the second day, it ordered a supplementary investigation, and returned the documents to the procurator general. Following this—apart from hearing Dr. József Szilágyi's segregated case—the People's Court held its next hearing more than four months later, on June 9, 1958, at which time the minutes of the previous hearings were read, but to a court with a different composition. In short, they continued the old court action rather than starting a new one. On the basis of the above-mentioned section of the Bp, in view of the length of time elapsed, and of the changes in the makeup of the court, the proceedings should have been started anew, beginning with the questioning of Imre Nagy and his associates. According to the contemporary judicial practices of the Supreme Court, and according to law, the above in itself constitutes a procedural violation of the kind from which the reversal of the judgment follows (section 201, item a of the Bp; section 202, item b of the Bp; Criminal Law Casebook, 1953-1963: cases 1,977 and 1,978).

9.) The People's Court committed another procedural violation by ordering closed sessions throughout the trial, the sentencing included. The public was barred from the entire proceedings, although the preconditions for this (as set out in section 7 of the Bp) did not obtain, nor was any reason given subsequently to warrant it.

Even on the contemporary interpretation of the law, the question of whether the public was to be barred from the courtroom was not to be decided by considerations having to do with the nature of the proceedings, the particular requirements of the prosecuting body, or the type of court handling the case. The principle of publicity was to be the guideline in all cases, whatever the crime and whichever the court conducting the proceedings. Only the particulars of the material involved in the proceedings were to determine whether the trial was to be public or closed, and exactly which of the sessions were to be closed to the public, given that its exclusion was warranted. (*A Büntető Perrendtartás Kommentárja* [Commentary on the Code of Criminal Procedure], Közgazdasági és Jogi Könyvkiadó, Budapest, 1957, Dr. László Molnár et al.).

10.) Although the provisions of Law Decree No. 34 of 1957 allowed for accelerated proceedings with or without a written act of accusation having been presented, this, over and above the above-detailed circumstances, constituted a further infringement upon the right to defense, if we consider the manner in which the criminal proceedings were conducted in its entirety. It cannot be established from the documents of the proceedings what factors motivated the authorities to take these measures, which, in the absence of satisfactory reasons, were unwarranted.

The investigating authority wanted to close the investigation already in August-September of 1957. This is evidenced by the fact that the documents of the investigation were made available, and that measures indicating the end of the investigation were taken. The investigation was ordered to be continued and was concluded in January 1958. The procurator general filed a written act of accusation on January 28, 1958, and the People's Court Division of the Supreme Court held the first hearings on February 5 and 6, 1958. On the second day of hearings, the documents—at his own suggestion—were returned to the procurator general, pending supplementary investigation of matters immaterial to the essence of the case.

Subsequently, and in violation of the rules of procedure, the case of Dr. József Szilágyi was segregated, and brought to trial on April 16, 1958. As for the rest of the case, the investigation was continued, and the trial resumed on June 9, 1958.

B

The judgments brought by the People's Court Division of the Supreme Court, which—partially on grounds of the above-listed violations of procedure—are the subject of the remedial petition I am submitting, are also without foundation:

1.) The part presented as a "statement of facts" in Judgment no. 18 of the People's Court does establish certain facts and events, but cannot be considered a statement of facts, as it fails to establish in its argument which individuals are connected with those facts and events and in what manner. This means that the People's Court did not present a statement of facts in a part of its judgment.

2.) Some of the facts established by the judgments of the People's Court are not substantiated by any evidence.

3.) A number of the details of the "facts" established in the judgments, particularly those to the effect that violations of substantive criminal law had taken place, are based on faulty argumentation.

4.) The judgments of the People's Court, in establishing certain facts, often refer to information obtained and decisions rendered by the Supreme Court in connection with other cases, without these facts having ever been directly introduced into the proceedings of the People's Court, and without the People's Court having ever verified these facts. According to section 177 of the Bp, the court may base its judgment solely on evidence examined in the course of the trial. The People's Court did not satisfy this legal requirement; it should not have based its conclusions as to the facts of the case on these references.

5.) The judgment holds Imre Nagy and his associates responsible for developments which even the judgments being petitioned against concede to have been brought about by the conduct of others.

That the judgments were unfounded is particularly evident in the following: as regards the conduct of Imre Nagy, the judgment of the People's Court (Judgment Against Imre Nagy—June 15, 1958, pp. 67-116) states that particular attention was given to his own defense to the effect that his behavior had had a generally moderating effect. The judgment goes on to state, without foundation, that Imre Nagy's deportment had been a tactical move: he was more cautious and more circumspect than his associates in moving toward the seditious goals he himself had formulated, and took pains to cover his tracks.

The People's Court draws this unfounded conclusion from, among other things, its likewise unfounded establishment as fact that at the October 23, 1956, meeting held at the residence of Géza Losonczy, Imre Nagy disapproved of those present giving advice on how the demonstration was to be organized. The People's Court totally disregarded those of his statements and the many instances of his conduct which controverted not only the above assumption, but also that criminal offenses of the kind established by the People's Court were committed [by Imre Nagy].

Foremost among these [pieces of disregarded evidence] are Imre Nagy's writings. Individually and in their totality, they reflect that his aim was to eliminate the mistakes and shortcomings of the socialist system, and to bring about reforms within the framework of the [socialist] social order.

The documents clearly reflect that a number of the MDP's leaders telephoned Imre Nagy in the course of the day on October 23, 1956, asking him to go to the Parliament. He did not comply. Only in the evening, when they actually came to fetch him, did he agree to go, and only because they hoped that he would be able to temper or reverse the situation. This is how he came to make his speech in the evening in front of the Parliament. He agreed with the emergency measures ordered to restore public order, took steps to thwart the excesses, and in the days that followed instituted further measures to this end.

There is absolutely no grounds for the self-contradictory statement established as fact in the judgment, namely, that all the while that he was instituting these measures to safeguard the social and economic order of the People's Republic, he was also obstructing their taking effect.

To substantiate the above statement, the People's Court makes unfounded reference to Imre Nagy's objecting to the annihilation of the armed insurgent group at Corvin Alley. The trial documents reveal quite clearly that a variety of military actions (bombardment, the blowing up of the theater building, artillery attack) were contemplated as possible means of liquidating the armed insurgent group. It was not the group's annihilation as such that Imre Nagy objected to; he only asked that it be done some other way, without causing further bloodshed among the population. It can also be ascertained from the documents that it was not Imre Nagy's fault that the action planned against the armed group did not take place; circumstances quite outside his control made it impossible.

Likewise without foundation is the statement in the judgment (Judgment Against Imre Nagy—June 15, 1958, pp. 67-116) that Sándor Kopácsi distributed twenty thousand arms at Budapest Police Headquarters on the orders of Imre Nagy. In addition to this statement being unfounded, the judgment of the court goes on to establish a further—contradictory—version of this incident. In another section of the judgment, it is recorded as established that orders for the distribution of these arms came from the minister of the interior, the orders specifying that 75 percent of the arms be given to industrial workers, and 25 percent to the young people. The documents of the proceedings unequivocally show that Sándor Kopácsi got his orders for distributing the arms from the minister of the interior, and Imre Nagy had had nothing to do with the matter. Still, the statement of facts in the section of the judgment pertaining to Sándor Kopácsi links the distribution of the arms with the meeting between Imre Nagy, Sándor Kopácsi, and Béla Király.

The People's Court holds Imre Nagy responsible also for the cease-fire ordered on October 28, 1956. The People's Court disregards the fact that this measure was taken on the basis of a decision made by the Party leadership and the government; nor does it take into account the extraordinary circumstances at the time. I will deal with the matter of responsibility for government orders later, in the course of showing cause for my protestation. Apart from the fact that in this matter, too, the proper approach would have been to examine the matter in terms of political and moral responsibility for a government measure, the People's Court totally failed to consider whether, in the given situation and in the light of the circumstances as a whole, there was indeed any other alternative open to the government for the restoration of social harmony. The judgment of the People's Court does not address itself in this connection to the question of whether the armed forces and security forces at the order of state's, and therefore at Imre Nagy's, disposal were at all competent at that time to secure public order.

Another matter tied to the efforts to establish public order is that of the national guard. The earlier-mentioned large quantity of arms were to be distributed in the prescribed manner in order to prevent them from finding their way into extremist hands. The efforts to organize the national guard were aimed at drawing its members into the closed structure of the army and the police force. In evaluating the nature of the national guard, one has to take into consideration the stand taken by the representatives of the various national guard units at the October 31, 1956, meeting held at the Kilián barracks. In summing up the opinions voiced at the meeting, Béla Király said that there was no room in the national guard for advocates of the old regime. The [national guard's] activities were not aimed at the restoration of the past regime; they stood by the socialist order of state (minutes of the October 31, 1956, meeting, vol. V-150.000/5).

According to the judgment, the declaration issued by the conspiracy's "front organization," the Revolutionary Committee of Hungarian Intellectuals, expressed dissatisfaction with the above-mentioned radio address of October 28, 1956, calling for a cease-fire. There is no foundation for the assertion in the judgment that this committee was an illegal institution of the government fulfilling the role of a front organization. The statement that Imre Nagy, on the one hand, would call on the population to stay calm and would call for a cease-fire, and on the other, would use the above committee to have a declaration issued against himself is a self-contradiction.

Of the defendants other than Imre Nagy, Zoltán Tildy and Pál Maléter were members of the order of state. A subsequent section of my petition dealing with the ascription of responsibility for government actions applies to the People's Court's findings against them as well.

The separate section of the judgment petitioned against which pertains to Zoltán Tildy reproaches him for his role in connection with József Mindszenty's radio address. The judgment, however, disregards in this respect the facts which are most significant from the standpoint of responsibility. Namely, that on the basis of a realistic evaluation of József Mindszenty's behavior, Imre Nagy and his associates expected that the address would have a calming effect on the people. It was in an effort to ensure this desired effect that Imre Nagy insisted—and took steps to make certain—that Mindszenty's speech be prerecorded, and only the approved text be allowed to go on the air. This is how he wanted to make sure that the address would play a positive part in the consolidation.

The separate section of the judgment pertaining to Pál Maléter states without foundation that he had prior knowledge of the siege of the Party Headquarters building, and contributed to its success. The judgment bases this statement on the fact that on October 30, 1956, he (Maléter) kept János Virágh, believed to be a plant by the Ministry of Defense, prisoner for a day. This, purportedly, to keep him from reporting the attack planned on the Party building. The account in itself is without foundation. There is no evidence to the effect that János Virágh had any knowledge of this kind, or that this was the purpose of keeping him in detention for a day.

The People's Court Division found Pál Maléter and Sándor Kopácsi guilty also of the crime of mutiny in a position of leadership in violation of section 29 of the KTBTK, and classified as such in section 30, paragraph /2/. The judgment does not give a detailed explanation as to what in their behavior constituted this criminal act. With regard to Pál Maléter, it states only that he committed this crime by announcing that he would no longer carry out the orders of the minister of defense.

The court did not examine the circumstances under which Maléter made this statement. Maléter had tried repeatedly to contact the responsible head of the Ministry of Defense, that is, the minister, but was unable to reach him. His reason for trying to contact the minister was to get information partly on the situation in general, and partly on the course of action to be taken. A statement made under these circumstances—and considering some others to be discussed later—does not constitute adequate basis for establishing that a criminal act was committed.

Furthermore, the court did not examine the de facto conduct of either Pál Maléter or Sándor Kopácsi. In their actions, they both followed the government's position of the moment.

The conduct of the other defendants named in the criminal proceedings tied in with the government's activities. Consequently, the observations made in my petition in connection with the government's activities apply to them as well.

The judgment reflects that the sense of personal responsibility expressed by the defendants and others was taken by the People's Court as evidence that it was Imre Nagy and his associates who provoked the events which began to unfold on October 23, 1956. The simple fact that all the participants in these events felt personally responsible for all the developments which dealt such a heavy blow to [Hungarian] society as a whole does not, in itself, mean that they either brought about those developments or played a negative part in them.

Judgment No. 12 of the People's Court Division found Dr. József Szilágyi guilty of the crime of leading a conspiracy, as entered in section 1, paragraph /1/ of the BHÖ.

The conduct adduced as grounds for the judgment does not constitute such a crime. The judgment itself does not state what conspiracy Dr. József Szilágyi was supposed to have led. The bulk of the statement of facts consists of statements Dr. József Szilágyi made, or intended to make, at various locations, and provides insufficient evidence of conspiracy or of any other criminal act. His deportment at the October 22, 1956, meeting at the University of Technology and after October 23, 1956, at the Budapest Police Headquarters was of the same character. The People's Court—without further ado—classified both of the above as leading a conspiracy. Neither in the above two instances, nor on any other occasion cited in the statement of facts did Dr. József Szilágyi's behavior constitute this criminal act. Given that his conduct met none of the legal criteria of leading a conspiracy, his committing a criminal act of this kind should never have been established.

C

The above-listed procedural violations and the facts pointing to the unfoundedness of the protested judgments would, in themselves, constitute sufficient grounds for their reversal. But it can also be established, and this is the crucial point in connection with the attached judgments, that the People's Court Division of the Supreme Court, in the course of its proceedings, gave an unlawful interpretation of substantive criminal law when it classified as criminal conduct which, given the proper application of the provisions of substantive criminal law, would never have resulted in the establishment of criminality. Essentially, it was on such grounds that the attached judgments of the People's Court established the guilt of Imre Nagy, Dr. Ferenc Donáth, Miklós Gimes, Zoltán Tildy, Pál Maléter, Sándor Kopácsi, Dr. József Szilágyi, Dr. Ferenc Jánosi, and Miklós Vásárhelyi of the crimes enumerated therein.

At the time that the acts subject to the written act of accusation occurred, the substantive criminal law in effect was contained in the Hatályos Anyagi Büntetőjogi Szabályok Hivatalos Összeállítása (BHÖ) (Official Compilation of Substantive Criminal Law Provisions in Force), and in Act 62 of 1948 pertaining to the Military Criminal Code (KTBTK).

Section 1, paragraph /1/ of the BHÖ states the following: "Liable to punishment for a criminal act is whoever commits an act aimed at subverting the people's democratic order of state or the People's Republic as defined in the constitution of the Hungarian People's Republic, initiates or leads a movement or conspiracy, or provides substantial financial assistance thereto."

Paragraph /2/ of the same section states further: "A criminal act is committed also by whoever assumes an active role in, or abets, a movement or conspiracy as defined in paragraph /1/."

The quoted letter of the law leaves no doubt that criminality is constituted by conduct "aimed" at subverting the people's democratic order or the People's Republic.

The sentencing practice of the time was established in Decision No. 216 of February 1957 of the Criminal and Military College of the Supreme Court, which was not binding for the courts, but which they followed. According to the above decision, it is not an element of the letter of the law defining the crime in section 1 of the BHÖ that the perpetrator carry out the action with the purpose of subverting the people's democratic order of state. The College explained the position taken in this decision by noting that the word "aimed" contained in the letter of the law was not synonymous with "purpose," but was, rather, a basic substantive element of the criminal act itself; that is, the conspiracy had only to be de facto capable of overthrowing the people's democratic order of state. According to this decision, the criminal act [entered in section 1, paragraph /1/ of the BHÖ] can be committed without any particular political purpose. The matter of whether the perpetrator was or was not subjectively led by the purpose to subvert the order of state is, at most, to be considered in determining the severity of the appropriate punishment.

My position is the following: concluding that the letter of the law applies only to the objective element of the crime is stretching the interpretation of the law to an unacceptable limit. This element of the definition of the offense is a subjective, not an objective, element. If it were the other way around, any behavior deemed to be threatening to the political, social, or economic order could be construed as the gravest of crimes against the state, on the sole basis that independently of its purpose, it is capable of leading to such results.

It follows that the only lawful interpretation of the law is that by its very nature, a crime of this sort cannot be considered to have taken place—it is conceptually impossible—without striving for the achievement of one of the results specified by the law, that is, purpose. Thus, in the case of Imre Nagy and his co-defendants, too, it would have been absolutely essential for the proper application of the law to examine the question of precisely what their intentions were, whether they indeed intended to achieve a result specified by the law. This the People's Court Division of the Supreme Court failed to do.

I must further point out that the People's Court's judgments that I am protesting are unlawful even if we accept the Criminal College's above interpretation, since the People's Court, in arriving at its unlawful decision, disregarded innumerable circumstances and drew a great many fallacious conclusions when it established that a crime had been committed.

In its statement of facts, Judgment No. 18 of the People's Court broke the time frame down to three periods, but examined the actions as an organic whole. The time periods were the following:

1. The period between the second half of 1955 and October 23, 1956;
2. The period between October 23, 1956, and November 4, 1956;
3. The period after November 4, 1956.

Part A of Judgment No. 18 of the People's Court (Judgment Against Imre Nagy—June 15, 1958, pp. 67-116) deals with some of the events which took place within the first period. The statement of facts in itself reveals the fallacy of the judgment that Imre Nagy, Dr. Ferenc Donáth, Miklós Gimes, Dr. József Szilágyi, Dr. Ferenc Jánosi, and Miklós Vásárhelyi created a political power group which was in the nature of a movement or conspiracy aimed at overthrowing the order of state. The facts that they kept in contact with one another, that they carried on various political discussions, that they debated different articles, including those of Imre Nagy's writings specified in the judgment, are a far cry from having committed a crime. Criticism of the existing social order, discussion of how to find solutions, especially if these are rooted in the existing situation and remain within the framework of the social order determined by the constitution, do not constitute a crime against the state.

The People's Court Division of the Supreme Court attributed definitive significance to the writings referred to in the judgment. Contrary to the findings of the People's Court, these writings, considered both individually and collectively, are such that neither having written them nor discussing them can, in any way, be taken as undermining the social order, even on the interpretation that purpose is an objective element of conduct in terms of the letter of the law. The conduct in question objectively lacked the criteria essential for establishing the commission of a crime.

The statement of facts contained in the judgment brought by the People's Court establishes without foundation as a formal feature of the action that the activities of Imre Nagy and the people around him were systematic, coordinated, and conspiratorial. Imre Nagy and the people who at the time were in contact with him met at random. There is no data to indicate that their get-togethers were planned, scheduled, or organized. The mere fact that these meetings took place repeatedly does not constitute a valid basis for the conclusions taken as established facts in the judgment. Likewise without foundation is the statement in the judgment that their conduct was of the conspiratorial nature characteristic of this type of criminal act. The fact that they met on a one-to-one basis, or with third persons, does not make their behavior conspiratorial.

Part B, section 1, paragraph g of Judgment No. 18 (Judgment Against Imre Nagy—June 15, 1958, pp. 67-116) deals with the events which took place on the morning of October 23, 1956, at Géza Losonczy's residence. According to the statement of facts in the judgment, the discussion centered, among other things, on whom those present considered to be illsuited to be members of the MDP's Central Leading Body and of the Political Committee, and who should be co-opted to take their place. In another section of the grounds given for the judgment, it is noted that other people, too, considered personnel changes within the leadership of the Party a necessity. Elsewhere in the judgment, the statement of facts censures them [the Imre Nagy group] for divulging the party's internal problems to non-Party members. Farther on, the judgment goes on to state that while residing on the premises of the Yugoslav Embassy, the Imre Nagy group acted as the Executive Committee of the MSZMP.

[The group's] conduct while engaged in Party-related activities or while acting as a Party organ does not, in itself, constitute a crime.

I consider it of prime importance that the Presidential Division of the Supreme Court pronounce as a matter of legal principle that—whether the party in question is in power or not—criticism of a party's actions, statements made as to the suitability or otherwise of any person for a position of leadership, debate over a given party's ideological or political platform, judgment of any grouping or faction formed on ideological or any other grounds within a party, and evaluation of disputes between parties all fall outside the competence of criminal justice. The same applies when a person/group considers himself/itself the leader/leading organ of that party. None of this can fall within the realm of criminal justice, but must remain the internal affair of the particular party itself.

Approval or disapproval of any given party's policy or ideology, expressing one's opinion about party leaders, and formulating and expressing one's views—either within or outside the party—on one party's relationship to another or on cooperation between them cannot, objectively speaking, subvert, undermine, or weaken the order of state.

These are the matters at issue in the above-cited parts of the judgment delivered by the People's Court. In their discussions, Imre Nagy and his associates voiced their opinions on the leadership of the MDP of the time. During their stay at the Yugoslav Embassy, they considered themselves the interim Executive Committee of the MSZMP only because they had been elected to that post. It is one of the basics of legal theory as applied to criminal law that conduct of this sort and expressions of opinion having to do with the Party cannot be construed as criminal acts. This is what follows also from the provisions of the constitution of the Hungarian People's Republic in force at the time.

Part B, section 2 of the judgment deals with the events which took place between October 23, 1956 and November 4, 1956. The judgment of the People's Court—ignoring even the pertinent facts that the Court itself established—disregards the circumstance that during this period, from October 24, 1956, Imre Nagy was the country's duly elected prime minister. The judgment also disregards the fact that the others were also members of the order of state, or held responsible positions in various government organs. The establishment of facts as recorded in the course of the proceedings was not directed at clarifying either how events in Hungary changed from one interval to the next during this period, or whether the government or the different government organs were in a position to do more or act differently than they actually did. The judgment makes absolutely no attempt to determine the extent to which some of the steps that Imre Nagy and his associates were censured for in fact served the purpose that had motivated them, that is, prevented events from taking an extremist turn.

Apart from all this, evaluating the actions of a given order of state, and weighing whether some of the measures taken were right or wrong—particularly under extraordinary circumstances—is not really the business of criminal law. A government bears primarily a political and moral responsibility to the constitutional organs to which it is subordinated. From this it follows that mistakes made in the course of carrying on the business of government, violations of certain operating procedures out of necessity or otherwise, do not constitute a crime against the state. The court's claim that the government functioned at the time "as a private body" is totally unfounded.

As concerns the legality of the government's operation, the judgment repeatedly asserts that it was illegal. In the course of examining the legality of the proceedings and of the judgment, I acquired the documents of the Presidential Council of the People's Republic and of the Council of Ministers pertaining to decisions on personnel changes between October 23 and November 4, 1956. The documents are attached to my petition. These documents prove that all decisions regarding personnel changes within the government came from the Presidential

Council of the People's Republic, and that personnel changes within other government bodies originated with the Council of Ministers. It was the Presidential Council which elected Imre Nagy to be prime minister, and later confirmed him in that position. It was likewise the Presidential Council which elected Zoltán Tildy, Pál Maléter, and Géza Losonczy to be members of the government. The constitutionality of this government is further confirmed by the fact that the Presidential Council issued Resolution No. 33/1956—dated November 4, 1956, and published in the November 12, 1956, issue of the Official Gazette—to dismiss it. Therefore, the assertion of the judgment to the effect that the cabinet acted for the Presidential Council and for Parliament as a private body is both unfounded and contrary to the facts.

The documents also show that the uninterrupted functioning of the entire government was impossible.

The criminal evaluation of the events that took place in the period after November 4 (part B, section 3 of the judgment delivered by the People's Court) is likewise unlawful. The charge of conspiracy has to be repudiated in this instance, too, and not only on the grounds that there was no purpose to overthrow the order of state. The fact that the persons temporarily residing at the Yugoslav Embassy were in contact with the representatives of that country was a necessary and unavoidable result of the events, and cannot be construed as conduct contrary to the interests of the Hungarian state. Nor can the facts that the idea of going abroad occurred to the persons temporarily residing at the Yugoslav Embassy, and that they let their whereabouts be known be considered subversive acts. The judgment provides absolutely no justification for treating these natural human reactions to social and political isolation as a crime.

Just as unlawful was the classification of crime for the established fact that a questionnaire was sent out [from the Yugoslav Embassy by the Imre Nagy group] around November 10. Not one of the constitutional regulations in effect at the time was violated by the circumstance that a group that was still a significant factor in the nation's political life wished to obtain information on the latest political situation and on the possible mode of their continued activities.

It was a mistaken conclusion on the part of the People's Court to establish as fact that the questionnaire had the effect of prompting the formation of the "Hungarian Democratic Independence Movement" on November 13, 1956, and the publication of the newspaper *October 23rd*. The documentation contains no evidence of such a cause and effect relationship, and we have absolutely no data whatsoever to indicate that Imre Nagy and his associates while at the Yugoslav Embassy meant to encourage anyone to do either of the above.

The only fact which can be established in this connection is that independently of the questionnaire, the forming of the "Hungarian Democratic Independence Movement" was discussed on November 13, 1956, at the residence of Róbert Bohó, where Miklós Gimes and others decided to form the movement (Judgment Against Imre Nagy—June 15, 1958, part B, section 3, p. 93). The aim of the movement, however, as Miklós Gimes and all the others present perceived it, was not the subversion of the people's democratic order of state or of the People's Republic. Rather, its purpose was to find some means of paving the way to rapprochement between the government of János Kádár and the political group staying at the Yugoslav Embassy, and thereby to consolidation (statements of Péter Józsa, György Ádám, and Róbert Bohó at the June 11, 1958, hearing). For lack of [evidence of] the purpose required by law, Miklós Gimes's participation in the publication of unauthorized material did not provide sufficient grounds for the People's Court to find him guilty of the crime of leading a conspiracy aimed at subverting the people's democratic order of state.

Judgment No. 18 of the People's Court Division of the Supreme Court, which is the subject of this legal petition, found Imre Nagy guilty also of the crime of treason, as defined in section 35, paragraph /1/ of the BHÖ. According to the judgment, the reason that some of his actions—that is, withdrawal from the Warsaw Pact, the declaration of neutrality, and his radio address of November 4, 1956—were so classified was that "his having contacted foreign powers was not only an attempt to commit them to taking some action, but created the imminent danger of their doing so." Beyond this, the People's Court did not offer any detailed explanation as to why the above actions should be classified as instances of the above crime.

The offense entered in section 35 of the BHÖ was declared a crime under Hungarian criminal law by Act 3 of 1930. It specifies that any person who "forms an alliance with, or establishes contact with the government of a foreign power or with a foreign organization with the aim of inducing it to take hostile action against the Hungarian state, moreover any person who incites a foreign power to war or forcible measures against the Hungarian state" is guilty of the crime of treason.

The letter of the law is clear, and its ministerial interpretation further emphasizes that the law differentiates between foreign governments and foreign organizations. The judgment [brought against Imre Nagy for violation of this law] speaks of contacts having been established with foreign powers. Neither by withdrawing from the Warsaw Pact, nor through the declaration of neutrality did Imre Nagy establish contact with any foreign power. The verbal communication which, on November 2, 1956, the president of the Council of Ministers, in his capacity as acting foreign minister addressed to the heads of the foreign embassies accredited to Budapest does not meet the criteria of establishing contact with foreign powers, and therefore by no means establishes the commission of the crime. It is also clear from both the contents and the wording of the communication that it was merely a statement of how matters stood, and contained absolutely no requests of those to whom it was addressed. For a government to inform the foreign embassies accredited to the country of the situation of the country at the time without asking anything of them is well within the parameters of everyday [diplomatic] communication.

Further documentation of the proceedings establishes that Imre Nagy turned repeatedly to the United Nations on behalf of the Hungarian government, requesting of the four great powers (undoubtedly of the members of the Security Council) that they protect the country's neutrality by putting the matter on the agenda of the General Assembly scheduled to open at that time. The second letter sent to the U.N. differed from this only in that it requested the Security Council to instruct the governments of the Soviet Union and Hungary to continue negotiations.

In this connection, I wish to point out that the People's Court did not examine whether or not the United Nations organization qualified as a "foreign" organization. The Hungarian People's Republic was, by then, a member of the United Nations organization, having enacted its charter into Hungarian law with Act 1 of 1956. The Hungarian government's actions were in keeping with the regulations of that charter. It is obvious that no international organization of which Hungary is a member—the United Nations organization included—can be considered a "foreign organization" in the sense that the term occurs in the [above-mentioned] law. An organization of this kind cannot be called "foreign" as concerns the Hungarian People's Republic.

Furthermore, establishing contact with a foreign power can be considered an instance of treason only if the person establishing the contact does so with the aim of inducing the foreign power to take hostile action against the Hungarian state. The letters forwarded to the United Nations organization are available in the documentation, and they leave no doubt that the aim was to secure protection for Hungary's declared neutrality, and to ensure the continuation of negotiations with the government of the Soviet Union.

The government's proclamation of withdrawal from the Warsaw Pact merely stated the government's purpose to do so. This is supported by the fact that at its November 2, 1956, meeting, the government appointed a delegation to conduct negotiations to this effect. In doing so the government was taking action that followed from its constitutional position, and was in keeping with the principles and rules of international law. Consequently, it, too, fails to meet the criteria of treason according to the letter of the law.

Nor does Imre Nagy's radio address of November 4, 1956—a factual report on the situation for the information of the population and of international public opinion—constitute the crime of treason.

In sum, the judgment of treason brought by the People's Court Division of the Supreme Court is unlawful: none of the "facts" established by the court as grounds ever actually took place.

Judgment No. 18 of the People's Court Division found Pál Maléter and Sándor Kopácsi guilty of the crime of mutiny in a leadership capacity, in violation of section 29 of the KTBTK. According to the above section, "Mutiny is committed by soldiers if they, as a group, openly defy military regulations."

The letter of the law makes clear—without the need for further analysis—that mutiny, if committed, is committed by a group of soldiers. Not even the judgment alleges that a military group defying military regulations was ever formed with the participation or leadership of either Pál Maléter or Sándor Kopácsi. Given that no such group existed, neither Pál Maléter nor Sándor Kopácsi could have been its leaders. Therefore no crime [of mutiny] had been committed.

It also becomes evident from the documentation of the proceedings that Pál Maléter always acted as a supporter of the socialist system, both before and after October 23, 1956.

After October 23, 1956, Pál Maléter carried out his responsibilities as best he could under the circumstances. He cleansed, and than secured the Kilián barracks, and organized its defense according to his orders. He fought against the insurgents of Corvin Alley. It was under orders that, following the cease-fire, he established contact with the insurgents, and tried to use his influence to establish peace and order, and to prevent extremism.

His actions, as described in the judgment, cannot be considered "going over to the other side," or mutiny against lawful authority for the simple reason that he was following the directions of the lawful government in all he did. Throughout the period, Pál Maléter acted in the political spirit represented by the government. As deputy minister, and later, as minister, he acted on behalf of the government and represented its political direction.

Sándor Kopácsi's conduct was similar. On October 23, 1956, and in the days that followed, he personally took part in armed confrontations with the insurgents until such time as the government changed its position.

The documentation of the proceedings discredits the statement of the judgment (part C, section 6) that he issued a blanket order to the district police headquarters prohibiting resistance. He ordered a halt to resistance only in cases when the situation seemed hopeless, and further resistance would only have raised the number of casualties.

Finally, the proceedings conducted by the People's Court Division of the Supreme Court was unlawful also because it did not extend its investigation to the international conditions with a direct bearing on the case, either for between October 23 and November 4, 1956, or for the following period. Thus, it did not take these into consideration in reaching a judgment.

One of the undeniable facts in connection with the events between October 23 and November 4, 1956, is that the Hungarian and Soviet governments agreed on the withdrawal of the Soviet troops from Budapest. No subsequent negotiations or agreements followed to the contrary. When, on November 1, 1956, the cabinet decided on the matter of neutrality and of the [country's] withdrawal from the Warsaw Pact, the Soviet ambassador to Hungary was also present at the meeting. Following the session, Prime Minister Imre Nagy continued his discussions with the Soviet ambassador. Given that there were no other negotiations concerning the activities or the utilization of the Soviet troops stationed here, neither the government or its leader can be faulted for objecting to [Soviet] military activity [within the country] that went beyond the provisions of the Warsaw Pact. In taking measures [to express its objection], the government, or, rather, the prime minister, was fulfilling his constitutional obligations, and consequently committed no crime.

The other international aspects weighing on the case but neglected by the People's Court have to do with the agreements the Hungarian government reached with the governments of Yugoslavia and Romania on November 21 and 22, 1956. The documentation of the proceedings contains no data regarding the Romanian agreement. It is the agreement reached with the Yugoslav government that has a more direct bearing on the case. Although the agreement itself could not be found in the course of the review of the case, it was established on the basis of a variety of records of the proceedings, and substantiated by documents obtained from the Hungarian Ministry of Foreign Affairs, particularly by Verbal Communication No. 007810/1956 made by the Hungarian side and dated December 1, 1956, that such an agreement was, in fact, made. Some points of the agreement with a direct bearing on the criminal case can be ascertained from this document.

It can be established, for instance, that on the night of November 3, and/or on the morning of November 4, 1956, Imre Nagy, Ferenc Donáth, Dr. Ferenc Jánosi, Miklós Vásárhelyi, Dr. József Szilágyi, and others took the opportunity offered to them by the government of Yugoslavia to move into the building of the Yugoslav Embassy. During the time Imre Nagy and his associates were staying at the Embassy, discussions were held between the Yugoslav and the Hungarian governments concerning the situation and the future of the Hungarian group. The documentation of the proceedings leaves no doubt that on November 21, 1956, an agreement was reached by the two governments that the Hungarians staying at the [Yugoslav] Embassy could leave the building where they enjoyed extraterritoriality with the Hungarian government guaranteeing that they would not be held criminally responsible for their earlier actions.

According to section 7 of Act 2 of 1950 (Btá) in force at the time of the proceedings conducted by the court of first instance, but ignored by the People's Court, what is decisive in matters of the criminal responsibility of persons enjoying personal immunity is the provisions of the international agreement, settlement, and so on. The above rule of the Btá does not differentiate between Hungarian citizens and foreign nationals in cases of personal immunity by international agreement. It simply provides exemption from the principal rule, that is, from the territorial and personal jurisdiction of the law. The Hungarian People's Republic had signed a great many international agreements curtailing the territorial and personal jurisdiction of the law over both Hungarian and non-Hungarian citizens. Some of these agreements provided partial, others provided complete immunity from criminal accountability. From this it follows that the authorities conducting the criminal proceedings [against Imre Nagy and his associates] should have acquired and considered the agreements relevant in this instance, and should have established the nonexistence of Hungarian jurisdiction. This matter should not have escaped the attention of the authorities conducting the criminal proceedings, especially since particularly Imre Nagy and Dr. József Szilágyi both pointed it out to them emphatically and repeatedly.

Thus, over and above the fact that the establishment of guilt in these proceedings was unlawful on a number of other grounds, in the case of Imre Nagy, Dr. Ferenc Donáth, Dr. Ferenc Jánosi, Miklós Vásárhelyi, and Dr. József Szilágyi, the existence of an international agreement guaranteeing their personal immunity should in itself have proven an impediment to prosecution.

In view of the foregoing, and in accordance with paragraph /1/ of section 284 of the Be, I hereby submit a remedial petition against Judgment No. TB. NB. 003/1958-12 and Judgment No. TB. NB. 003/1958-18 of the People's Court Division of the Supreme Court of the Hungarian People's Republic, which judgments became final on April 22, 1958, and on June 15, 1958, respectively, and in favor of Imre Nagy, Dr. Ferenc Donáth, Miklós Gimes, Zoltán Tildy, Pál Maléter, Sándor Kopácsi, Dr. József Szilágyi, Dr. Ferenc Jánosi, and Miklós Vásárhelyi.

I move that the Presidential Division of the Supreme Court establish that in the course of reaching its Judgments No. TB. NB. 003/1958-12 and No. TB. NB. 003/1958-18, the People's Court Division of the Supreme Court committed procedural violations, and that the judgments are without foundation;

that it further establish that the People's Court, in its judgments, applied the rules of substantive criminal law in an unlawful manner, and that it therefore set aside the attached judgments of the People's Court Division of the Supreme Court and, on the basis of section 214, paragraph 3, item a of the Be, on the grounds that the actions for which they were indicted were not criminal acts, acquit

Imre Nagy, Dr. Ferenc Donáth, Miklós Gimes, Zoltán Tildy, Pál Maléter, Sándor Kopácsi, Dr. József Szilágyi, Dr. Ferenc Jánosi, and Miklós Vásárhelyi.

Lastly, I move that the statement of facts related to Géza Losonczy in the attached judgments be disregarded.

I wish to state that in accordance with section 139, paragraph 1, item a of the Be, I have terminated the investigation initiated against Géza Losonczy. A copy of the decision to this effect is attached.

I have returned to Erzsébet Nagy Imre Nagy's "Thoughts and Recollections," dated Snagov, 1957, along with his handwritten notes from Snagov, and the outline of his autobiographical "Turbulent Generation."

Budapest, June 9, 1989.
Dr. Károly Szijártó
circular stamp of the procurator general of the Hungarian People's Republic.

Decision of the Presidential Division of the Supreme Court
July 6, 1989

Presidential Division of the Supreme Court of the Hungarian People's Republic
Eln. Tan. B. törv. no. 660/1989/6

IN THE NAME OF THE REPUBLIC!

The Presidential Division of the Supreme Court, at its public session of July 6, 1989, passed the following decision:

Judgments No. TB. NB. 003/1958/12, and No. TB. NB. 003/1958/18 of the People's Court Division of the Supreme Court are unlawful. For this reason, they are quashed.

In the absence of any crime having been committed, the Presidential Division of the Supreme Court hereby acquits Imre Nagy, Dr. Ferenc Donáth, Miklós Gimes, Sándor Kopácsi, and Dr. József Szilágyi of the charge of leading a conspiracy aimed at subverting the people's democratic order of state; Imre Nagy of the charge of treason; Sándor Kopácsi of the charge of mutiny in a leadership capacity; Zoltán Tildy of the charge of abetting a conspiracy aimed at subverting the people's democratic order of state; Pál Maléter of the charge of taking action aimed at subverting the people's democratic order of state, and of the charge of mutiny in a leadership capacity; and Dr. Ferenc Jánosi and Miklós Vásárhelyi of the charge of taking an active part in a conspiracy aimed at subverting the people's democratic order of state.

The costs incurred in the course of adjudicating the remedial petition are to be borne by the state.

GROUNDS

I

In its judgment No. TB. NB. 003/1958/18, of June 15, 1958, the People's Court Division of the Supreme Court sentenced Imre Nagy, defendant no. 1, to death, and confiscation of all his property, for the crimes of leading a conspiracy aimed at subverting the people's democratic order of state, and of treason; Dr. Ferenc Donáth, defendant no. 2, to 12 (twelve) years of imprisonment, 10 (ten) years of prohibition from exercising of certain rights enumerated in the Criminal Code, and to confiscation of all his property, for the crime of leading a conspiracy aimed at subverting the people's democratic order of state; Miklós Gimes, defendant no. 3, to death, and confiscation of all his property, for the crime of leading a conspiracy aimed at subverting the people's democratic order of state; Zoltán Tildy, defendant no. 4, to 6 (six) years of imprisonment, 6 (six) years of prohibition from exercising of certain rights as enumerated in the Criminal Code, and confiscation of all his property, for the crime of abetting a conspiracy aimed at subverting the people's democratic order of state; Pál Maléter, defendant no. 5, to death, degradation, and the loss of all medals and decorations, and confiscation of all his property, for the crimes of taking action aimed at subverting the people's democratic order of state, and—as a leader—of mutiny; Sándor Kopácsi, defendant no. 6, to life imprisonment, removal from office, 10 (ten) years of prohibition from exercising of certain rights enumerated in the Criminal Code, the loss of all medals and decorations, and confiscation of all his property, for the crimes of leading a conspiracy aimed at subverting the people's democratic order of state, and—as a leader—of mutiny; Dr. Ferenc Jánosi, defendant no. 7, to 8 (eight) years of imprisonment, 10 (ten) years of prohibition from exercising of certain rights enumerated in the Criminal Code, and confiscation of all his property, for the crime of taking an active part in a conspiracy aimed at subverting the people's democratic order of state; Miklós Vásárhelyi, defendant no. 8, to 5 (five) years of imprisonment, 5 (five) years of prohibition from exercising of certain rights enumerated in the Criminal Code, and partial confiscation of his property in the amount of 1,000 Ft., for the crime of taking an active part in a conspiracy aimed at subverting the people's democratic order of state.

In its Judgment No. TB. NB. 003/1958/12 of April 22, 1958, the People's Court Division sentenced Dr. József Szilágyi to death and confiscation of all his property, for the crime of conspiracy aimed at subverting the people's democratic order of state.

Against these judgments, which became final immediately upon their pronouncement, the procurator general filed a remedial petition (Bfl. 21 206/1989) on the grounds of procedural violations, lack of foundation, and groundless application of the rules of substantive criminal law. In judging the petition, the Presidential Division arrived at the following general conclusions: Parliament, the government, the MSZMP, and the Hungarian people see the events of 1956—and specifically the historical role of Imre Nagy and his associates—radically differently today than even a few months ago. Their political and moral rehabilitation has, in effect, already taken place. The responsibility of the Presidential Division of the Supreme Court is to reexamine the case, the proceedings and the judgments from the legal point of view.

The statement of facts on the basis of which Imre Nagy and his associates were sentenced cannot be changed by the petition, and the initiation of new proceedings is not possible; nor is it necessary. The Presidential Division's examination was directed primarily at whether or not the evaluation that the People's Court Division gave of the facts was legally proper, and whether or not the actions that were the subject of the proceedings in fact constituted crimes on the proper interpretation of the law. By comparison, the matter of whether procedural rules were adhered to or violated—while symptomatic of the period and of the contemporary attitude toward legality—is of secondary importance.

The same holds for the matter of the unfoundedness of certain "facts," or of certain conclusions based on these "facts." Today, this is relevant only from the point of view of whether it influenced the legal interpretation of the actions subject to the proceedings, and if so, how. All that the Presidential Division can do in the course of this reevaluation to redress the balance of objectivity is to take into consideration certain well-known facts publicized by the media at the time, in the light of which the actions ascribed to the defendants must be very differently evaluated from the way they were by the People's Court Division, and to point out the contradictions in the grounds cited in the judgments.

In view of the above, the Presidential Division deems it unnecessary to detail the statement of facts given in the judgments, and elects to limit itself to a brief summarization of those facts which are significant from the point of view of this legal review.

II

A brief summary of the statement of facts as given in
Judgment No. TB. NB. 003/1958/18 of the People's Court Division

The People's Court Division limited its examination of facts significant from the point of view of criminal law to answering the following questions:

A. Did the political power group which formed around the person of Imre Nagy constitute "a conspiracy or movement aimed at subverting the government" as defined in section 1 of the BHÖ?

B. If it was, in fact, such a conspiracy (movement), what criminally relevant role did their collective activities play in:

1.) The October 23, 1956, eruption of the counterrevolution;
2.) The course the counterrevolution took between October 23 and November 4, 1956;
3.) The fight to frustrate the consolidation of the dictatorship of the proletariat after November 4, 1956?

C. Did the individual defendants' activities fit into the collective activities of the seditious conspiracy (movement), and if so, to what extent?

== A ==

1.) From the second half of 1955, a coterie of bourgeois intellectuals gathered around the person of Imre Nagy. At Imre Nagy's initiative, the group planned to take collective action within the party to block Imre Nagy's expulsion. Later, at the initiative of Miklós Gimes, Ferenc Jánosi, and Miklós Vásárhelyi, they organized another collective action against what were real shortcomings in the MDP's cultural policies at the time. They drew up what became known as the "writers' memorandum," and solicited signatures for it. These actions went beyond what was still within the scope of an "in-Party factional grouping," and took on the complexion of a conspiracy to undermine the state. This is how the influence of Imre Nagy and his associates was increased within the cultural mass organizations (Writers' Association, Journalists' Association, etc.).

2.) During the same period (late 1955, early 1956), Imre Nagy put his political ideas in writing, and secretly circulated them among the members of his inner circle. "Timely Moral and Ethical Issues in Hungarian Public Life," "Some Timely Questions about the Application of the Theories of Marxism-Leninism," and "The Five Basic Principles of International Relations, and the Timely Issue of Our Foreign Policy" were some such works. In them, he stated, among other things, that the Party leadership had bankrupted the country, and that it was a degenerate Bonapartist power which was to be done away with. He indirectly denied the leadership role of the working class and its Party, and could envision a return to the multiparty system. He equated the aggressive political bloc with the defensive alliance formed to counterbalance it, and suggested that participation in the alliance formulated to counterbalance the aggressive imperialist political bloc violated Hungary's independence and sovereignty.

3.) As of the spring of 1956, Imre Nagy's "inner circle" began using its earlier-attained and growing political influence to spread Imre Nagy's ideas among the intelligentsia in general, and the intellectual youth in particular. They enlisted the Petőfi Circle, the TTIT, and other cultural fora for this effort. They discussed and coordinated their activities, and made contemplated speeches the subject of advance discussions. Imre Nagy and his associates—primarily Géza Losonczy and Miklós Vásárhelyi—exerted their influence [on the youth organizations] through Gábor Tánczos and László Kardos.

4.) It took József Szilágyi almost a year to recruit Sándor Kopácsi into the group. In early October 1956, Szilágyi arranged his personal introduction to Imre Nagy.

5.) In the summer of 1956, Miklós Gimes suggested that they form an "illegal committee" to direct and supervise the group's activities. Imre Nagy rejected the idea, as he wanted to maintain an appearance of legality, as well as his personal leadership.

6.) Imre Nagy commissioned Miklós Gimes, Ferenc Jánosi, and Miklós Vásárhelyi to deliver to Georgievich, first secretary of the Yugoslav Embassy, writings of his which he carefully kept secret from the leaders of the party and the [Hungarian] government.

7.) In mid-October 1956, Géza Losonczy and Sándor Haraszti arranged a conspiratorial meeting with Anna Kéthly, to discuss what position the right-wing Social Democrats would take vis-à-vis a new Imre Nagy government which would realize the above-mentioned goals.

On the basis of the above, the People's Court Division came to the conclusion that, by the end of 1955, the political power group forming around Imre Nagy had taken on the character of a conspiracy aimed at subverting and overthrowing the government.

== B ==

1.) The members of the conspiracy escalated their propaganda activities to involve also other organizations. A concerted attack was started to discredit the policies of the Party and the government. They found themselves unable to contain the movement they had created. By September and October of 1956, the movement itself obliged Imre Nagy and the members of his conspiracy to carry their proclaimed principles to their practical conclusion.

In the period immediately preceding, and in the initial stages of, the counterrevolution, the various groups attempted to establish a common political platform against the MDP. They condensed their political programs into points and circulated them as such. They called for "a changing of the guard" and the extension of democracy to a point which, in essence, was aimed against the leading role of the working class and of the Party, and the declaration of the country's "neutrality," and its withdrawal from the Warsaw Pact.

On October 22 and 23, 1956, at meetings attended by Imre Nagy, Géza Losonczy, Ferenc Donáth, Miklós Gimes, and others, they began to draft the all-inclusive program of the future Imre Nagy government. Those gathered in the evening of October 22, 1956, at the home of László Kardos discussed how the followers of Imre Nagy would take over the crucial posts within the DISZ leadership.

On the evening of October 22, 1956, József Szilágyi appeared and spoke twice at the student rally at the University of Technology. He took a stand for the fight against Stalinism, and for proceeding with the demonstration. Later he got in touch with Sándor Kopácsi, asking him that the police not interfere with the demonstration.

On the morning of October 23, 1956, members of the group who were gathered at the residence of Géza Losonczy maintained contact with Gábor Tánczos, organized the demonstration on behalf of the leadership. Tánczos kept them abreast of the situation as it unfolded, and they provided him with instructions.

On the basis of the above, the People's Court Division arrived at the conclusion that the result of the agitation of Imre Nagy and the other members of the conspiracy was that it was the movement they created, that is, the campus auxiliary circles of the Petőfi Circle, which sparked the October 23, 1956, demonstration with the purpose of overthrowing the existing order and carrying Imre Nagy's ideas to victory.

2.) Between October 23 and 28, 1956, the members of the conspiracy and of the movement they created concentrated around three different nuclei, which maintained close contact with one another. These nuclei were located in the MDP Central Leading Body building around the person of Imre Nagy, in the Budapest Police Headquarters building around the person of Sándor Kopácsi, and on the premises of the Writers' Association.

Initiatives and directives came from the nucleus established around the person of Imre Nagy, although—especially after October 25—the Deák Square nucleus, and József Szilágyi in particular, showed an inclination to take over. Between October 23 and 25, the members of the conspiracy and some of its leaders organized a variety of delegations to urge Imre Nagy that the leadership of the MDP assume leadership of the "revolution," and trust itself to the armed forces of the "insurgents." Thus it was that József Szilágyi and Miklós Gimes were among those in the "workers' delegation from Angyalföld."

On October 28, 1956, the concerted action of the conspiracy compelled the MDP leadership to compromise. They called together the members and followers of the conspiracy, or, rather, of the movement, and formed the Revolutionary Committee of Hungarian Intellectuals. The committee issued a "Declaration," and was of the opinion that "the danger of a left-wing restoration" was growing. They discussed what party or movement to organize should the MDP be dissolved.

Imre Nagy's "Government Proclamation" did not satisfy the members of the conspiracy. The most serious discrepancy between the proclamation and their declaration was that while the proclamation called on the population to surrender all arms, and implied that a new police force including members of the military and contingents of armed workers and young people had already been set up, the declaration called for the establishment of such a police force "to safeguard the achievements of the revolution."

Following the radio broadcast of the proclamation, they launched a campaign to popularize Imre Nagy. They alleged that to that point, Imre Nagy had been "a prisoner of the ÁVH," and had been forced to make the statements he made. On October 30, it was announced on radio that Imre Nagy had had no knowledge of the Soviet troops having been called in, nor of martial law having been declared.

Imre Nagy never again convened the Council of Ministers, and took no measures to prevent the lynching and other extremist actions. They began organizing the national guard from among the members of the armed groups. At the Budapest Police Headquarters alone, following the orders of Imre Nagy, Sándor Kopácsi distributed over twenty thousand arms among the counterrevolutionaries.

Imre Nagy conducted negotiations with the leaders of various groups, and appointed Béla Király to be the commander of the national guard.

After October 28, 1956, Imre Nagy did not convene the Council of Ministers. In place of the lawful government, he instituted a smaller coalition "cabinet." The cabinet took over the competence of the Council of Ministers and of the Presidium, and assumed decision-making power in all matters of government. It was the cabinet that decided on the restructuring of the government, the withdrawal from the Warsaw Pact, and the declaration of neutrality, and sent telegrams to the U.N., asking the great powers to "guarantee" the country's declared neutrality.

There was no truth in the official statement that members of the Council of Ministers had been relieved by the Presidential Council of office and replaced with individuals already participating in the meetings of the cabinet at their own request.

On November 4, 1956, following the appearance of the Soviet troops, Imre Nagy made a radio appeal protesting against the reestablishment of order, and then the majority of his group took refuge at the Yugoslav Embassy.

3.) In the building of the Yugoslav Embassy, the members of the group continued their conspiring. Calling themselves "the Executive Committee of the MSZMP," they started establishing contact and/or negotiating with leaders of the Yugoslav government, with their coalition partners, indirectly with Radio Free Europe, and with members of the conspiracy who had stayed outside the Embassy concerning the steps that were to be taken to prevent consolidation, and the reestablishment of the dictatorship of the proletariat.

Encouraged by the response they got to their opinion poll—the questionnaires sent out from the Embassy around November 10, 1966—on November 13 they formed the "Hungarian Democratic Independence Movement," which was later to publish the counterrevolutionary paper *October 23rd*.

═ C ═

1.) The "facts" of Imre Nagy's personal activities have already been given in sections A and B; thus, the only part of the statement of facts in the judgment which needs to be looked at here is that pertaining to how the People's Court Division evaluated Imre Nagy's role, or rather his line of defense.

The court rejected the line of defense that Imre Nagy had had a "moderating" effect on his associates, and determined that the differences between them had been merely tactical ones: Imre Nagy had simply been more careful in trying to achieve his subversive goals than some of his associates.

The court rejected the line of defense that Imre Nagy had abided by the decisions of the MDP's leadership. His behavior, it conceded, had been generally passive. He voiced no opinion on the contemplated measures, yet he obstructed them (he lifted the curfew, opposed the military action being planned to annihilate the Corvin Alley counterrevolutionary core, etc.). In the final analysis, his behavior had been equivocal.

His line of defense that he had acted in his capacity as the president of the Council of Ministers was taken to be without foundation. At any rate, the establishment of the national guard had had nothing to do with either the in-Party compromise, or with the government proclamation. He had not submitted for the Party leadership's preliminary approval either his plans for the restructuring of the government, or for the withdrawal from the Warsaw Pact, or for the declaration of neutrality. Even to the cabinet, he had presented these measures as *faits accomplis*.

2.) Ferenc Donáth joined the already-established subversive movement grouped around Imre Nagy in the spring of 1956, and began to take part in the group's organizational and propaganda activities.

In the evening of October 23, 1956, he took part in the meeting held to set up Imre Nagy's new program, and offered to work out its agricultural section.

The Central Leading Body had co-opted Ferenc Donáth to be a member as their secretary. On October 24, he resigned from his functions, stating that what was needed was "decisive and fundamental change." At the October 25-26 meetings of the MDP's central leadership, he demanded that the counterrevolution be evaluated as a "democratic movement," and that the armed counterrevolutionaries be consolidated into the armed forces. Since his demands were not met, he reiterated his resignation. On October 28, he was present at the meeting drafting the government proclamation. He also attended the introductory meeting of the Revolutionary Committee of Hungarian Intellectuals.

On November 4, at dawn, he took part in drafting Imre Nagy's radio address; then he, too, took refuge at the Yugoslav Embassy, where, as a member of the "Executive Committee," he had a part in deciding on the above-outlined actions.

3.) Journalist Miklós Gimes was one of the first, in 1955, to join the Imre Nagy group. He spread Imre Nagy's ideas also through his own articles, and it was he who had proposed that they form the illegal committee.

On October 22, 1956, he took part in the meeting to draft the new program, and undertook to work out the section pertaining to foreign affairs.

Between October 23 and 27, he worked at the editorial offices of the *Szabad Nép*, where, in essence, he assumed editorship. On October 27, he went to the Budapest Police Headquarters building, where he took part in the meetings of that nucleus of the conspiracy. He was a member, and one of the spokesmen of the "workers' delegation from Angyalföld," and also participated in drafting Imre Nagy's radio address.

On October 29, with several other persons, he started a new daily, the *Magyar Szabadság*, and he wrote the editorial for the first issue. In his article, he took a stand for return to a democracy "representing the people." After November 4, when he alone of the general staff remained outside the Yugoslav Embassy, he produced handbills—between November 6 and 8—calling on the people of Hungary to keep fighting so as to force the Soviet officials to negotiate with Imre Nagy.

On November 13, he attended several meetings, and stated that "the legal government was Imre Nagy's government," and that the fight should go on until such time as this fact was recognized.

After that, he conferred with several other people at the residence of Róbert Bohó. It was to this meeting that Balázs Nagy had delivered the message from the "Executive Committee" headquartered at the Yugoslav Embassy transmitted by Gábor Tánczos.

At the meeting, they formed the Hungarian Democratic Independence Movement, an illegal, subversive organization, and decided to start an organization paper, *Október Huszonharmadika*, under the editorship of Miklós Gimes. They published four issues of the paper before Miklós Gimes was apprehended. The articles called the workers to resistance against the government and against the Soviet troops.

4.) Zoltán Tildy had returned to the political scene after October 23, 1956. At the request of the Party leadership, he delivered a calming radio broadcast, then became minister of state in the Imre Nagy government. He supported Imre Nagy's conspiracy, demanded the abolition of the one-party system, and the inclusion of the coalition parties in the business of government. By November 2, the cabinet consisted of members of the Smallholders' and other parties, and they had succeeded in ousting the communist ministers from the government.

Zoltán Tildy played an active part in freeing Cardinal József Mindszenty, in bringing him to Budapest, and in "reinstating him in his rights." He took part in the preparation of the "rehabilitation announcement," conferred with Mindszenty, and, in essence, made it possible for Mindszenty to deliver his memorable "address" unsupervised, in a direct broadcast.

In his radio broadcast of October 30, he unilaterally announced the immediate recall of Hungary's representatives to the United Nations, and on November 2, in a statement to the press, he declared that "we want to live as a neutral country," and therefore Hungary had withdrawn from the Warsaw Pact.

Following Imre Nagy's November 4 radio appeal, it was Zoltán Tildy who gave orders to have the text forwarded to the secretary general of the United Nations, and it was he who gave permission to Gyula Háy to broadcast the Writers' Association's statement appealing for help.

5.) Pál Maléter had had no connection with Imre Nagy's group prior to October 23, 1956. On October 25, 1956, as a professional soldier, he faltered in the course of carrying out his orders to clear the Kilián barracks, and got in touch with the counterrevolutionary group at Corvin Alley. At that time, his conduct reflected elements of duplicity and ambivalence, for even while he conducted negotiations with the Corvin Alley group, he and his units were engaged in armed action in an attempt to clear the Kilián barracks. Somewhat later, he declared that he was no longer willing to obey the orders of the minister of defense, and he and his units went over to the side of the "insurgents."

Imre Nagy appointed him, as the leader of the "insurgents," to be first deputy minister, and later, minister of defense.

The People's Court Division came to the conclusion that Pál Maléter had prior knowledge of the siege of the Party building, and contributed to its success. While the siege was being carried out, he held detained a person (János Virágh) accused of being a plant likely to have exposed the plans for the siege of the Party building.

Pál Maléter consolidated various armed units under his own command to fight against the Soviet troops, and made preparations to hold the Kilián barracks against the Soviet troops.

6.) Sándor Kopácsi, as the head of the Budapest Police Headquarters, came to adopt the views of the conspiracy immediately prior to the October 23, 1956, demonstration. At the request of József Szilágyi, he promised that the police would not fire at the demonstrators.

Between October 23 and 26, his behavior, too, was somewhat equivocal. He opened the Police Headquarters building to his associates in the conspiracy, and permitted the establishment of a counterrevolutionary nucleus around his own person. On the other hand, at that time he was still fighting against the counterrevolutionaries, and ordered his subordinates to do the same. On October 26, however, he ordered the district headquarters not to engage in armed confrontation, and to retreat if they were attacked.

Following this, it was with his participation that preparations were made for setting up the "national guard." On October 30, Imre Nagy appointed Béla Király to be the commander, and Sándor Kopácsi the deputy commander, of the national guard, and ordered the latter to provide it with arms. Accordingly, Sándor Kopácsi distributed over twenty thousand arms among counterrevolutionaries and hooligans.

After this, Sándor Kopácsi played very much a minor role, as compared to Béla Király and Pál Maléter. On November 5, he also attempted to take refuge at the Yugoslav Embassy, but was captured.

7.) Ferenc Jánosi was Imre Nagy's son-in-law, and, as such, worked for Imre

Nagy as secretary and coordinator. He was a liaison between Imre Nagy and the members of the conspiracy, and had a part in getting Imre Nagy's writings to the Yugoslav leaders.

It was as Imre Nagy's "associate" that he got into Party Headquarters, which he left on October 25, to go organize a delegation from the Writers' Association. He forwarded information from Imre Nagy on proposed measures and policy matters to other members of the conspiracy, including the persons at the Deák Square nucleus. On November 2, Imre Nagy reinstated him in the rank of brigadier general, and appointed him to head the Education Department of the Ministry of Defense. On November 4, he also took refuge at the Yugoslav Embassy.

8.) Miklós Vásárhelyi was one of the first to join the Imre Nagy group. He took part in transforming the group into a conspiracy ("writers' memorandum"), and continued to work to expand the conspiracy and propagate its aims.

After October 23, 1956, he helped to prepare the text of Géza Losonczy's and Ferenc Donáth's second resignation, and had a vital role in the debate over the text of the declaration of the Revolutionary Committee of Hungarian Intellectuals.

Later he acted as "public relations chief" for Imre Nagy and Géza Losonczy. On November 4, like his associates, he tried to flee to the Yugoslav Embassy, but could not get there, and took refuge at the residence of one of the Embassy employees. He, too, was polled when the "Executive Committee" sent out its questionnaire.

III

A brief summary of the statement of facts according to judgment No. TB. NB. 003/1958/12 of the People's Court Division

Dr. József Szilágyi had joined the Imre Nagy group at the end of 1955. In mid-1956, he participated in the propaganda activity the group engaged in at the meetings of the Petőfi Circle.

He persuaded Sándor Kopácsi to accept the political views of the Imre Nagy group, and arranged for his meeting Imre Nagy in person.

On October 20, 1956, speaking to leading county officials in Kecskemét, he declared that the Stalinist elements must be eliminated from the Party and government leadership.

On October 22, 1956, he spoke at the student rally at the Budapest University of Technology, where he urged the participants to go ahead with the demonstration. First he telephoned Sándor Kopácsi, then personally intervened with him, asking that the police not interfere with the demonstration.

After October 23, he went to the Budapest Police Headquarters once again, in order to persuade Sándor Kopácsi and his high-ranking officers not to take action against the "insurgents."

On October 27, he was part of the delegation from "Angyalföld" which tried to persuade Imre Nagy to dissociate himself from the MDP's central leadership, and support the demands of the counterrevolutionaries.

From October 29 to November 4, he worked in close proximity with Imre Nagy, urging him to be more consistent in effectuating his political ideas. On November 4, he, too, took refuge at the Yugoslav Embassy.

IV

Legal review

In his protestation, the procurator general—after quoting verbatim the facts of the cases as established by the judgments—enumerates the violations of procedural and substantive law which, in his opinion, make the judgments of the People's Court Division unlawful. He groups the violations into three categories.

In Part A of the petition, he recounts the procedural violations. He points out that basic procedural principles and procedural rules have repeatedly been violated, seriously hindering Imre Nagy and his associates in exercising their right to defend themselves, and making the evidence one-sided, with emphasis only on the incriminating circumstances.

Part B of the petition states that, due partly to the procedural violations, the facts of the cases as given in the judgments are wanting: several "facts" are unsubstantiated, or are based on erroneous conclusions. The petition enumerates the instances of lack of foundation, and points out other self-contradicting elements within the supporting arguments.

As a result, the People's Court Division held Imre Nagy and his associates responsible for events for which they were not to blame, or, to put it another way, the court judged several circumstances mistakenly, and in such a way as to incriminate them.

The procedural violations and lack of foundation would, in themselves, be sufficient—emphasizes the petition—to set aside the judgments, but what is even more significant is the improper application of the rules of substantive criminal law. The People's Court Division classified as criminal certain actions which are not, in fact, crimes.

In Part C, the petition goes into a detailed argument as to why political disputes and criticism of political parties fall outside the competence of criminal law, and cannot be considered as initiating a conspiracy or movement, and so on. It points out that the People's Court Division disregarded the fact that, on October 23, 1956, Imre Nagy became Hungary's lawful prime minister, though this has substantial bearing on how his actions—and the actions of his associates—are to be evaluated from the point of view of criminal law. It also demonstrates why

Imre Nagy was not guilty of treason, and Pál Maléter and Sándor Kopácsi were not guilty of mutiny.

The Presidential Division found the remedial petition, in its entirety, to be well-founded. In the course of the legal review—as already stated in part I—it will examine, first of all, the legality of the application of the rules of criminal law. Within this, it will refer to the lack of foundation in the establishment of certain facts, then, in a separate chapter, to the procedural violations. In some aspects—not affecting the case as a whole—the Council's opinion differs from that reflected in the petition. The reasons for the differences will be dealt with in the appropriate passages.

Legality of the application of the rules of criminal law

1.) The rules of criminal law applicable at the time the events subject to the indictment were adjudicated are set down in the Official Compilation of Substantive Criminal Law Provisions in Force (BHÖ), and in Act 62 of 1948 on the Military Criminal Code (KTBTK). Imre Nagy and all his associates were found guilty of conspiracy as defined in section 1, paragraphs /1/ and /2/ of the BHÖ, that is, as defined in section 1 of Act 7 of 1946. The rules normative at the time of the trials read as follows:

a.) "Liable to punishment for a criminal act is whoever commits an act aimed at subverting the people's democratic order of state or the people's republic as defined in the Constitution of the Hungarian People's Republic, initiates or leads a movement or conspiracy, or provides substantial financial assistance thereto."

b.) "A criminal act is committed also by whoever assumes an active role in, or abets, a movement or conspiracy as defined in paragraph /1/."

The Presidential Division had first of all to examine whether the actions of Imre Nagy and his associates were, in fact, aimed at "subverting the people's democratic order of state or the People's Republic."

Act 20 of 1949 on the constitution of the Hungarian People's Republic guarantees freedom of speech, freedom of the press, freedom of assembly, and other civil rights. However, in the political structure which had developed in Hungary by the early 1950s, civil rights were violated in practice, or were respected only in certain particulars. Any expression of opinion, any activity which in the least differed from the Rákosi/Gerő leadership's "official" stand was likely to be considered an attack on the people's democratic government, and the legal system was regularly manipulated to deal a fatal blow at political foes and people with differing views with the iron fist of criminal law.

In the opinion of the Presidential Division, in any legal review of the actions considered criminal acts at the time the point of departure must be not the perverted political and judiciary practices of the time, but the proper interpretation of the constitution. It is on this basis that it must be determined whether an action was, or was not, directed against the "people's democratic government." This is the principle that applies in the case of Imre Nagy and his associates as well.

2.) In 1955 and 1956—prior to October 23—Imre Nagy and his associates fought for reforms within the Party, government, and institutions of the time, taking a stand against the shortcomings and crimes of the Party leadership. They propagated their views both verbally and in writing, and also made use of political means in the effort to realize their goals. They stayed within constitutional boundaries, and their actions were not aimed at subverting the people's democratic order of state.

The Presidential Division hereby declares as a general principle that criticism of the ruling party, government, and prevailing social institutions cannot be considered an attack on the system of government, nor can any political activity conducted—within the bounds of the constitution—with a view to bringing about changes in them.

From the point of view of evaluating the events that were the subjects of the indictments, it is totally immaterial whether Imre Nagy and his associates carried out their ideological activities individually or as a group, whether they were highly or loosely organized, or whether they acted from within or outside the Party. None of this alters the fact that they did not conspire to subvert the system of government, but, on the contrary, were working to improve it. The petition, however, is correct in noting—in contradiction to the unfounded statement of facts presented by the People's Court Division—that their activities were not "planned, coordinated, and conspiratorial," but were devoid of these formal features of collusion.

Therefore, the Presidential Division attaches no particular importance to the legal issue of whether Decision No. 216 of the Criminal College of the Supreme Court had interpreted the cited law correctly when it stated that the crime of conspiracy can be committed without any particular political intent (petitionation, p. 127). Given that the actions of Imre Nagy and his associates could not, de facto, overthrow the system of state, the question of intent does not even enter into play. It is also totally immaterial whether, in the course of the proceedings, any of the defendants felt that they were "responsible" for any given action or event.

3.) a.) The People's Court Division convicted Imre Nagy and his associates for organizing and touching off the October 23 demonstration, and for working out the policies of the future Imre Nagy government.

It is a historical fact that the October 23 demonstration and the events that followed were, in essence, the spontaneous reaction of a number of very different social groups to a long-festering crisis, an outburst of protest against the obdurate inflexibility of the Party and government leadership. The views and aims of the Imre Nagy group, and the direct action taken by some of its members were, naturally, part of the events leading up to the demonstration; and certainly the insurgent masses pinned their hopes of change mostly on Imre Nagy's again coming to head the government.

Given that the demonstration was authorized in the end, the fact that some members of the Imre Nagy group participated in its organization cannot be considered a criminal act.

As for their working out the policies of the future government—something not against the law even in itself—this was very much a necessary step at a time when it was evident that the earlier leadership would be unable to maintain its hold, and would, in all probability, ask Imre Nagy to form the new government.

b.) The statement of the judgment of the People's Court Division that after October 23, the conspiracy and the movement it created gathered around three tightly coordinated "nuclei," disregards the fact that what Imre Nagy was heading was not some kind of "nucleus," but the lawful government installed with the prior consent of the MDP leadership.

Contrary to the statements of the judgment, the subsequent changes made within the government were also entirely within the law. The decisions were made by the Presidium of the People's Republic. The functioning of the "cabinet" was likewise constitutional; under the circumstances at the time, there was no possible way for the full governmental body to operate on a regular basis.

Its post facto recognition as a constitutional government is indicated by Resolution No. 33/1956 of the Presidium, dated November 4, 1956, and published in the November 12, 1956, issue of the *Magyar Közlöny*, which relieved the [Imre Nagy] government of office.

The actions of a government are not for criminal law to evaluate. A government has a political responsibility to the appropriate constitutional institutions, and a moral responsibility to the entire nation, but its members cannot be held criminally responsible for carrying out their official functions within constitutional parameters. Thus, the official activities that the Imre Nagy government, or any member of that government, engaged in while in office cannot be considered conspiratorial.

c.) The People's Court Division—ignoring the arguments as well as the well-known facts—took into consideration neither the extraordinary circumstances under which the Imre Nagy government operated, nor the actions they took in order to maintain law and order.

It was at the request of several leaders of the MDP that Imre Nagy delivered his October 23 speech at the Parliament building, for the leadership hoped that he could pacify the masses. He also took measures to ensure public order in the days that followed.

The judgment is wrong in faulting Imre Nagy for opposing the elimination of the Corvin Alley group. What he really wanted was to find a solution without further bloodshed.

The judgment also disregards the fact that the October 28 cease-fire was decided on jointly by the Party leadership and the government.

Contrary to the statement in the People's Court Division's judgment, the establishment of the national guard was meant not to "arm the counterrevolutionaries," but to restore public order by integrating the armed groups into the military and the police force, thereby putting them under government supervision and military discipline.

d.) The People's Court Division found Imre Nagy guilty also of the crime of treason as defined in section 35, paragraph /1/ of the BHÖ—section 58 of Act 3 of 1930. It specifies that the crime of treason is committed by a person who "forms an alliance with, or establishes contact with the government of a foreign power or with a foreign organization, with the aim of inducing it to take hostile action against the Hungarian state, as well as a person who incites a foreign power to war or forcible measures against the Hungarian state."

According to the judgment, this crime was perpetrated with the withdrawal from the Warsaw Pact, with the declaration of neutrality, and with the November 4 radio address, since, by having contacted foreign powers, Imre Nagy not only attempted to commit them to taking forceful action, but created the imminent danger of their doing so.

It is the opinion of the Presidential Division that the government, by its declaration of neutrality and by stating its intention to withdraw from the Warsaw Pact—the November 2 cabinet meeting did no more than appoint a delegation to conduct the negotiations—did not overstep the scope of its authority; therefore, its members committed no crime. Whether these actions were expedient or timely is a matter outside the competence of criminal law.

The same applies to Imre Nagy's radio address of November 4, which was meant only to inform the Hungarian people and the world at large of the latest developments.

As prime minister and acting foreign minister, Imre Nagy had the legal right to contact any foreign government or organization, or the United Nations. Therefore, neither the November 2 communiqué he addressed to the foreign embassies accredited to Budapest, nor the letters he sent to the United Nations can be considered "contacting the governments of foreign powers" as described in the cited law. Besides, their intent was certainly not to induce them to take hostile action against the Hungarian state. Thus, Imre Nagy did not commit the crime of treason.

e.) Zoltán Tildy and Pál Maléter were also members of the lawful government, and their actions in that capacity, like those of Imre Nagy's, did not constitute criminal acts.

Zoltán Tildy's demand to replace the one-party system with a government incorporating the coalition parties was a lawful political move aimed at widening the government's basis of support, and at strengthening national unity. The fact that he helped "reinstate" cardinal Mindszenty "in his rights," and arranged for the broadcasting of his address was held against him in the judgment. Tildy's aim was to normalize the situation, for—on the basis of Mindszenty's conduct—his speech was expected, realistically, to have a calming effect on the masses.

Imre Nagy, by the way, had issued specific instructions that the speech was to be prerecorded and edited before being broadcast.

f.) The People's Court Division found Pál Maléter and Sándor Kopácsi guilty of mutiny as well, each in their capacity as leaders, in accordance with section 29 of the KTBTK. The section states that "mutiny is committed by soldiers if they, as a group, openly defy the rules of military conduct." Not even in the judgment is it alleged that a military group defying the rules of military conduct was ever formed with the leadership of either Pál Maléter or Sándor Kopácsi.

In accordance with the orders he received, Pál Maléter cleared the Kilián barracks of the armed insurgents, and secured the premises. After the cease-fire, he was again following orders when he got in touch with the insurgents and tried to reestablish order. He acted in accordance with the objectives of the lawful government, and then, as a member of that government, he carried out his duties in keeping with its policies. He did not commit the crime of either conspiracy or mutiny. He made the announcement, which was held against him, that he would no longer obey the orders of the minister of defense after a series of unsuccessful attempts to contact the persons in charge of the Ministry of Defense. This, in itself, is not sufficient grounds for establishing guilt.

The assertion by the People's Court Division that Pál Maléter had advance knowledge of the siege of the Party building and contributed to its success is without foundation, and is based on faulty conclusions. There is no proof that János Virágh knew of the plans, and that his day-long detention was to keep him from disclosing them. Thus, Pál Maléter committed no crime by holding him prisoner.

g.) Sándor Kopácsi's actions must be evaluated in the same light. On October 23 and in the days that followed, he personally took part in the fight against the insurgents, until such time as the government changed its position. He did not issue a blanket order to the district police forces not to resist, but ordered withdrawal only if resistance seemed hopeless, and would result only in further bloodshed.

The statement of the judgment that Sándor Kopácsi, on orders from Imre Nagy, distributed over twenty thousand arms among the counterrevolutionaries is without foundation. According to data amassed in the course of the proceedings, it was the minister of the interior who gave Sándor Kopácsi the order for the distribution of arms. Furthermore, the arming of the national guard was a government decision, and was legal.

Sándor Kopácsi, therefore, was involved neither in conspiracy nor in mutiny.

h.) Nor can the activities between October 23 and November 4 of the other two "nuclei," and of the persons not yet mentioned, be considered conspiratorial.

Activities directly connected with the operation of the Imre Nagy government (for example the secretarial and organizational activities of Ferenc Jánosi, the press secretarial work performed by Miklós Vásárhelyi, Ferenc Donáth's assistance in the wording of Imre Nagy's government proclamation or of his radio address, etc.) cannot be considered criminal acts, for they served the proper functioning of the lawful government.

Likewise, other political activities carried out within or outside the so-called nuclei no more constitute a conspiracy aimed at subverting the government than do the actions prior to October 23, 1956 (see the arguments advanced in the preceding sections).

The persons convicted for [subversive] activities of this kind did not always, and in all respects, agree with the position of the Imre Nagy government and of the Party leadership. This is borne out by the declaration of the Revolutionary Committee of Hungarian Intellectuals (MÉFB), Ferenc Donáth's address to the Central Leading Body and his resignation, the demands of the workers' delegation from Angyalföld (with Miklós Gimes and József Szilágyi among its members), and so forth. No crime was committed with these political activities either.

At this point, the Presidential Division wishes to point out the inherent contradictions in the judgment delivered by the People's Court Division. On the one hand, it makes a point of noting these discords within the "conspiracy," and on the other, it holds Imre Nagy responsible even for those activities of his "associates" which were counter to the activities of the government.

4.) a.) After November 4, Imre Nagy and most of his associates took refuge at the Yugoslav Embassy. There, "declaring themselves the Executive Committee of the MSZMP," to quote the judgment of the People's Court Division, they continued their "subversive" activities. What is true is that most members of the Executive Committee resided at the Embassy at the time.

The fact that the group established contact with the representatives of the Yugoslav government was, in the first place, unavoidable under the circumstances. Secondly, given that they kept up their political activity (see the questionnaires sent out on or around November 10 from within the Embassy), establishing contacts of this kind cannot be considered a criminal act. Such activity was not an attempt to overthrow the government, but the continuation of a yet-undecided political battle.

b.) As opposed to the conclusions of the judgment, it cannot be established as fact from the data presented in the course of the proceedings that the establishment of the Hungarian Democratic Independence Movement and the publishing of the newspaper *Október Huszonharmadika* was "prompted" by the [Executive Committee's] opinion poll. Both had been independently agreed upon by Miklós Gimes and others.

The post-November 4 activities of Miklós Gimes were also part of the above-mentioned political battle, were not aimed at overthrowing the government, and do not constitute a criminal act.

——— V ———

In summary, it has been established that none of the activities on which the People's Court Division passed judgment constitutes a criminal act. Therefore—having found the remedial petition well substantiated—on the basis of section 209, paragraph /3/ of the Be, the Presidential Division hereby sets aside the unlawful judgments in full, and, on the basis of section 214, paragraph /3/ of the Be, acquits all the defendants, as none of the activities made subject to the accusation constitute a criminal act.

The decision concerning costs is based on the closing sentence of section 290, paragraph /5/ of the Be.

The application of the procedural rules

The Presidential Division went on to examine the manner in which the procedural rules were applied by the authorities conducting the proceedings, and found—in agreement with the contentions of the petition—that they violated several of the basic rules of criminal procedure. It must be reiterated, however, that from the standpoint of the outcome of the proceedings these were of secondary importance.

The criminal proceedings against Imre Nagy and his associates were conducted according to the repeatedly modified Act 3 of 1951, and Law Decree No. 34 of 1957 on the People's Court divisions. In the course of examining the manner in which the procedural rules were applied, the Presidential Division found that several parts of the judgment of the People's Court Division are without foundation (they contain faulty conclusions), and that the Court violated the procedural rules as well: it did not fulfill its obligation to present proper argumentation, and/or its argumentation contained contradictions. Exception must be taken also to the style in which the judgment was pronounced: along with establishing the facts—and often in lieu of them—the Court is satisfied with "characterizations."

1.) The legal position of the persons brought under indictment was not clarified until January 20, 1958. They were pronounced defendants only immediately prior to the end of the investigation, although according to section 91/B, paragraph /1/ of the Bp, the investigating authorities should have brought a substantiated resolution in this regard as soon as they obtained sufficient data to determine the nature of the crime. The resolution should have contained a brief description of the criminal act. This procedural violation limited the above persons' right to proper defense, as they were not informed of the facts upon which the proceedings were based, and it was only on January 20, 1958, that they were given the opportunity to exercise their right to name a defense counsel of their own choosing. Furthermore, proper charges should have been brought prior to ordering their being put under preliminary detention (see section 97 of the Bp), or the order should not have been given.

2.) Section 3 of the Bp, whereby both the incriminating and the extenuating circumstances are to be ascertained and considered in every phase of the proceedings, was violated in the course of both the investigation and the trial. Imre

Nagy and his associates made a number of references to circumstances and evidence which were not followed up, or taken into consideration, by the People's Court. The procedure of emphasizing only the incriminating circumstances resulted in the Court's establishing facts without foundation, and in erroneous applications of the criminal law.

In the course of the proceedings, Imre Nagy and his associates were not given the opportunity to present a comprehensive defense (see section 94, paragraph /2/ of the Bp), or to elaborate on the background or the international ramifications of certain events, and on the actions and role of others.

3.) According to section 2, paragraph /3/ of Law Decree No. 34 of 1957, the presiding judge of the People's Court Division was to be appointed by the president of the Supreme Court. Although formally this was done, "recommendations" as to the person of the presiding judge, the people's judges, the prosecuting attorney, and even the court clerk came from the Ministry of the Interior. The proceedings were, in fact, conducted by the people the Ministry "recommended."

Mrs. Péter Lakatos was a member of the People's Court Division in both proceedings. Her husband was one of the victims of the events at Köztársaság Square. Since the indictment holds Imre Nagy and his associates responsible for the eruption of the October 23 events, and states that Pál Maléter had prior knowledge of the siege of the Party building, and contributed to its success, a cause for exclusion (bias, as per section 13, item e/ of the Bp) was present. Mrs. Lakatos should have reported this fact without delay, and should have been disqualified from taking part in the proceedings.

4.) The People's Court Division committed another procedural violation by barring the public from the entire proceedings, the pronouncement of the judgment included. The preconditions for this ruling, as specified in section 7 of the Bp, did not obtain. Without doubt, the defendants could have presented a more effective defense in an open court, where the public would have followed the developments.

5.) The People's Court Division held the first hearings on February 5 and 6, 1958. On the second day of the hearings, the Court ordered a supplementary investigation, and returned the documents to the procurator general. Not counting the hearing of Dr. József Szilágyi's segregated case, the next hearing was held over four months later, on June 9, 1958, by a Court of different composition.

According to section 153, paragraph /2/ of the Bp, a new trial should have been started on June 9, 1958, because of the change in the composition of the Court, and because more than one month had elapsed since the last hearing. The People's Court Division, however, did not conduct a new and thorough interrogation, but continued the hearings after the minutes of the previous hearings were read. This constituted a procedural violation of the kind which, in accordance with section 202, item b/ of the Bp in force at the time, should, without a doubt, have set aside the judgment of any court.

6.) The procurator general presented an accusation against Pál Maléter and

Sándor Kopácsi to the Military College of the Supreme Court, as early as February 28, 1957. As reflected in the documentation of Katf. I. 125/1957, the Court held a preparatory session, and set a trial date. It subsequently postponed the trial, and then, on August 29, 1957—without commenting on the points of the accusation—had the case filed in the archives. (The whereabouts of the records of the investigation are unknown.)

7.) There were no legal grounds for segregating the case of Dr. József Szilágyi, and for bringing a separate judgment against him.

VI

In the light of the acquittal of Imre Nagy and his associates, as to the violations of procedural law, the Presidential Division limits itself to stating that both the investigation and the proceedings were conducted in violation of the law even in terms of procedure. It needs to be emphasized that by the provisions of the constitution and the rules of law on the courts in force at the time, judges were to be independent, and [their decisions] subject only to the law. In practice, however, these laws were seriously curtailed. There were no adequate guarantees—as is borne out by these proceedings—that the provisions of the constitution would be put into practice, especially in political cases. It would be a mistake to lay the blame for this at the door of some erroneous contemporary scientific theory. On the contrary, it was theory that was, on occasion, hard put to "justify" the warped practices of that time.

VII

The remedial petition maintains that in accordance with section 7 of Act 2 of 1950 (Btá), the People's Court Division should have examined whether the persons taking refuge at the Yugoslav Embassy were entitled to personal immunity. On November 21, 1957, the Yugoslav and Hungarian governments signed an agreement in which the Hungarian government guaranteed that Imre Nagy and his associates would not be held criminally responsible for their earlier actions. According to the petition, Hungarian citizens could enjoy personal immunity by international agreement. The Court, thus, should have obtained a copy of the agreement, and established its own lack of jurisdiction.

In the opinion of the Presidential Division, however, Imre Nagy and his associates were not entitled to diplomatic or other immunity based on international law, as the necessary legal conditions did not obtain.

Section 7 of the Btá states that the matter of criminal responsibility of persons enjoying extraterritoriality or personal immunity is governed by international treaty or agreement, or in the absence of this, by international precedent. The above regulation does not state that personal immunity applies only to foreign nationals, but this is what follows from the nature of our entire legal system. Thus, the Hungarian government could not validly have granted [Imre Nagy and his associates] such indemnity. On the correct interpretation of the agreement, it promised only that Imre Nagy and his associates would not be charged, and criminal proceedings would not be initiated against them. That this promise was not kept is both politically and morally exceptionable.

In accordance with section 144, paragraph /1/, item b/ of the Bp—the procedural rule in effect at the time—in cases involving extraterritoriality or personal immunity, where a decision by the minister of justice was required, the Court was to suspend the proceedings. In this case, however, this was unnecessary, because it was the government's position—published even in the daily papers—that was guiding, according to which Imre Nagy and his associates were not entitled to immunity. The People's Court Division, therefore, did not have to examine the matter, but was obliged to try the case.

VIII

On the basis of section 139, paragraph /1/, item a/ of the Be the procurator general terminated the investigation of Géza Losonczy, who died before the accusation was preferred. The Presidential Division disregards all statements of fact pertaining to him, declaring however, that they are inadequate for establishing guilt.

In closing, the Presidential Division notes that the procurator general submitted all pertinent documents necessary for the evaluation of this case.

Budapest, July 6, 1989.
Dr. Jenö Szilbereky, president of the Presidential Division.
Dr. Gyula Czili, reporting judge.
Dr. György Berkes, Dr. Jenö Domokos, Dr. István Fehér,
Dr. György Pálinkás, Dr. Ede Rabóczky, members of the Presidential Division.

Conclusion

The Political Background of the Imre Nagy Trial

György Litván

The long crisis in Hungarian communism that culminated on June 15, 1958, with the conviction and sentencing of Imre Nagy and his associates, apparently began exactly five years earlier.

The fact is, however, that in the early summer days of 1953, barely three months after the death of Stalin, the signs of trouble that manifested themselves in several countries within the Soviet bloc—in the GDR as well as in Hungary, and to a certain extent even in the Soviet Union itself—were indicative of a latent crisis that had been brewing, for a long time, in consequence of Stalin's inability or unwillingness to use the victory and prestige he gained in World War II to "open" the system, to democratize and modernize it after the war. While he lived, he had managed by dint of his authoritarian presence and his despotic methods to delay the manifestations of crisis; but after his death it became immediately clear to his successors that changes had to come about in domestic policy, "imperial" policy, and foreign policy alike.

The changes began in East Germany, as early as May 1953. In that month, the Central Committee of the Communist Party of the Soviet Union issued a resolution judging the situation in the GDR so alarming that Walter Ulbricht and his comrades were summoned to Moscow and directed to temporarily abandon the effort to build socialism in Germany. In the next month, Hungary became danger area number two. In mid-June, Hungarian party and government leaders were summoned to Moscow and subjected to a humiliating dressing-down for their Stalinist economic policy and violations of law, which, they were told, were pushing their country into increasing poverty and despair. Instead of enforced industrialization, they were directed to develop agriculture, to improve living standards, to consolidate legality, and to pay more attention to the needs of the population. Mátyás Rákosi, who held all the highest party and government positions, was instructed to pass the position of prime minister without delay to Imre Nagy, who until then had been forced into the background because of his moderate views.

Thus, on June 16, 1953, Imre Nagy returned to Budapest as prime minister, with a mandate to work out and implement reforms beneficial to the people. With this, he started on the road that would lead to his execution exactly five years later to the day.

The Historical Role of Imre Nagy and the Imre Nagy Group

In Imre Nagy the masters of the Kremlin found the best man for the job they thought they wanted done. They neglected, however, to factor two major considerations into their decision. On the one hand, Imre Nagy's assigned task coincided perhaps too closely with his conviction, indeed his obsession, that socialism could and should be created not in spite of the people but with their accord. On the other hand, in the case of Hungary they were dealing with a Western-type society which, unlike their own, might react unpredictably, even explosively, if presented with an alternative to the experienced realities of Stalinism, particularly if the alternative was dramatically presented.

Imre Nagy believed firmly in the government program he announced in a live radio broadcast July 3, 1953. The tone of his speech made clear even to less sophisticated listeners that this was not a mere modification of the old policy but a rejection and replacement of that policy. His words electrified with hope a population sunk in suffering and apathy, and the new, little-known prime minister at once became the most popular, in fact the only, generally accepted communist politician in the country. His initial impact was further enhanced by economic, political, and administrative measures that were taken during the next few months (the elimination of the so-called kulak lists, the abolition of internment camps, the modification of state plan directives, the permitting of small private enterprises in the service sector and the disbanding of some cooperatives, etc.), and even more by the firmness of his dedication to his ideas and program after he was dismissed in the spring of 1955, when he refused to exercise Bolshevik "self-criticism" for his alleged rightist, "opportunistic," and altogether erroneous ways. From that time on, Imre Nagy stood as a symbol of possibility for a more human, a more national and reasonable socialist order. He stood also as the model of an enlightened communist, one who could accept that noncommunists lived in his country (in fact in Hungary they form the majority), and who cared enough about his alternative program to defend it against the Stalinists in Moscow as well as at home.

Notwithstanding his courage and dedication to principle, Imre Nagy acting alone might have ended his days as just another ex-member of the Party, doomed to isolation, loneliness, and political impotence, but for the fact that his program and his conduct were seen as a viable alternative among the more astute of the disillusioned Party intellectuals. For after the first, albeit thwarted, communist reform attempt, a revolt against Stalinism no longer seemed necessarily tantamount to a suicidal leap into darkness.

Beginning in the spring of 1955, well-known, respected, and influential members of a once-enthusiastic Party intelligentsia (most of them former correspondents for the Party press and some of them victims of preconceived trials who were newly released from prison) gathered around Imre Nagy, became more and more active, and drew numerous younger activists closer to him and to his ideas. In this way the so-called Imre Nagy group was formed, its inner circle including journalists Géza Losonczy, Sándor Haraszti, Miklós Gimes, Miklós Vásárhelyi, and György Fazekas; such once-illegal communists as Ferenc Donáth, Ferenc Jánosi, Szilárd Ujhelyi, and József Szilágyi; and several literary writers, among them Tibor Déry, Tamás Aczél, and Tibor Méray. They were soon joined by almost the entire membership and Party organization of the Writers' Association, by writers for the literary weekly *Irodalmi Ujság* and for certain other cultural publications, and finally by the Petőfi Circle, a highly vocal and tempestuous debate forum founded by communist-reared young intellectuals.

This aggregation, at first only a few dozen strong, later a few hundred and finally several thousand, was held together without formal organization, merely by links of friendship, sympathy, and shared opinion. It was a unique phenomenon within the Soviet bloc, and the Stalinist leadership under Mátyás Rákosi did its best to eliminate this "revisionist" Party opposition. Be that as it may, when the Twentieth Soviet Party Congress convened in Moscow, it was in Hungary and in the Hungarian Communist Party alone that there existed a more or less coherent, unified, purposeful and determined opposition, capable of taking advantage of the situation, of the historic opportunity.

Of course, the group and the trend it represented were not aimed at overthrowing the communist system, but rather at renewing it, reforming it, making it a fit system to live in. The group, however, was fighting for its aims with real vehemence, aware that it had broad-based support across the society; and with the Stalinist leadership stubbornly resisting (with the support of Moscow), in October 1956, when masses of students declared for the cause and were later joined by workers as well, the tensions erupted in revolution.

Thus would-be reformers unintentionally prepared a genuine popular revolution. Its waves quickly engulfed them and, as a group, they had little control over what happened afterward.

However, their roles as individuals were far from over. Hemmed in by the old regime and the forces of the revolution, Imre Nagy, elected prime minister again, attempted to mediate between the ruling Party and the people, between the Soviet Union and the Hungarian nation, in order to put an end to the bloodshed. Meanwhile, his followers, the reform opposition, tried to win him over to the side of the national democratic revolution, and in a few days they succeeded. Imre Nagy first acted to forestall the use of military force to destroy the strongholds of the uprising, which would have endangered the population. He then declared that the democratic and nationalist aims of the movement were rightful. Finally, he initiated a multiparty system and declared the country politically neutral. By these moves, he created the preconditions and the possibility for a democratic consolidation against leftist (Stalinist) and rightist (ultraconservative or fascist) extremes. And although the situation also raised the danger of a possible shift to the right, the chances of consolidation appeared favorable in view of the support of leaders of the army (Pál Maléter), the police (Sándor Kopácsi), and the national guard (Béla Király).

There can be no question that by this point Imre Nagy and his followers had stepped over the borderline between communism and democracy. And when the Soviet invasion started on November 4, the break became final: in his radio appeal, the prime minister called the attack an action aimed at overthrowing the lawful government. He did not resign; he did not lend his name to the violent and bloody measures under way to crush his nation's attempt at liberation. Rather, with the aim of carrying on the struggle from Belgrade, he took refuge with some of his closest followers in the Yugoslav Embassy. With this, as a culmination of their "heresy," Nagy and his colleagues broke all the written and unwritten rules of the communist movement. Setting every reservation aside, they had chosen to identify with the nation and its revolution instead of with Moscow, thereby authenticating the fundamentally democratic and freedom-seeking force behind the great popular upsurge.

Crushing the Revolution and Stabilizing the "Camp"

Soviet Party and government leaders seemed to hesitate for a while in their assessment and handling of the events in Poland and Hungary. The explanation may be found in three factors: the ongoing process of de-Stalinization, tactical considerations with respect to Yugoslavia, and conflicts within the Soviet Politburo.

For example, the role played by Anastas Mikoyan in the removal of first the Stalinist satrap Rákosi then his closest collaborator and deputy Gerő and in supporting Imre Nagy's October policy suggests that the Soviet leadership, or at least its moderate wing, did not consider the existence of a more independent and (for internal arrangements) more democratic Hungary altogether inconceivable. On balance, however, it appears that the dominant consensus for Moscow, and at least to the same extent for the Stalinist leadership in East Germany, Czechoslovakia, and Romania, judged such a breach of unity and discipline within the camp to be patently intolerable.

Khrushchev reckoned with the necessity of an intervention in Hungary (and possibly Poland) as early as the summer of 1956. After the Moscow conference on June 22-23, he sent a message to Tito stating: "If the situation in Hungary continues deteriorating, all means will be used to eliminate the crisis. The Soviet

Union can under no circumstances permit any breach of the lines within the camp."

This long-running trend was present in Kremlin policy in late October as well, particularly after the American president and secretary of state gave the Soviet leadership to understand that they did not consider the United States to be directly concerned with developments in Hungary and Poland.

The decision to intervene was made no later than October 31, and during the next two days Khrushchev and Malenkov (by this time Mikoyan was not involved) informed the leaders of the "sister parties" of the region (in Brest, in Bucharest, and on the Isle of Brioni) of what was to follow. The ensuing meeting with Tito, to Khrushchev's surprise and gratification, was marked by an atmosphere of mutual understanding, and it was a particularly important point that Marshal Tito took it upon himself to get Imre Nagy and his associates (it is not clear whether this meant Nagy's government or his group) out of the way.

It seems that the precise nature and extent of the Yugoslav involvement were not clarified; at least subsequent disagreements and mutual reproaches suggest this was the case. At the Hungarian Socialist Workers Party (HSWP) Central Committee session of December 2, 1956, János Kádár recalled that in Moscow on the night of November 2, in a conference with the representatives of several sister parties, the "Yugoslav comrades promised to send their ambassador to Budapest, Comrade Soldatic, to inform Imre Nagy and Losonczy of their position and to urge them, as communists, to stop associating [read: hallmarking] the counterrevolution with the names of communists and to clear the way for the reestablishment of revolutionary government." At a later date, Kádár even asked Yugoslav Deputy Foreign Minister Vidic and Soldatic himself why this promise had never been fulfilled, which was embarrassing for all. Allegedly, Vidic did not answer the question but admitted that it was not out of a fear of white terror that Imre Nagy and his associates had sought refuge.

More recently, even some Soviet historians support an as yet uncorroborated (but quite plausible) version of the story which holds that by the time of the Soviet intervention, the idea on both sides was that the Nagy government would have ceased to exist. In this scenario Nagy would have admitted he could not control the counterrevolutionary chaos and at that point external assistance would arrive and Kádár would supply the solution. Politically and from an international perspective, that would indeed have been the optimal outcome. Later, Moscow actually reproached Belgrade for its breach of the alleged promise.

It is a fact that the Yugoslav Embassy took no action before the morning of November 4, and even then it was done indirectly. Although the details are still uncertain, it is known that Imre Nagy, his associates, and their family members were invited, or lured to, the Yugoslav Embassy with the collaboration of Zoltán Szántó and Péter Erdős. According to Szántó's later statement to the police, he was asked to meet with Ambassador Soldatic at 1:00 a.m. on November 4, and the ambassador informed him that on the basis of an earlier request his government would grant political asylum at the Embassy to Nagy and any others he chose to designate. Soldatic stressed there was no time for delay, the danger was grave, and urged them to accept the offer immediately. Reportedly it was as late as 5 a.m. before Szántó relayed the message to Nagy in the Parliament building. In the next few hours, then, a trap closed on the group of almost forty people.

Early the same night the entire Hungarian governmental negotiating delegation, led by Pál Maléter and Ferenc Erdei, had been arrested in Tököl (Erdei would be released in a few weeks). The next day, another leader of the armed forces, Colonel Sándor Kopácsi, Budapest chief of police, was arrested, too. (The third military leader, General Béla Király, put up a resistance for a few days before fleeing to the West.)

Now, after months of indecision, the Soviet power machinery went into action with firm and frightening determination. The difficult and complex (military, police, and political) task of consolidation could be left neither to the yet-untried Hungarian leaders (Kádár and Münnich returned from Moscow and Uzhgorod only on November 3) nor even to Soviet generals. As if to redress Mikoyan's many errors, this time three members of the hard-line faction of the Politburo, Malenkov, Suslov, and Aristov, arrived in Budapest in complete secrecy and settled in at a villa next to the Soviet Embassy, a mere 150-200 meters distant from the Yugoslav Embassy compound that sheltered Imre Nagy and his followers. The presence of the Soviet leaders was known only to two or three members of the Hungarian leadership. Without doubt everything that happened during the next weeks to Imre Nagy, to his group, and to the country was controlled from that villa, the one-time residence of Marshal Voroshilov, on Andrássy Avenue. And just as obviously, the police activity that aided in the implementation of it all was coordinated by General Serov, head of the KGB, who also stayed at the villa.

The plan formulated on the Isle of Brioni to "remove" Imre Nagy succeeded only in part. His removal from the Parliament building, where Kádár and his people dared to move in only on November 7, proved possible in the physical sense but not in the political one. The legitimate prime minister of the country, the man who until November 3 had been recognized as such not only by the Hungarian people but by foreign governments in both the West and the East, was still Imre Nagy.

When Nagy arrived at the Yugoslav Embassy, he found a message from Tito and Rankovic calling for his resignation as prime minister. He refused their advice, and after discussions with his colleagues (five of the seven members of the original temporary Executive Committee of the HSWP were present at the Embassy, with only Kádár and the already-arrested Kopácsi missing), he responded in the same way to repeated Belgrade attempts to exert pressure.

One might say that Nagy's recalcitrance at this time was what sealed his fate (although it seems inconceivable that he could have escaped retribution in any case once the process of establishing responsibility for the uprising had been initiated and focused on the political level). According to György Aczél, when some three decades later the subject of the Nagy trial and execution came up in a conversation with Kádár, Kádár remarked tersely but intensely that everything had hinged on one sentence (that is, on a simple statement of resignation from Nagy).

This was the same message that Kádár kept repeating when, his mind unbalanced, he made his last speech before the Central Committee in 1988. He had made similar remarks earlier, both in speeches before the Party leadership and during negotiations with Yugoslav Deputy Foreign Minister Vidic. For Kádár, in an uncertain position and under pressure from two directions, found it simply unbearable not to have the legitimacy that Nagy's resignation would have conferred. "This is the single most sensitive issue both internationally and within the Party" he told the Central Committee at its meeting as early as on November 11, 1956.

Not surprisingly, the intransigence of Nagy and his associates brought about a deterioration of their relations with the Yugoslav government. The Yugoslavs now found themselves caught in their own trap. Like Khrushchev and his associates in 1953, Tito and his people had neglected to give due consideration to Imre Nagy's character and the intellectual independence of such people in the group, as for example Géza Losonczy. They believed that although Nagy and his associates had gone too far under the pressure of events during the revolution, a little comradely talk and persuasion would suffice to bring them back into line.

They had to confront their mistake when they realized there was no fair means by which they could get rid of Imre Nagy and the others—not physically, because they could not be sent home or taken to Belgrade, and not politically and morally either, because whatever their fate might be, it was bound to have negative consequences for Yugoslavia.

At the first meeting of the Central Committee since his accession to power, on November 11, 1956, Kádár reported on his talks the previous day with Ambassador Soldatic: ". . . the bottom line was that we should agree to their taking the group to Yugoslavia. . . . I said we could not agree under any circumstance to their leaving the country. I suggested they must be told they should declare in writing that they no longer consider themselves to be ministers and they should make a [supportive] statement concerning the present government. They should declare unconditionally that they will never take action against this government. As long as they will not say this, there is nothing to discuss."

When the negotiations with Soldatic produced no satisfactory solution, Deputy Foreign Minister Vidic was sent to Budapest to continue the talks and to find a solution that would also satisfy Yugoslavia's prestige concerns. Fortunately, the minutes from those talks remain intact and are among the few documents that were obtained from Belgrade (see Tibor Zinner's communication in *Társadalmi Szemle*, No. 12, 1989, pp. 72-89). Kádár himself reported to the Central Committee on December 2 that he had made it clear to the Yugoslav diplomats that Nagy and his associates could neither go home nor go to Belgrade because either solution would pose too great a danger. Anna Kéthly, the prominent Social Democratic politician who left Hungary in November 1956, for one, was already making noise abroad about the legitimacy of the Nagy government. And if they were to go home freely, they could unintentionally become a center for "incitement," which could lead to their arrest, which in turn would lead to new diplomatic complications even for the Yugoslavs. Since Vidic nevertheless—cynically but understandably—demanded a written guarantee that his protégés would be allowed to return safely to their homes, as Kádár put it, "After three and a half hours of negotiations—I do not know what they thought of us since we had told them we could not under any circumstances allow them to stay at large in this country—we finally included it [that is, included Vidic's stipulation in the agreement whereby Nagy and the others left the Embassy compound]."

Thus, when the bus left the Embassy building on November 22, Vidic and Soldatic had to know the "protégés" would not be taken to their homes. (If further proof is needed, the Yugoslavs knew that György Lukács, Zoltán Szántó, and Zoltán Vas, who had left the compound a few days earlier, were apprehended less than a block away by the KGB—a fact the diplomats "forgot" to pass on to Nagy and his associates.) The further activities of the Yugoslav government in the affair were restricted to expressions of surprise and consternation in a flurry of diplomatic notes of protest over the abduction and the subsequent sentences.

The "solution" found thereafter was obviously directed by Soviet leaders from behind the scenes, but they had Kádár declare it: "Romania is the best solution: there no harm will come to them . . . there they can have a rest, calm down, think things over. They are not exiled for good."

Publicly, of course, there was no mention of exile. For two days after the kidnapping, only silence and speculation surrounded the fate of the group. Then, on November 24, the following official statement appeared in the press: "More than two weeks ago, Imre Nagy and his associates asked permission from the Hungarian government to leave the territory of the Hungarian People's Republic and travel to another socialist country. With the consent of the government of the Romanian People's Republic, Imre Nagy and his associates left for the Romanian People's Republic on November 23."

Here is what actually happened.

Under guard by Soviet armored vehicles, the group was taken to the KGB headquarters at Mátyásföld, where the families were separated. The same day, Romanian Party Secretary General Gheorghiu-Dej arrived in Budapest in the company of Walter Roman, a former Muscovite communist émigré and old acquaintance of Imre Nagy who, obviously under instructions from Moscow, had already conducted lengthy talks with Nagy on November 3, the eve of the Soviet invasion. On November 23, Roman again visited the now captive Nagy to try to persuade him on behalf of Kádár and Gheorghiu-Dej to retire from public affairs "for a few months" and leave the country. Nagy, however—as he informed

Ferenc Donáth in a smuggled letter— refused to leave voluntarily and declined to make any kind of statement.

At the same time or soon thereafter, Ferenc Münnich, the number two man in the Kádár regime, offered each member of the group, one at a time, the option of declaring a political turnabout. Since all of them refused, all were placed that very same day aboard Soviet military aircraft and flown to Romania, where they were to be given accommodation at Snagov, a resort near Bucharest.

From the outset, their reception in Romania and the way they were treated there added up to a curious mixture of hospitality and imprisonment. Romanian Party leaders were on hand to extend a welcome, but Nagy, Losonczy, and Donáth were immediately separated from rest of the group. And immediately upon their arrival, the philosopher György Lukács made his feelings known. "Let's not try to be diplomatic," he said, "come right out and say it. We are not here of our own free will!"

This the "hosts" knew perfectly well—so well that they placed listening devices in every room in the resort houses in order to audit the conversations of their guests. The service staff consisted mostly of security people who understood Hungarian. The treatment, particularly after the beginning of 1957, came more and more to resemble that of in an internment camp. And all pretense of validity in the "right of asylum" ended at the moment when Kádár, in a brief letter to the Romanian government, asked that it end owing to some newly found "incriminating evidence." The Romanian government apparently saw no violation of its sovereignty in a situation where officers of the Hungarian Ministry of the Interior arrived to arrest, handcuff, and, one by one, drag off by airplane the same guests whom it had earlier treated as "comrades."

The Stations to the Trial

Even allowing for a historical period abounding in turnabouts, it was with unprecedented speed that the government and the Party leadership, and János Kádár himself, reevaluated the role and activities of Imre Nagy and his associates over the few months following November 4, 1956.

In his first report on November 11, Kádár almost identified himself with the group, whose good intentions he seemed to take as a given: "I personally am convinced," Kádár declared, "that Imre Nagy, Géza Losonczy, and the other comrades who were members of the government did not want to help the counterrevolution." The consensus during those days is reflected in the fact that many speakers at the meeting considered it natural, indeed necessary, to pursue negotiations and seek cooperation with Nagy and his associates, even on the basis, as György Aczél put it, that "if an agreement can be reached on the fundamental issues, they should be allowed to form a separate party." Lajos Fehér went so far as to put this idea in a draft resolution, suggesting that negotiations with Imre

Nagy could begin with Tito acting as a mediator.

By November 24, however, Kádár was asserting that he had been forced to break relations with the Nagy group because after a time they "took the internal issues of the Party outside the Party, and they took the internal issues of government to the streets." As he put it, "two trends existed" within the leadership of the Party and within the government: ". . . this was manifest in judging the uprising and also later, during the counterrevolution." In his opinion, the Nagy group had hindered the struggle against the uprising even within the Party center.

In his report of December 2, Kádár placed the time of the Nagy group's lapse into sin at a yet earlier date: "A part of the opposition within the Party which was under the control of comrades [sic] Imre Nagy and Losonczy, in the spring of this year, went beyond the limits within which the struggle was being waged to correct mistakes and . . . remove the Rákosi and Gerő clique." It was at that point, he claimed, that the group became the "ideological sire," even organizer, of the armed revolt, and formed a separate center within the Party center.

In January 1957, the Executive Committee of the HSWP sent Gyula Kállai to Romania to assess the general situation at Snagov, sound out the positions of the group's various members, and prepare a report and recommendations on the basis of his experience. Kállai presented his report at the January 29 session of the Executive Committee. According to the minutes, he had "talked with those who might be steered away from the group—with Zoltán Szántó, György Lukács, and Szilárd Ujhelyi—and finally, with Imre Nagy (to learn how the head of the group thinks of the issues, because his opinion throws light on the opinion of the group as a whole)."

The report indicated that Zoltán Szántó had denounced Nagy and his followers as "an anti-Party and anti-Soviet political group." Although with some reservations, Zoltán Vas and György Lukács declared themselves in solidarity with the revolution and the group, while Szilárd Ujhelyi went beyond that to express his total disagreement with the policies of the Hungarian Party and government. "He [Ujhelyi] predicts there will be some judicial proceedings to determine responsibility, which he says will be a sham and amount to a second Rajk trial. He declared he would not leave the group; he would not make any statement to their detriment . . . [he would not] buy his freedom 'at that price.'"

About Imre Nagy: "He does not feel he did anything wrong." Nagy apparently said that the measures taken were the right ones, and in his opinion those measures would have served to stabilize the situation.

In Kállai's judgment, the group was treated "royally," and it was agreed that "a stricter regime should be introduced." Szántó and Lukács should come home, Vas should not. "In the case of Imre Nagy and Jánosi, it should be considered whether going to court is advisable. The group should not be readmitted to the Party." The Executive Committee accepted the report and declared: "The collection of facts relating to the October and November activities of the group (recollections, statements of counterrevolutionaries, minutes of governmental sessions, etc.) is necessary. In charge: J. Kádár."

It appears this was the first time the idea of bringing Imre Nagy to trial was voiced.

The next step was taken at a meeting of the Political Committee on February 22, which was held to prepare for the Central Committee meeting scheduled on February 26. Here Gyula Kállai was again involved. According to the minutes, Kállai said in connection with the Imre Nagy question: "We have been handling the whole Imre Nagy group issue with kid gloves. We have gone no further than our first statement, which said only that they had made a mistake, and our later [statement] that they had opened the way for the counterrevolution. It is not right to put the problem in this way. We must go beyond this [and say] Imre Nagy perpetrated *treason*, and we also have to show how this manifested itself. Such issues as neutrality and national communism must be raised not only in a general way, but as a trend, a manifestation, which has existed within the Party." (Kállai proposed that the report of the trip to Romania should not be presented at the Central Committee session, so that it would not become too widely known. But a political unmasking of the group should be started, he said, because otherwise "it will not be possible to cope with the hostile and confused views existing in the Party.")

The top-secret internal resolution dealing with the question reads as follows: "2/ The CC charges the Executive Committee with ensuring an accurate investigation and systematization of the facts related to the anti-Party activity of the Nagy-Losonczy group and with making a report at the appropriate time."

All this seems to refute allegations or assumptions that the Hungarian leadership was forced primarily by external pressures (from the Soviet Union and/or East Germany) to initiate the Imre Nagy trial in particular and the whole brutal scourge of reprisal in general.

At the meeting of the Central Committee on February 26, 1957, the construction of the accusation proceeded on the basis suggested above. According to the report to the CC, the Imre Nagy group had been an organized faction since the summer of 1955; in October 1956, acting through the government and other organizations, it engaged in counterrevolutionary activity and continued to do so even after November 4, when it established contact with American and Yugoslav authorities and with Radio Free Europe. At this time the CC passed a resolution to initiate proceedings against the group, for the time being, in the spirit of gradualism—not criminal proceedings, but an "accurate exploration and systematization of the facts." It also approved separation of the cases of Szántó, Lukács, and Vas from the rest of the group.

The final decision was made between March 21 and 27, 1957, on the occasion of an official visit by Kádár to Moscow. In public addresses delivered there, Kádár attacked Imre Nagy and his associates with striking vehemence. In all probability, his tone was part of a balancing act aimed at averting pressure from Stalinist chiefs (Voroshilov, Molotov, Suslov, etc.). He wanted to establish once and for all that the members of the Moscow émigré group headed by Rákosi were "politically dead," but as a price he had to make a show of his own leadership zeal. It is not known yet who actually took the initiative in the Nagy affair. When Kádár reported on his Moscow trip at the April 21 session of the Central Committee, he conspicuously claimed responsibility: "The question of Imre Nagy and his associates was discussed. We raised the issue. The comrades [the leaders of the Soviet Communist Party] agree that we should be severe in calling them to account. In the opinion of the comrades, it may be a matter for some debate as to whether it should take place in a short time or later, but they agree that it will have to take place." He added his own view on the question of timing: " In my opinion, we have to demonstrate to the Hungarian people, to the enemies of the people, and to the world that it is not possible to organize a counterrevolution in the socialist system without punishment. I am for starting the work and making a decision within a foreseeable time; one does not wait eight or ten months to extract a poisonous fang."

In fact, at the moment when Kádár was delivering his report, three members of the group deported to Romania—József Szilágyi, Gábor Tánczos, and György Fazekas—were already in the custody of Hungarian state security forces who for the time being were acting out of the Bucharest prison of their Romanian colleagues. (Thus, they did not even wait for the consent of the Central Committee, of which in any case, they could have no doubt.) In the course of the first two weeks of April, there were other arrests as well. On April 8 and April 11, the two separately housed "deputy chiefs," Ferenc Donáth and Géza Losonczy, were taken into custody; on April 14, Imre Nagy himself was arrested, together with Ferenc Jánosi, Sándor Haraszti, and Miklós Vásárhelyi. On April 17, handcuffed and blindfolded, all of those in custody were flown to Hungary in secrecy and installed in the state security prison on Gyorskocsi Street, where the "regular investigation" of their case began. The leader of the so-called special unit was police Colonel Sándor Rajnai, while the investigation was directed by Lieutenant Colonel József Szalma.

It was on June 22 that Kádár informed the Central Committee of the investigation under way, and "as to further steps," he would present the matter again "when the fundamental facts are clear." But he already knew and acknowledged that the Imre Nagy group would be treated as "a group that went over to the enemy camp." And it was at the same meeting that the Central Committee expelled two of its members, József Köböl and Antal Gyenes, who had earlier displayed sympathy toward Nagy and his associates. This of course was a clear advisory and warning to the other CC members concerning their conduct in the future.

The "investigation" was essentially completed by the end of the summer, but the trial did not commence in the fall. According to some speculations, the delay was occasioned in part by the upcoming U.N. General Assembly agenda, which called for a report on the Hungarian issue by a special five-member committee, and partly by the Moscow meeting of communist sister-party leaders scheduled for November in conjunction with the fortieth anniversary celebration of the October Revolution. There Kádár reportedly told the international communist gathering that "we are going to determine their (Imre Nagy and his group's) responsibility in this spirit." Back in Budapest, Kádár informed his Central Committee about the Moscow events on November 29 and stressed that all the sister parties (with Togliatti, Gomulka, and the Yugoslavs expressing some reservations) agreed that Nagy and his group should be deemed "despicable traitors."

In December, after careful political preparations, Kádár and his associates made up their minds to go ahead with a trial. On December 21 the Central Committee convened for a closed session with a single item on the agenda: "criminal policy." The speakers were János Kádár and Interior Minister Béla Biszku. On the basis of their recommendations, the Central Committee "decided," among the cases of Nagy group members already in custody in Hungary or still in Romania and of other arrested or suspected politicians and high-ranking military and police officers—twenty-five people in all—calling them by their names, those for whom "the legal process *must* be allowed to take its unhampered course" and those for whom "procedural clemency *must* be granted" on the basis of their lesser offenses. Of all those on whom they passed judgment, Géza Losonczy alone evaded their power: the man intended as defendant no. 2 in the Nagy trial died that very day while in detention in Hungary. According to Kádár, no one was responsible for Losonczy's death, and the precise circumstances of the matter still have not been determined. What is certain, however, is that Losonczy first suffered a total physical and nervous collapse and waged a desperate hunger strike.

The enumeration of charges and the characterizations of the defendants contained in the report Kádár and Biszku presented to the Central Committee were completely divorced from reality. By their account, Imre Nagy had for years been the leader of a veritable conspiracy, plotting together with his associates to restore the multiparty system and withdraw Hungary from the Warsaw Treaty, maintaining contact with Western imperialists and Hungarian fascist rebels, and so forth.

At length, after nearly all the most influential members of the Central Committee, including many hitherto known for their reform sympathies, had either expressed agreement or voiced even harder positions than those of the Political Committee itself, and the two absent members (György Marosán and the philosopher Béla Fogarasi) had endorsed the expected decision in a letter, the closed session of the Central Committee passed its resolution "on the unlawful acts of certain Hungarian citizens." In this resolution not only was the group in Romania divided into two camps according to their alleged culpability, but the leading personalities of 1956 who had been arrested in Hungary were similarly sorted out. Thus, those in Hungary who were to stand trial with Imre Nagy were named (Zoltán Tildy, Pál Maléter, Sándor Kopácsi, Miklós Gimes, the journalist Péter Erdős, and the "escaped" Béla Király), as were those who were to receive procedural clemency (Tivadar Pártay, Colonel Miklós Szücs, and others).

The resolution classified the whole case as top-secret for the duration of the proceedings, with the provision that the Ministry of Justice would issue a communiqué after the conclusion of a closed trial. Finally, in a guarded and rather roundabout manner, the resolution addressed the Yugoslavs' concerns about the diplomatic aspects of the case. On the one hand, it directed the Central Committee to inform President Tito that "facts which have come to light subsequently have rendered the bilateral agreement of November 19, 1956, null and void." On the other hand, it ordered that no reference to the Yugoslav connection should appear in the trial records or be introduced in any other way.

It was on the basis of this Party resolution that one month later, on January 28, 1958, a written act of accusation, signed by Procurator General Géza Szénási, was issued "against Imre Nagy and his associates for conspiracy aimed at subverting the people's democratic order of state and other criminal offenses." Only the members of the People's Court, the defendants themselves, and those defense counsel who had been chosen from an officially approved list were allowed to see and study the written act of accusation, and that for only one week. For on February 5 the secret trial began in tightly sealed chambers at the Military Court in Fő Street, before the People's Court Division of the Supreme Court, with Dr. Zoltán Radó presiding.

The ten defendants were selected—quite arbitrarily—as representative of the various factions deemed most responsible for the revolution. Even without Géza Losonczy, the former in-Party opposition was assigned the leading role (Imre Nagy, Ferenc Donáth, Miklós Gimes, József Szilágyi, Ferenc Jánosi, Miklós Vásárhelyi) in terms of sheer numbers, indicating that their responsibility was seen as graver than that of government members or military personnel, even though one (Gimes) had held no Party position, and another (Donáth) had been active only within the Party.

In an apparent attempt to "put things into proportion," however, other arrested members of the Nagy group were tried in separate proceedings. For example, from the Snagov group, the veteran reformer Sándor Haraszti; Gábor Tánczos, secretary of the Petőfi Circle; and the journalist György Fazekas were co-defendants in one case, although their activities had been completely unrelated. Tibor Déry had been convicted in an earlier trial along with three other writers; while journalists Pál Löcsei, Sándor Novobáczky, and Péter Erdős were all tried individually.

The Nagy trial had also to demonstrate a degree of conspiracy within the government. For this reason, in addition to the prime minister, his most important minister in the coalition, former President of Republic Zoltán Tildy of the Smallholders' Party was named as co-defendant, as was Pál Maléter, minister of defense in the last cabinet. Moreover Maléter; Sándor Kopácsi, the chief of Budapest police, who was next after Maléter in the ranking of defendants; and the absent General Béla Király were named to represent the revolutionary leadership within the armed forces.

On February 6, the second day of the trial, following a cursory examination of the defendants, the proceedings were interrupted and adjourned to allow for the collection of additional evidence. When the trial resumed more than four months later, a different judge, Ferenc Vida, presided. In a radio interview some thirty years later, Vida claimed that Radó had been unable to control the trial, that he had been weak and allowed the defendants to gain the upper hand. According to other versions, Radó fell unexpectedly ill, suffered a heart attack or something of that nature—or at least used that excuse to wriggle out of presiding over the trial and rendering a judgment. But minutes from the sessions of the high Party councils indicate clearly that the main reason for the delay was something quite different.

The Political Committee in its session of February 5, 1958, the opening day of the trial, passed a resolution that declared, "Judgment over the main criminals of the counterrevolution in Hungary must be subordinated to an issue vital to the whole of humanity, the issue of peace. . . . The Political Committee holds that proceeding with the trial now would provide an excuse for leading imperialist circles [that are] looking for a way out of the negotiations." In other words, the trial was brought to a standstill by Moscow out of concern for the forthcoming summit conference, and at the request of Togliatti, in consideration of the forthcoming elections in Italy.

It was with singular candor that Kádár laid the dilemma before the Central Committee at its closed session of February 14. The main objective, he said, was to bring about a thaw in the Cold War. "What can we do?" he asked, referring to the trial. "One, we can postpone it. Two, we can bring it to a conclusion, but influence the outcome so that the judgment brought will not increase international tensions. This, however, would be a very bad choice." He proposed that the Central Committee "acknowledge this assessment and agree to postponing the conclusion of the trial."

These few sentences reveal more about the responsibility of the Hungarian Party leadership in the Imre Nagy trial than any other document discovered so far. First of all, they make it clear that it was not the Soviet leaders who forced Kádár to stage the trial. Second, here Kádár unmistakably admits a fact later denied to the end by him, by his lieutenants, by his judges and his in-house Party historians: that the Party could "influence" the outcome of the trial (and, evidently, not only in the direction of leniency). Third, the February 14 session and its recorded discussions reveal beyond question the acquiescence of the entire Central Committee, some one hundred members strong, in the prosecution of the Nagy trial and in its outcome. For if the Central Committee at its session of December 21 had agreed in principle that "the legal process must be allowed to take its unhampered course," this time it accepted, even endorsed the idea that judgments should be rendered at the price of a few months' delay in order not to be lenient and therefore "unprincipled" but rather, as Kádár put it, "true to principle." This euphemistic phraseology, which was taken up and repeated by a majority of the Central Committee members, unmistakably implied that death sentences would be imposed after the trial. (After all, to anyone politically informed it would have been obvious that no mere prison sentence, even a sentence of greater than usual length, could produce a seriously adverse effect on the international scene!) In this way, Kádár very astutely prepared the ground for a "favorable" reception of the dreadful terror trial within the Party leadership, and at the same time, implicated them in the responsibility.

By all indications, no further discussion of the issue in such a broad forum was needed. Kádár and the Political Bureau were given the authority to work out the "details" and to make the necessary decisions. They soon put this authority to use by having József Szilágyi, whom they saw as the most dangerous defendant in the case and a man likely to imperil the running of the trial, convicted in a separate procedure. His case was moved forward to be tried April 16-18, 1958; he was executed on April 24. No official statement followed. (Deceptively, the news of Szilágyi's sentence was included in the communiqué of June 17 concerning the Nagy trial.)

The final details of the trial staging and the judgments to be rendered presumably were decided in late May or early June. At the May 27 session of the Political Bureau, where János Kádár reported on his Moscow negotiations of the previous week (a convention of the political consultative body for the Warsaw Treaty), a resolution was passed, whose last two items read as follows:

> 6.) On Monday, June 2, an informal session of the Political Bureau shall be held without a planned agenda. Premises ensuring undisturbed discussion shall be secured by Comrade Biszku.
>
> 7.) The trial of the Imre Nagy group shall be allowed to take its unhampered course. The preconditions for this shall be ensured on the government level by Comrades Münnich and Biszku, on the Party level by Comrades Kádár and Marosán. [Author's note: In the top-secret minutes, prepared in duplicate, Kádár with his own hand rendered the name of Imre Nagy illegible, and the copy in the "top-secret" archives now reads "X group."]

The "informal" session of the Political Bureau was held, so far as we can determine, at the Party's resort hotel in Leányfalu. Although there are no written records of the meeting and all those present seem to have suffered a memory lapse in this regard, it is probable that the sentences to be imposed by the People's Court were determined then and there. There can be no doubt even in the absence of evidence that, in the view of the Kádár regime, such a highly political issue involving international repercussions could no more be left to judicial lackeys than the earlier decision as to whether György Lukács, Zoltán Vas, and Julia Rajk should be brought to trial. We may even presume, and the timing supports it, that

Kádár obtained advance approval from Moscow for the trial date and at least for the death sentences of Imre Nagy and Pál Maléter (for it was foreseeable who would draw international blame for the executions). It is conceivable, though less certain, that the sentences to be imposed on the internationally less known Miklós Gimes and József Szilágyi also had to be discussed in advance with Moscow. At any rate, according to certain Moscow sources, Interior Minister Béla Biszku made at least one trip there to present the results of the investigation to "competent" Soviet authorities.

At the closed session on February 14, 1958, János Kádár told the members of the Central Committee that there had already been "three starts" in the Imre Nagy case. First, he said, "When we could have closed the case, we did not have the strength. Last September, too, there were political considerations. With the international conference of workers' parties just ahead of us, should we have declared war on Yugoslavia? The Poles are not great supporters of retribution either, and the Italians were preparing for elections and the judgment would not have been a help to them."

Thus, after the February postponement, the mid-June date constituted a fourth "start." This time neither internal nor international political obstacles were seen on the horizon. What is more, state security and the Party apparatus were by now itching for revenge for their humiliations of 1956; alongside the Soviet, East German, Czech, and Romanian Party leadership they were demanding that the Kádár group, which they considered to be "centrist," take strong steps to demonstrate that there had been no weakening of resolve.

Action now was demanded by the "logic" of the bloody postrevolution reprisals as well. By mid-1958, the courts had handed down thousands of judgments and hundreds of death sentences, a number of them involving politicians, military men, and intellectuals who were in direct contact with the Nagy group or the government in the course of the revolutionary events. The perceived interrelation of cases was pointed out by István Bibó, a minister without portfolio in the Nagy government, in his recollection: "I did not feel I was under the shadow of a death sentence, primarily because I had no idea that Imre Nagy had been sentenced to death, and by the time I was brought before the court, had even been executed. I even told my cell mate, István Marián, who was in a state of despair and fearing the worst, that there was no way he would be sentenced to death, because for that they would have first to sentence Maléter, who had been apprehended in his capacity as negotiating partner with the Soviet army. . . . And Maléter could not possibly be executed, said I in my total naiveté, because for that Imre Nagy would first have to be executed, and that was patently impossible."

All these political and tactical considerations were present behind Kádár's laconic and simplifying formulation in the resolution of June 6, 1958, the last resolution dealing with the issue: "The Central Committee concludes that, against the special counterrevolutionary group guilty of overthrowing the lawful order of the People's Republic, lawful process must be allowed to take its unhampered course."

Objectives and Tactics in the Imre Nagy Trial: Accusation, Judgment, and Remedial Petition

The nearly one and a half years spent in preparation for the trial, and its repeated disruptions in response to domestic and foreign policy developments working against its staging or at least demanding consideration, virtually rule out any assumption that it was a phenomenon recklessly conceived out of political passion or vengeance. Indeed, recently discovered data and documents suggest and substantiate the notion that the trial and its outcome were manifestations of a deep and tragic inevitability.

In ten speeches lately found to have been delivered by János Kádár in 1957 and 1958 at sessions of the Central Committee of the HSWP, one sees clearly that he and his fellow leaders, evidently under pressure from the Soviets and from their own secret police but also driven by the logic of power and by guilty conscience, simply could not be at ease, could not feel legitimate and secure so long as Imre Nagy and his associates, the nucleus of an alternative leadership and politics, remained alive. This is the primary explanation for their willingness to accept the moral consequences of the trial after they had effected a successful consolidation of power. Developments in 1988 and 1989, and the role played in those events by the revolution of 1956 and by the Nagy trial victims and survivors, in a sense confirm the fears of Kádár and his comrades. (It is noteworthy that Kádár displayed almost the same dedication, but used less brutal means, in the political liquidation of another power alternative, the Stalinist group headed by Rákosi.)

In their guidance of the preparation, approval, and public acceptance of the trial and judgments, Soviet leaders were directed not so much by passion or vengeance as by a cold determination to weed out the seeds of national independence and ideological heresy springing up in satellite soil. The progression in Hungary from reform and a quest for intellectual freedom to armed insurrection, then to the establishment of a multiparty system and a declaration of neutrality, convinced them that the road indicated by the Twentieth Party Congress of the Soviet Union in fact could not be followed, and that attempts on the part of countries in the region to find separate paths, particularly in the case of Yugoslavia, could be discouraged by impaling the heads of Imre Nagy and his associates up on the ramparts. And because they did not fully trust Kádár either, they hit upon complicity in murder as the best way to bind him to their cause.

Naturally, Khrushchev and Kádár and their respective cliques, not to mention the police ideologist who conducted the "investigation," understood from the beginning the effective roles played by the Nagy group: to intellectually undermine and morally paralyze a totalitarian regime before the revolution, to mediate between Nagy and the populace during the time of the revolution, and to champion the revolution after the Soviet invasion. From the Soviet perspective and that of communist power, all this could justifiably be considered reprehensible. It might even have been called ideological treason with some justification—*if* (1) Nagy's ideological transformation and that of his associates had not come about by an open and logical process, and *if* (2) Kádár and the centrists who supported him had not taken for tactical reasons the same turn that the Nagy group took out of conviction.

As it was, the perfectly legal and unconcealed activities and opinions endorsed by Imre Nagy and his associates were supported and shared at the time by Kádár and his people; and while in retrospect all this might be politically condemned, no legal grounds existed even in the extant "socialist" system of laws to establish criminal liability. For that, the whole problem had to be shifted from its true ideological and political plane to the conceived plane of conspiracy. This was accomplished in two ways: through a gradual reassessment of the opinions and actions of Nagy and the others, as reflected in the quoted Kádár speeches of 1956 and 1957 and in other like presentations; and through an allegation which perhaps even the accusers themselves came to believe, namely, that the facts of a conscious conspiracy by the Nagy group came to light only as a result of the investigations.

The construction of the charge with its deliberately mendacious language and the judgment itself were based on this "shift," which drew upon mostly tangible evidence (oppositional articles, speeches, reports of discussions) to arrive at totally false conclusions (deliberate conspiracy against the regime, conspiracy to seize power, illegal foreign connections, collusion with right-wing groups hostile to the people's democracy).

According to the written act of accusation, "In the period prior to October 23, 1956, the defendants formed a hostile group and, through their destructive activities displayed in various social organizations, launched an assault against the people's democratic state system; then, after the outbreak of the counterrevolution, assuming its leadership, they made a direct attempt at disrupting the alliance of the socialist states, at overthrowing the people's democratic order of state." If possible, the judgment departed still farther from historically verifiable facts to include every step the defendants took in 1955 and 1956, every statement and every contact they made, in the category of "conspiracy."

Péter Kende, editor of *Az Igazság a Nagy Imre Ügyben* ("The Truth About the Nagy Affair," Széckes and Warburg, Paris, 1959), stated in his foreword to the 1989 edition:

> As we can see, the charges [in the Nagy case] had not even the faintest connection with the actual doings of the defendants, with their political motivations before and during the revolution, with the real role they played during the events. They did not aim to overthrow the people's

> democratic order of state, they did not spark an armed insurrection, they did not ally themselves with the "imperialists," did not betray their country or the government positions they were asked (we know well by whom) in that critical situation to fill. . . . Of course, dropping these charges would not prevent anyone [so disposed] from adjudging Imre Nagy to be a bad communist, a poor strategist, a traitor to the Stalinist party and state idea. This might well be the opinion, or even legal formulation, [propounded by] a historian, but it could not serve as legal grounds to initiate criminal proceedings against Imre Nagy and his comrades, not to mention [Zoltán] Tildy, who was not even a comrade but merely a fellow minister at a critical moment. Such legal grounds did not exist even under the laws in force in 1958. The so-called rehabilitation must be addressed in this sense and only in this sense. Otherwise, Imre Nagy needs no "rehabilitation."

But rehabilitated he was, on hurried orders from an old regime trying to preserve and justify itself in 1989. The rehabilitation took the form of a remedial petition, and based on that, a judgment of the Presidential Division of the Supreme Court. The remedial petition presented by the procurator general contains a detailed substantive and procedural analysis of the legal violations committed by the People's Court and assails the determination of facts and conclusions underlying the judgment. Indeed, reading it today, one gains the impression it could have served as a closing argument for the defense before the so-called People's Court of the communist party state (though, to be sure, most of the attorneys registered in the "double O" lists would not at the time have dared to question either the accusation or the judgment, not even partially).

The remedial petition, however, does not expose the fundamental lies contained in the charges and the judgment but instead tries to find excuses for Imre Nagy, for his associates, and for the revolution itself, and in the process it strays in certain instances even farther from the historical truth than the written act of accusation or the judgment—but in the opposite direction.

For while the accusation claimed that Nagy for some time had been deliberately working to subvert the system, according to the remedial petition his highest priority on October 23 and during the following days was to save the regime: this was why he undertook to address the crowd of demonstrators and agreed to take "extraordinary measures" (read: martial law and Soviet intervention?) to restore public order.

Whereas the accusations claimed that Imre Nagy sabotaged and actively prevented an armed extermination of the revolutionary group at Corvin Alley, according to the petition the prime minister merely hoped to find a "different solution" to accomplish the same purpose. In this particular case the accusation certainly came closer to the truth than the subsequent vindication.

The People's Court placed heavy blame on Imre Nagy for ordering the cease-fire on October 28, since it worked to the advantage of the revolutionary forces and not the government. The petition seeks to excuse Nagy's order by claiming that the armed and security forces at his disposal were in all probability inadequate to the task of securing public order.

Finally, contrary to the accusation, the remedial petition stresses, inter alia, that the aim of the Hungarian Democratic Independence Movement initiated by Miklós Gimes in November 1956 was not to subvert the people's democratic order of state which had just been restored with the help of Soviet tanks, but to "promote rapprochement, and by that, consolidation" between the government and the group sequestered at the Yugoslav Embassy. This preposterous claim is signally based on testimonies and statements that were motivated by self-interest. In fact Gimes's intention in creating this illegal organization was not to overthrow the system, an unrealistic aim, but to hamper political consolidation following the military restoration of order without making any concessions to the puppet government.

Thus, we are dealing with distortions in two directions. While the pliant jurists of 1958 made insidious counterrevolutionaries of Imre Nagy and his "accomplices," their 1989 successors tried to recast them as exemplary, faithful communists. Neither representation is correct. The defendants in the trial (with the exception of Zoltán Tildy) were former communists who, as result of exposure to the crimes of Stalinism, had lost their faith in communism (and even Marxism) and who, influenced by the revolution, identified with the democratic and national independence aspirations of the Hungarian people. Their historic role was to open the way for democracy, and with that, for all the varied tendencies, democratic and antidemocratic, which democracy might entail.

Supplemental Notes

In November 1992, well after this chapter was completed, Boris Yeltsin, president of the Russian Federation, visited Budapest and handed over to the Hungarian government a valuable collection of Soviet foreign policy, military, KGB, and Party documents. Some of these documents relate directly to our topic and cast the described and analyzed series of events in a somewhat different light owing to new facts and perspectives, although basically they strongly confirm all that we knew and almost everything we presumed.

A report by Firiubin, Soviet ambassador to Belgrade, dated November 4, 1956, conveys a message from Yugoslav Vice President Eduard Kardelj to the Soviet Party leadership which unequivocally proves the complicity of the Yugoslav leadership in the events surrounding the Soviet invasion. Specifically, it shows that the Yugoslavs undertook at the Brioni talks to effect a smooth removal, if possible, of Imre Nagy and his government/group, and to prevent

Nagy from making a statement on behalf of his government against the forthcoming Soviet invasion and persuade him instead to declare his resignation and his support for the Kádár government. Surprisingly, however, the Soviet leaders responded to the effect that they no longer needed a statement from the overthrown prime minister. This can only mean that Imre Nagy had already been "written off" with finality in Moscow.

As to the actual preparation of the trial, the "Yeltsin dossier" includes two important documents: reports of August 26 and August 29, 1957, to the Soviet Central Committee from Yuri Andropov, then head of the East European Department of the Central Committee of the Soviet Communist Party. The first document fully confirms our information that Minister of the Interior Béla Biszku took a trip to Moscow at that time and reported on the preparations. It also reveals that by August 1957 the draft of the written act of accusation was ready, that eleven (not ten) defendants, including Béla Király, had been selected, and in fact that the Political Committee of the HSWP had decided on the imposition of *seven* death sentences (Imre Nagy, Géza Losonczy, Ferenc Donáth, Miklós Gimes, Pál Maléter, József Szilágyi, and Béla Király); in the event, of course, Donáth and Király escaped their intended fate. The reports further indicate that the Soviet leadership, beyond obviously giving consent to the Hungarian plans, were greatly concerned for the international ramifications and timing of the trial because, first, they hoped to avoid an undue deterioration of relations with Yugoslavia, and second, they feared that too great a scandal at the U.N. General Assembly would sink the chances of a summit conference. On these considerations, they asked for a postponement of the trial originally scheduled for late September (after the U.N. General Assembly session) until December 1957 or January 1958. (As we have seen, the trial, which in fact began in early February 1958, would again be postponed on another Soviet "request" for a further four months.)

The Andropov reports also make it clear that mention of the Yugoslav role in the last days of the Nagy government was omitted from the trial on Soviet instruction. But when the Yugoslav government later expressed public indignation over the sentences and the breach of promises made in 1956, the Soviet Presidium summoned the Hungarian leadership and directed them to publish the compromising data concerning the Yugoslav leaders in a diplomatic note.

In light of all this, the role of Moscow in the Nagy case seems rather less significant, or at least more passive, than first surmised. This picture, however, is somewhat modified by a Party document recently discovered in Warsaw, which includes the minutes of a meeting involving a sharp dispute between Khrushchev and Gomulka in May 1957. Gomulka spoke emphatically against the trial in preparation in Hungary and defended Imre Nagy; Khrushchev, in turn, accused and deplored in tones that leave no doubt about his views concerning Nagy's fate.

Appendices

About the Author

Alajos Dornbach was born in Ózd, Hungary, in 1936. He was educated at the Cistercian College in Eger and at the Piarist College in Kecskemét, Hungary. After graduating in law from Budapest University, he was an articled clerk, and after 1964, practiced his profession, at first in Gyöngyös and then in Budapest between 1973 and 1990. In October 1956, Alajos Dornbach was a member of his university's revolutionary committee and the revolutionary national guard. Because of these activities, he was briefly under arrest after the defeat of the revolution and was barred from membership in the Chamber of Attorneys until 1964. Right from the start of the opposition activities, Alajos Dornbach acted as the legal advisor of organizations such as SZETA (Poor Aid) as well as representing signatories to the Charter 77 protest in litigation against their wrongful dismissal.

In 1983, on behalf of the philanthropist George Soros, Dornbach successfully negotiated with the Hungarian government to establish the Soros Foundation Hungary, acting as the foundation's legal advisor in Budapest until 1990. He is still a member of the Foundation's Board of Trustees, acting as a personal representative of the founder. In 1988, Dornbach was one of the founding members of the first independent Hungarian trade union, the Democratic Scientific Workers' Trade Union. That same year, Dornbach also joined the Network of Free Initiative, the forerunner of the Alliance of Free Democrats, Hungary's liberal party. In the spring of 1990, in Hungary's first free elections, Alajos Dornbach was elected to Parliament to represent Budapest, and was elected deputy speaker. He is a member of the Executive of the Alliance of Free Democrats.

In January 1988, at the request of Miklós Vásárhelyi, the only survivor among those accused in the Imre Nagy trial, Alajos Dornbach started the process of rehabilitating Imre Nagy and his co-defendants. In June 1988, Dornbach became head of the legal section of the Historical Justice Committee. This commission initiated the reexamination of the records of the political show trials and has worked for the rehabilitation of Imre Nagy and other victims of communist repression. Dornbach is currently a member of the Hungarian Parliament and serves as Vice President of the Parliament's Local Government Committee.

His wife, Zsófia Zachár, is deputy editor of *The Hungarian Quarterly*. They have two children.

Short Biographies of the Defendants

IMRE NAGY (1896-1958)

Born into a family of farmers and artisans, he was trained as a locksmith. Nagy was drafted into the Austro-Hungarian army in 1915 and became a POW in Russia in 1916. After the revolution, he joined the Red Guards and in 1920, the Bolshevik Party. From 1921 to 1927, he lived in Hungary and was active in the Social Democratic Party, and later in the semilegal cover organization of the Communist Party. After spending 1928-1930 in exile in Vienna, Nagy went to Moscow in 1930 and lived in the USSR until 1944 as an agricultural scientist and later as editor of Radio Moscow's Hungarian program. Returning to Hungary with the Communist Party leadership, Nagy became minister of agriculture and was instrumental in implementing the 1945 radical agrarian reform. In the subsequent years, he served in the government, was speaker of the Parliament (1947-1949), and was a member of the Party's top leadership. As he opposed the forced collectivization of agriculture, Nagy came into conflict with the Party, and even though he admitted his mistakes, he was for a while "exiled" to a university post. In 1951, he again became member of the Politburo, minister, and deputy prime minister. After Stalin's death, the Moscow leaders selected him to implement the "New Course" in Hungary. As prime minister from June 1953 to April 1955, Nagy attempted reforms that went far beyond the cosmetic changes planned by the Kremlin. His adversaries (Rákosi and his group) managed to oust him from the government and the Party leadership; however, this time Nagy did not practice self-criticism but worked on his reform plans (later published as *Imre Nagy on Communism: In Defense of the New Course*, New York, 1957) and became the focus of an in-Party opposition. Called by the people on October 23 as the only credible communist leader, he was torn between Party loyalty and the program of the street, but finally, on October 28, he accepted the revolution's demands and stood at its helm until the Soviet invasion on November 4. Having obtained asylum in the Yugoslav Embassy, Nagy and his entourage were kidnapped by the Soviets on November 22 and taken to Romania. Arrested there on April 14, 1957, he was brought to trial, sentenced to death, and executed on June 16, 1958. His ceremonial reburial thirty-one years later became the symbolic event of the fall of the communist regime in Hungary.

GÉZA LOSONCZY (1917-1957)

The son of a Protestant minister, Losonczy graduated from Debrecen University and soon joined the antifascist resistance, having contacts with the communists. Arrested in 1940 as a journalist of the socialist daily *Népszava*, he had to spend most of the war years in hiding. In 1945, he became an editor of the central organ of the Hungarian CP, *Szabad Nép*, and in 1948, he was appointed political secretary in the prime minister's office. From 1949 to 1951, Losonczy was deputy minister of education. Arrested in 1951 and convicted as part of a frame-up trial, he spent three years in prison. When released under Imre Nagy's government, he was so ill that he had to spend a year in the hospital. Thereafter, he became editor of the Popular Front's daily *Magyar Nemzet*, and a central figure in the in-Party opposition around Imre Nagy. Although co-opted by the leadership on October 23-24, Losonczy refused to accept the Party's position against the revolution and was instrumental in winning over Nagy to the side of the uprising. On October 30, he became minister of state in the revolutionary government. Having shared the fate of the group around Nagy—Yugoslav Embassy, Romanian detention—he was arrested and brought to Budapest for trial. In prison, his health deteriorated, and he died on December 21, 1957, as a consequence of his illness and the maltreatment suffered in connection with a hunger strike.

FERENC DONÁTH (1913-1986)

The son of a lawyer, Donáth was also trained in the law. He joined the antifascist movements and the underground Communist Party in the 1930s. From 1945 to 1948, he worked in the Ministry of Agriculture, then for three years as head of the secretariat of the CC of the CP. Sentenced to fifteen years in prison in one of the frame-up trials, he was freed in 1954 and worked as an economist. He was active in the in-Party opposition and was a speaker at several meetings of the prerevolutionary Petőfi Circle in 1956. Just like Losonczy, he was co-opted by the leadership on October 23-24 but opposed the Party's position against the revolution and was instrumental in winning over Nagy to the side of the uprising. On November 1, he became a member of the Executive Committee of the newly founded anti-Stalinist Communist Party. With Nagy in the Yugoslav Embassy and later in Romania, he was tried and sentenced to twelve years in prison. Released in 1960, he resumed his work on agrarian economics and rural policy. In 1977, he signed the declaration of solidarity with the Prague Charter 77, and from then on became a leading figure of the opposition. Thanks to his personal qualities and political skills, he was able to unite the different oppositional circles at the now famous meeting in Monor in 1985. On July 15, 1986, he died in Budapest after a long illness.

MIKLÓS GIMES (1917-1958)

Born in a medical family, Gimes studied medicine himself but preferred other intellectual fields. Drafted into a labor battalion, he escaped in 1944 and joined the Yugoslav partisans. From 1945 to 1953, he was on the staff of the daily *Szabad Nép*. As an advocate of the reforms of Imre Nagy, he left the Party paper in 1954 and joined the staff of *Magyar Nemzet*. He demanded the rehabilitation of the victims of the show trials at several meetings and came to be one of the most radical members of the in-Party opposition. During the revolution, he launched the daily *Magyar Szabadság* and did not give up even after the Soviet invasion. As editor of the underground paper *Október Huszonharmadika* [October 23rd] and leader of a resistance group, he was arrested by the Soviets in December 1956, and later transferred to the group of defendants with Imre Nagy. Sentenced to death, he was executed on June 15, 1958.

ZOLTÁN TILDY (1889-1961)

Having studied at the Protestant Theological Academy of Pápa and the University of Belfast, Tildy became a Calvinist (Presbyterian) minister. Beginning in 1917, he was politically active in the Smallholders' Party, in 1930, was one of the founders of the Independent Smallholders' Party, and was an M.P. between 1936 and 1944. As leader of his party, which had joined the antifascist resistance, Tildy became prime minister after the first free elections in November 1945 and subsequently the first president of the republic on February 1, 1946. Forced to resign in 1948, he was under house arrest until 1956. On October 28, 1956, he joined Imre Nagy's government and was among the last to leave the Parliament building on November 4. Arrested in 1957 and sentenced to six years in prison, he was released in 1959, a seriously ill man. He died in Budapest on August 3, 1961.

PÁL MALÉTER (1917-1958)

After medical studies in Prague, Maléter changed to a military career, and in 1943 graduated from the Ludovika Military Academy in Budapest. Sent to the Russian front, he became a Soviet POW, attended an antifascist partisan school, fought against the Nazis, and in 1945 became an officer in the new Hungarian army. Between 1946 and 1949, he was the commander of its Presidential Guard. In 1955, he was transferred to an engineering unit with the rank of colonel. After the outbreak of the revolution, Maléter was sent to the Kilián barracks to quell the uprising, but finally sided with the revolutionaries, and on October 31, was appointed deputy minister of defense in the Imre Nagy government. On November 3, he became minister of defense with the rank of major general. During the night of November 3-4, Maléter was arrested by the KGB while negotiating with the Soviet commanders on troop withdrawals. Handed over to the Hungarian authorities in 1957, he was tried, convicted, and executed with Imre Nagy.

SÁNDOR KOPÁCSI (1922-)

A factory worker in the industrial city of Miskolc, Kopácsi joined the CP in 1945 and became a police officer. He served first in Miskolc, later in Budapest, and after political training, became, as a colonel of the police, police chief of Budapest. Sympathizing with the demonstrators and later with the armed uprising, Kopácsi was instrumental in avoiding greater bloodshed during the revolution. On October 30-31, he became a leading commander of the revolutionary national guard. Arrested on November 5, he was tried with Imre Nagy and sentenced to imprisonment for life, but was released as part of a general amnesty in 1963. In 1975, he emigrated to Canada, where he wrote his memoirs, *In the Name of the Working Class.* In 1989, he returned to Hungary, was fully rehabilitated, and promoted to police major general.

BÉLA KIRÁLY (1912-)

After graduation from the Ludovika Military Academy and the General Staff Academy, Király saw action on the Soviet front and retreated with his unit to Köszeg, in western Hungary. Thereafter, he held high positions in the new Hungarian army; in 1950, he was commander of the Zrinyi Military Academy. Arrested in 1951 and sentenced first to death and then to life imprisonment on trumped-up charges, he was in jail until 1956. During the revolution, he was appointed commander in chief of the national guard. Fleeing from the Soviets, Király left for the West, where he became one of the leaders of the Hungarian 1956 exiles. He was charged in the trial against Imre Nagy, but later his case was separated. Király settled in the U.S.A., where he obtained a doctorate at Columbia University (1963) and became professor of history at Brooklyn College, New

York. In 1989, he returned to Budapest and was one of the speakers at the funeral of Imre Nagy and his fellow martyrs. Promoted to colonel general, Király became an M.P. in 1990.

JÓZSEF SZILÁGYI (1917-1958)

A graduate of the School of Law at Debrecen University, Szilágyi was an active member of the antifascist resistance and the underground Communist Party, for which he suffered three years in prison in 1940-43. In 1944, he became chief of police in Debrecen, and in 1947, moved to the Police Department of the CP Headquarters and became a member of the Party's Control Commission. In 1949, he was removed from his post, and because of his loyalty to Imre Nagy and the reform, he was expelled from the CP in 1956. During the revolution, Szilágyi headed Nagy's secretariat and shared his fate after the defeat. Arrested before the others, Szilágyi was interrogated in Budapest, where he refused to cooperate and went on a hunger strike. In April 1958, his case was separated from Nagy's and tried individually. Sentenced to death, he was executed on April 24, 1958.

FERENC JÁNOSI (1916-1968)

A graduate of the Universities of Debrecen and Halle-Wittenberg, Jánosi was ordained a Protestant minister and taught at the famous Sárospatak College. In 1943, he was captured by the Red Army as an army chaplain. He attended an antifascist school and edited a newspaper of the Soviet command. After 1945, he was employed first in the Ministry of Defense, later in the Ministry of Education, and joined the Communist Party. He married Erzsébet Nagy, Imre Nagy's daughter. Between 1953 and 1955, Jánosi was secretary general of the reorganized Patriotic Front. During the revolution, he worked with Nagy and followed him to the Yugoslav Embassy, to Romania, and into court. Having served part of an eight-year sentence, Jánosi was released in 1960 and given a post in the Pest county archives until his retirement.

MIKLÓS VÁSÁRHELYI (1917-)

Born in Fiume (today Rijeka, Croatia), Vásárhelyi studied politics and law in Rome and Debrecen, and was active in the antifascist resistance. After 1945, he became a journalist on the staff of the Communist Party's papers, and in 1953 joined the newly organized Information Office under Imre Nagy. Fired from his posts and expelled from the CP in 1955, he was an active member of the oppositional group around Nagy, at whose call he became what amounted to the government's spokesman during the revolution. Although not initially in the Yugoslav Embassy, Vásárhelyi was also taken to Romania and brought back to Hungary for trial. Having served part of his four-year sentence, he was released in 1960 and after 1972 was allowed to publish on the history of the press and to work on films. A central figure of the opposition in the 1970s and 1980s, Vásárhelyi was elected to the free Parliament in 1990.

Index

www.ingramcontent.com/pod-product-compliance
Ingram Content Group UK Ltd.
Pitfield, Milton Keynes, MK11 3LW, UK
UKHW020815290926
15470UKWH00003B/1180